AN ENQUIRY INTO PROGNOSIS IN THE NEUROSES

Photo: Aero Pictorial Ltd

SWAYLANDS

AN ENQUIRY INTO PROGNOSIS IN THE NEUROSES

by

T. A. ROSS, M.D., F.R.C.P.

Sometime Medical Director, Cassel Hospital for Functional Nervous Disorders. Author of The Common Neuroses, *and* An Introduction to Analytical Psychotherapy

CAMBRIDGE

AT THE UNIVERSITY PRESS

1936

CAMBRIDGE
UNIVERSITY PRESS

University Printing House, Cambridge CB2 8BS, United Kingdom

Cambridge University Press is part of the University of Cambridge.

It furthers the University's mission by disseminating knowledge in the pursuit of education, learning and research at the highest international levels of excellence.

www.cambridge.org
Information on this title: www.cambridge.org/9781107455887

First published 1936
First paperback edition 2014

A catalogue record for this publication is available from the British Library

ISBN 978-1-107-45588-7 Paperback

"It is the best thing, in my opinion, for the physician to apply himself diligently to the art of foreknowing. For he who is master of this art, and shews himself such among his patients, with respect to what is present, past and future, declaring at the same time wherein the patient has been wanting, will give such proofs of a superior knowledge in what relates to the sick, that the generality of men will commit themselves to that physician without any manner of diffidence."

HIPPOCRATES ON PROGNOSTICS. Translated by Francis Clifton, M.D., *Fellow of the College of Physicians and of the Royal Society, London*, 1752.

CONTENTS

PREFACE

Notwithstanding the exhortation of Hippocrates quoted on the fly-leaf, knowledge in prognosis has lagged considerably behind other medical knowledge. With regard to neuroses there has been a vague idea that these patients get better, but there has been little accurate information about the conditions which are favourable or otherwise for this. In July 1935 Luff and Garrod published a paper in the *British Medical Journal* summarizing the results in 500 adult patients. Their follow up reported on these patients for three years after treatment. This is, I think, the only attempt made to follow up a large number of these patients. The present volume deals with nearly twelve hundred patients, and the period of follow up has been considerably longer. The patients have all been observed by the author, though not all treated by him personally. Those whose cases are described in detail were treated by him. He has also read every letter on which the book mostly depends. Some of the reports were communicated by his colleagues, who had themselves seen their former patients.

This book does not profess to settle this question. It is hoped that it may help to stimulate further enquiries and that it may indicate certain errors of method in making such enquiries, so that others may avoid them.

I am indebted to Miss Morris, who was my personal secretary during all the years under review, for her help in arranging the lists of patients and for keeping them up to date, also for putting a human touch into the letters of enquiry, which made answers more likely to be obtained.

T. A. R.

November 1935

I

PRELIMINARY

By the use of statistical methods it is possible to arrive at an average prognosis for acute disease, especially if this disease is of epidemic nature. Thus it is possible to say that the mortality of a given epidemic is so much per cent., the complete recovery rate so much; the various sequelae also could be given a definite average figure. It is true that the prognosis of any acute disease may vary in different epidemics and at different periods of the one under investigation, that the prognosis of diseases like scarlet fever and measles is different now from what it was fifty years ago; these facts, however, do not invalidate the statement that the prognosis in these disorders is capable of statistical treatment. And on this possibility depends our ability to assess the value of treatment, which must otherwise be a matter of guess-work and prejudice.

In acute non-epidemic disease, if the disease is as definite a condition as, say, lobar pneumonia, the same possibility is present. In all these diseases one may obtain what may be called a *natural* prognosis, i.e. one unaffected by treatment. The diseases may be merely observed without being treated, and it is of importance to say that they may be so observed without this having any effect on the patient. This may sound a platitude, but indeed, as we shall see presently, one cannot always merely observe a disease process without affecting or altering it.

In chronic diseases factors are at once encountered which make the assessment of their prognosis a much more difficult matter. These are of different kinds. A patient with scarlet fever or measles will commonly be under the same observer throughout the illness and, if he be a specialist in these disorders, and thus can see many examples at one period of time, the requisites for accuracy of statistical results could not be bettered. In chronic disease, on the other hand, the patient will sometimes be under the care of a general practitioner, but not always the same individual, and sometimes he will be in hospital under a specialist. Either of these might apparently collect reliable statistics, but very soon objections to placing complete faith in them will become manifest. The general practitioner has the advantage of seeing his patients over many years, but he frequently labours under the disadvantage of not seeing a large enough number of examples of the disease in question to make his figures of much value. There have, of course, been exceptions to this, of whom the late Sir James Mackenzie was one of the most recent; but it is usually granted that he was an unusual person. To prevent the total loss of the large mass of clinical knowledge now in the minds of the general practitioners and of them alone, for it is they particularly who see after-results, something can be done by a combined enquiry such as was undertaken a few years ago on the results of operation for peptic ulcer, and it will probably be by such enquiries in the future that many questions of prognosis will be settled. The specialist, on the other hand, sees a large number of cases, but his difficulties in ascertaining what happens to them after they have left his care are very great. If they have done well, he seldom sees them again, for they do not need him, and frequently if they have done badly he does not see them either, for they are apt to go to someone else. He is therefore driven to trust to written reports, or the reports of a social worker; we shall see presently how many fallacies underlie the report of any kind, written or oral, in the absence of personal observation. Sometimes he will be able to interview the patient afterwards, but this will probably be exceptional for many reasons. The specialist, furthermore, because he is a specialist is subject to certain disadvantages which make it difficult for him to arrive invariably at just conclusions. He is apt, for instance, to take a pessimistic view of any treatment which he himself does not practise, for he is apt to see the failures of that treatment, whereas, as has just been stated, he does not see quite so many of his own failures. In parenthesis it might be stated that if this obvious fact were more frequently recognized, some of the heated denunciations of certain forms of treatment, so often heard, would cease, to the great advantage of the progress of therapeutics, which in truth cannot be discussed profitably in an emotional atmosphere. The specialist, however, because of this fact, gets a distorted view in favour of what he himself practises, and against what he himself does not practise.

He is led into this particular error because in a less degree indeed, but still in some degree, he suffers from the same difficulty as the general practitioner in that he does not see a large enough number of cases if he is trusting to his own experience entirely. No one man, be he specialist or general practitioner, ever sees quite enough examples to be dogmatic; and unfortunately the specialist is the more apt to be groundlessly dogmatic than is the general practitioner. Furthermore, the specialist obtains an unduly pessimistic view, apart from treatment, of the disease in which he specializes, because as a rule he is not asked to see the milder forms of any disease, but is called in only when the illness becomes so serious that the general practitioner wishes further help. Every general practitioner believes that on the whole specialists always take too grave a view; this is in part the explanation of the belief that they see their own speciality in every patient; every specialist thinks that the general practitioner is too light-hearted. Having practised in both capacities, I am inclined to think that the general practitioner is more often right; though when he is wrong the consequences are often more dramatic, and as he is less given to writing papers than the other it is usually he that is made the whipping boy when affairs are not going smoothly. A very obvious example of this kind of error will be found in the history of schizophrenia. The specialist tended to see patients who had already pronounced schizophrenic symptoms, and when he traced back their histories he found that in one way or another they had often had similar though milder symptoms in episodes for many years; under his observation they passed into dementia; but it must be noted that they were more ill when they came to him than they had been in earlier attacks; unless indeed they were of the kind who were deteriorating, he would probably not have seen them at all, but he did not so often see those with one such episode which cleared up and was never repeated. Therefore for years all patients presenting schizophrenic symptoms were looked on by specialists as doomed. It was difficult for the general practitioner to believe this, as he seemed to know people who had formerly fitted into the schizophrenic category, but who were now well. The general practitioner, however, especially in psychiatric matters, does not dare to lift up his voice. The history of the stethoscope is associated with a similar disaster. Many patients who were dropsical and about to die were found to have cardiac murmurs, therefore anyone with a cardiac murmur was bound soon to be dropsical and moribund.

The clinical research on prognosis which is so necessary could best be undertaken by teams of both kinds of practitioners working together, and having their work correlated by medical statisticians. This is a form of research which might be very fruitful of results, but it is not showy and will probably not be done, except occasionally as in the enquiry on peptic ulcer.

These remarks are applicable to all chronic disease, both organic and functional, but in the latter, that is in the neuroses, there are reasons whereby these difficulties are even greater. As has been stated, it is possible to observe organic disease without treating it, and in this way to establish a natural prognosis for the disease in question. But in the neuroses there is no such thing as a natural prognosis; it is quite impossible to observe psychogenic diseases *in vacuo*. For good or evil every interview with these patients alters the course of the illness. Every time they are seen by a doctor they are left with either more or less hope, and there can be little doubt that more or less hope profoundly affects the course of their illnesses. I have seen doctors who proposed merely to observe patients suffering in this way, but in a very short time they began to realize that they were doing nothing of the kind; they were either influencing the patient by telling him that his case was curable, or plunging him into despair by remaining judicially non-committal. To give an opinion that a case is curable may make the patient better or worse; it never leaves things as they are. It will make him better if he desires cure, worse, if, as is possible, he dreads the consequences of cure—which may entail return to a hated environment. To be non-committal is alarming because it is interpreted by the patient to mean either that the doctor does not understand the case or that he has some fearful possibility in his mind, such as cancer; and though the patient might not be averse to a little illness, he does not wish a very bad one any more than the rest of us. It would therefore be truer to say that the prognosis of psychogenic disorders can be only the prognosis of the case as far as that case has been modified by the doctor in charge; in this book it will be a prognosis of the neuroses as modified by contact with the total environment of the Cassel Hospital for Functional Nervous Disorders, in itself a somewhat complex factor, which must be split up into its component parts if possible. The modifications which this complex induced in the neuroses were sometimes for the better, but sometimes they must have been for the worse. On the whole, it is hoped that they were for the better. Before we go further in our study of prognosis it would be well to give some account of this modifying environment, and also to assess if possible the value either plus or minus of the various factors.

II

THE ENVIRONMENTAL FACTORS

The Cassel Hospital for Functional Nervous Disorders was founded in 1919 by the late Sir Ernest Cassel, and was opened for the reception of patients in May 1921. He had been deeply moved by the pitiable state to which men were reduced by so-called shell shock. On learning that similar conditions were common among the civilian population, and that the means of coping with them were meagre, he expressed the desire to found a hospital which should help to deal with these problems.

In the materialization of this idea he was assisted chiefly by the late Sir Maurice Craig, who had for long wished that there should be a hospital for the special purpose of investigating and treating the neuroses.

Sir Ernest bought a large country house, Swaylands, near the ancient and historic village of Penshurst, Kent—Penshurst Place was the birthplace of Philip and Algernon Sydney, and was also closely connected with Robert Dudley, Earl of Leicester.

After certain alterations had been carried out accommodation was provided at Swaylands for fifty-two, and later with subsequent alterations for sixty-four patients. All the patients except seven have separate bedrooms, but there are also two small wards of four and three beds respectively.

After purchasing and equipping the house there was still a large sum of money left over from Sir Ernest's endowment. Because of this, patients can be received at a figure which is considerably less than cost price, the standard sum being five guineas a week. The ward patients pay three guineas, and patients who are better off pay seven guineas and upwards. These figures are inclusive of board and lodging, medical attendance, all necessary medicaments; indeed there are no extras of any kind whatever. It was Sir Ernest's wish to assist chiefly educated persons of slender means, as he knew that they formed a class which received almost less help than any other. The hospital is placed in a very beautiful garden. It has a private golf course, tennis courts, a cricket field and all the other amenities of a large country house.

The management consists of a committee for general superintendence of finance, repairs, alterations and so on, and a medical committee for purely medical affairs. The local executive is in the hands of a medical director, but as it was considered most important that his time should be devoted entirely to clinical matters he delegates all the domestic management to the secretary and to the matron.[1]

A patient at Swaylands comes into active contact for certain with his doctor. The ratio of doctors to patients has varied: at first it was about one to sixteen or seventeen patients, later it was increased to one to twelve or thirteen. Opinions will differ concerning what is the right proportion; for reasons which will become obvious later, I do not consider that the first proportion need spell neglect of the patients, but I do not expect to find that many psychotherapists will agree with me. Some hold that even the later figures provide too few doctors. With sixteen patients it is not possible for the doctor to see every patient every day; again reasons will emerge whereby this is not always necessary or even desirable. With this number it is to my knowledge eminently possible for the doctor to be a potent influence in the life of each patient, to be quite the most important thing he comes across in hospital. There are three methods of psychotherapy employed at Swaylands—hypnotism, persuasion and analysis. That the neuroses are psychogenic and that their proper treatment is by psychotherapy is a subject which will not be entered into here. I have dealt fully with the question in a previous book—*The Common Neuroses*—and I have no wish to modify what I there wrote on this head. Of course any concomitant physical treatment which is necessary is carried out at the same time as the psychotherapy, but this is always undertaken for the sake of the physical condition in question in exactly the same spirit as it would have been in a non-nervous person, and not with any hope that physical treatment will modify a neurotic tendency, or remove a neurotic symptom, though indeed it often seems to do the latter.

Hypnotism has been employed only occasionally. On the whole

[1] All information regarding admission of patients etc. can be obtained from the Secretary, Cassel Hospital, Swaylands, Penshurst, Kent.

it is probable that it affects the prognosis adversely: it does not tend to enable the patient to stand on his own feet, but rather to make him more dependent. It is significant that many clinicians, who used it at one time, gave it up later. The names of Bernheim and of Freud occur to one at once in this connection; and this has happened although in the literature there are many records of its lasting beneficial action. No one who has used it doubts its immediate potency, but that is of little importance. Alcohol, cocaine, morphine could all be given with the happiest immediate result in the neuroses, but that does not make their use desirable.

Persuasion and analysis are best considered together. In this connection it must be stated immediately that the word "psychoanalysis" is not being used, as it has become a sort of hall-mark which is the private property of the Freudian school. There was complete belief at Swaylands about the actuality of an unconscious mind, a belief also that it could be explored, but not a complete belief that the Freudian description of it was true in detail. From time to time one or other of us would develop strong beliefs in Freud, and feel for a time that he was very right indeed; and then usually such beliefs weakened. If the word had not been seized on, and, as it were, registered by another sect, I should have said that our belief was largely in an individual psychology, i.e. that the patient's personal experience was the important thing; some of this when he came under observation was conscious, some of it had become unconscious; we were interested also in trends which had not yet become experience, and often not yet conscious. What we aimed at was to discover what experiences an individual had encountered and how they had affected him. Much of this is often repressed, and the exploring of such repressions is frequently, as it seems to me, of more value than following the development of the infantile mind through the various stages which have been described by the Freudians, but which were possibly invented by them.

The mere existence of the unconscious mind is still denied by many, but this is not the place to give proofs for the beliefs in it. I have given my reasons for believing in it in another book—*An Introduction to Analytical Psychotherapy.*

One of the things which will emerge from the following studies, however, is that in a considerable number of examples no exploration of the unconscious need be undertaken at all; the proofs of this and further discussion of it will come later.

The word "persuasion" also needs comment. It has nothing to do with suggestion; it is not persuading a patient to become well. The word as used was coined by Dejerine. It connotes a process of history taking at length, during which several things will come out of a limbo of forgotten things. After this comes careful examination by ordinary clinical and, if necessary, laboratory methods, followed by evaluation of the symptoms in the light of this examination, and the demonstration that most of them commonly accompany emotion in everybody. It is then pointed out that the methods of management of life in the past were bad. After this in many instances the patient's symptoms disappear seemingly spontaneously. Again this method was described in great detail in *The Common Neuroses* and therefore will not be repeated here; but it might be pointed out that the method has not had a very intelligent trial by the specialist psychotherapists in this country. I have seen it dismissed very curtly in the Freudian literature by writers who to my knowledge have never tried it, who said it could not succeed because all the investigations were conducted on the conscious level, which begs the question twice, once by suggesting that all neurosis must depend on repression, secondly by saying that Dejerine was ignorant of the dynamic unconscious because he did not use the expression.

The next contact for the patients at Swaylands was with the staff. Not all the patients had any contact to speak of with the staff; only those who were too ill or too timid to mix much with the other patients had much to do with the nurses. If a patient was well enough he got up in the morning for breakfast, was occupied one way or another till bedtime, and such a one really never saw the nursing staff. If he was in bed or could not, because of phobias or other difficulties, go down to meals, then he saw more of them. So far as was possible the effect of the staff was meant to be neutral. No one can be quite neutral, but the staff were encouraged not to treat patients themselves at all, but to recommend them always to bring their troubles to the doctor. This precaution was part of the wisdom of Weir Mitchell. In his isolation rest cure the nurses were instructed not to permit the patients to talk to them about their symptoms or their troubles. If they talked about them to the nurse they did so less to the doctor, and Weir Mitchell wished to keep complete control in the matter of that moral influence which was obviously, in his eyes, the most important thing in his treatment. Even though he described it as the adjuvant to rest, it is easy to see that he himself thought highly of it, and that no course of treatment could be regarded as efficient without it. In a materialistic age this aspect was wholly ignored by his readers and imitators, and Weir Mitchell's treatment was spoken of and regarded as wholly a physical treatment which rested the exhausted cerebral cells and recharged them with energy. When others more or less followed his detailed instructions, and often thought they were bettering them when they kept patients in the dark in solitary confinement and allowed them to be visited by the nurse, only when she brought their meals, they usually failed to get good results, for they forgot to use his moral teaching; indeed, though it was plain enough in his book, it is probable that they never saw that it was there, but repressed it in the act of reading it. They looked about for materialistic reasons for his successes, and, curiously, so obviously veracious was Weir Mitchell that they never accused him of exaggeration. The most amusing explanation ever given was Osler's, who thought it must have been due to the excellence of his nurses, the very people whom the master would not allow to do anything with or to the patients. Excellent they must have been, but it was the excellence of the deaf and dumb slave whose tongue has been cut out so that he should not blab secrets, which in fact he had never heard.

The next contact for our patients was with the other patients; here we come across one of the most potent influences in the treatment of these patients, an influence which is sometimes helpful, but which tends often to be baleful. The advantages of contact with other patients may be summarized as follows.

Each patient can relearn the value of co-operation. That is a social faculty that nearly every patient has lost. He has become more and more the centre of his universe; the family has learned that his whims are disregarded at their peril; he assists other people when it suits him; his case is one which puzzles the doctors and confers upon himself an antisocial uniqueness. Most of this is automatically undone by living in contact with other patients. However little yet the doctors may understand the case, it is evidently a rather common affair, its treasured rarity has disappeared. Other people with similar conditions seem to have fallen into line and become co-operative, and no one else seems greatly upset if one does lose one's temper and makes that kind of scene which in the past brought everyone to heel. There is also the spectacle of other people getting better, of people who were formerly under the sway of neurotic reactions becoming rather contemptuous of these reactions, and with all this there is a weakening of the attitude of complacency about illness. So potent are all these influences for good that certain patients who have strong reasons for wishing not to recover will refuse to meet the others; the fear of meeting other people may, of course, be a primary symptom of any patient's illness, but it is sometimes acquired as a defence against the infection of getting better.

Here too we may summarize one or two advantages which the institution confers over out-patient practice, either in private or at a clinic. It is cheaper for patients to be treated in an institution, mostly because the doctor's time is saved, and he has not the expenses of a specialist's rooms in the doctors' quarter of a town, all of which have to be paid for.

Again, almost every patient in the first week or ten days of treatment feels better and then falls back. Sometimes this is connected with a fear of cure, i.e. of the consequences of cure, for very often these illnesses have a value. If the patient is coming to the doctor for treatment it is easy for him at this point to develop symptoms, unwittingly usually, which prevent him leaving his house, and so the treatment can easily be broken off. In an institution this danger is less. The patient must leave the place if he is to escape from the doctor, but that requires effort, and it is less easy in the doctor's reassuring presence to insist on the impossibility of going on. The institution therefore so far tends to keep the treatment going.

It is, moreover, obvious that unless there are beds, the clinical material which comes under observation must be very limited. There are numbers of patients with neuroses, who have been bedridden for long periods; to invite them to come to an out-patient clinic or to a doctor's house as the sole method of treatment is to ensure that they get none. It may be true that for none of these patients is bed treatment essential, but it is necessary for the doctor to come into contact with the patient before the latter can believe that that is true; and many of these patients do not dare to get out of bed for fear of the consequences. There are also many extremely emaciated patients where a period of bed and generous feeding makes all other necessary treatment much easier.

The disadvantages of other patients being part of the environment are, however, serious and must be faced. Some of them skilfully handled may be turned into advantages.

If there is a contagion of getting better, there is, unfortunately, one also of remaining ill or getting worse. Patients who discuss their symptoms with one another may easily pass symptoms on to each other. Pessimists who have made up their minds that these illnesses are incurable can undoubtedly delay the recovery of the more impressionable of their fellows. And from this arises in a much more dangerous form the failure of the doctor to hear what the patient is thinking and feeling. In talking about the nurses, it was mentioned that if the patient talked of his case to them he would do it the less to the doctors: but at least the nurse will put the doctor on his guard, will inform him, if she is a good nurse, that she is hearing a great deal, whereas the patient who has been made a confidant will probably be on his honour not to tell the doctor. The patient who talks about symptoms knows he is going against the doctor's wishes, and the recipient is almost always bound over to silence. The honour which exists in this matter is the school code of the children against the master, of the family against a parent. It is not, however, merely a matter of dislike of the master—parents. The recipient of the confidence may be himself greatly pained, and his recovery retarded by keeping something from that parent substitute, the doctor, but the code is on the whole strict, and it forbids him to tell. This is indeed one of the proofs of the presence of *regression* as a factor in all neurosis. The effect on the recipient is indeed, therefore, as bad as on the original sinner, and although the doctor may be able to do nothing to that sinner if he is told about it, the telling in strict confidence may be of great value to the confidant who, by confessing, achieves once more that oneness with the doctor, which he may have lost when he listened to something which he knew he should not have listened to.

Another important adverse factor, however, in this environment is jealousy. The doctor may be more interested in one patient than in another; one patient may really need longer interviews than another, and the doctor may feel very properly that he should give his interviews as regards length and frequency in accordance with the needs of each individual patient. If he does so to any great extent there will be trouble. It is probable that this is the greatest objection which exists to treating these patients in an institution. The difficulty cannot be ignored in the sense that it is no use for the doctor to say that he does not mind, they can be as jealous as they like, he will see whom he pleases when he pleases. That attitude will not cure patients. Moreover, it may be that he will hear nothing directly about it for weeks after it has been raging in the patient's bosom and retarding his recovery. There are, of course, ways of dealing with it in accordance with the technique of management of these patients.

Yet treating people as out-patients will not get rid of the perpetual stream of adverse mental influence either. Where is the place where ailments are not discussed, and where is medical advice not given to people who talk about themselves? And all these people talk endlessly about themselves. Where is the household that is free from jealousy? The comments of the family on the treatment, their persistent curiosity to find out what passes at the interviews, are just as detrimental as the talk between patients in an institution, and on the whole they are harder to stop. The doctor in an institution, if alive to the danger, can read the riot act from time to time; he can do very little with the relatives, who if the patient is living at home may be hostile to him, because they feel that the patient should become a well and co-operative person much more quickly than is probably happening.

It is not quite germane here, but the further question arises whether such an institution should be a pleasant place or not. It seemed sometimes that the Cassel Hospital was too pleasant. For people who have been accustomed to luxury and beautiful gardens the matter was of little moment; indeed such people would not stay long enough if the standard of comfort were too low. But for people unaccustomed to these things there was a danger. The Cassel Hospital was apt to become Enchanted Ground in which pilgrims fall asleep, and so never get to the Celestial City towards which they should never cease to be striving. This is a hard thing to say but it has often been grossly evident.

The next point of contact which must be considered is what is often rather grandly termed occupational therapy. It is a matter of regret that such a word has crept into the terminology. If work or occupation were a remedy for the neuroses, the majority of the patients I see would never have fallen ill: the word seems to encourage the idea that neurosis is something which specially affects idle people, whereas it is true that neither idleness nor overwork are in themselves causal of neurosis. Either may be prominent in the history and probably both are important, but neither is an essential causal factor. It is, of course, true that people are better when they are occupied than when they are loafing; it is also true that most of these patients have acquired dreads about overstraining their brains or their hearts or their eyes or something, and so they have become afraid of work, and this is not really a subject for humour. I believe that most of them will work when they are cured. It is, however, helpful that there should be an officer among the staff who will encourage them to resume work, and teach them some interesting methods which they had not known before. The medical interviews provide the treatment, and if they do not, nothing will. The occupations officer encourages the return to work which the doctor makes possible, and prevents the idle hands being given work by a less desirable personage between the medical interviews.

Work has also a value in reintroducing the idea of co-operation. If the work is being done for the hospital, such as helping to keep the cricket pitch or the golf greens in order, its value is probably greater than if it is a piece of purely private work.

Associated with the work are the organized games, like cricket matches against neighbouring clubs, golf and tennis tournaments. By them the co-operative spirit is enhanced.

This then is a sketch of what modified the symptoms of these patients, and, as was said at the outset, it is the doctor who does most of the modification. If he is to get most of the credit he must also be prepared to explain why he failed if the patient did badly.

III

FOUNDATIONS OF PROGNOSIS IN THE NEUROSES

It has been stated above that it is impossible to observe these patients without treating them, and it has been suggested that the amount of hope which the patient takes from the doctor is very potent in abolishing symptoms. It is not a long step to say that so long as a patient is under and has easy access to a doctor whom he trusts, so long particularly as this position is not threatened, so long as he thinks he will not be turned away soon, so long will he remain well. It is, of course, true that patients have relapses of symptoms while they are under care, but this will probably be because the pleasant position has in fact been threatened, or at least that its perfection has been threatened; the doctor has been unkind or negligent or something of that sort has happened. So potent is this position while it lasts that I have little doubt that if a doctor who has been accepted as a friend took a single patient—single so as not to introduce jealousy—and was able to look after and cherish that patient completely for an indefinite period, he would remain indefinitely well. In that particular case the prognosis would be absolutely good. But, of course, this experiment could not be carried out; the flesh and blood of no doctor could stand it. Prognosis then does not in the least depend on the condition of the patient while he is undergoing treatment. While I was yet in a very elementary stage of my own knowledge, while I believed in "nervous exhaustion", a patient was sent to me with an hysterical paralysis of her arm. She was rested and reassured, and in a few days the paralysis had disappeared. The reassurance at this stage of my development consisted in telling her that her nerve centres were tired but not damaged and that rest would soon put them right—a wholly hypothetical statement and probably doubly wrong; perhaps her nerve centres were damaged, perhaps she had disseminate sclerosis, and I am sure they were not tired. She did a six weeks' rest cure in accordance with custom. On the day she was due to leave, the arm became again totally paralysed; in which state she went away and I saw her no more. This is a gross example of the truth of the statement that the apparent condition during nearly all the treatment is no criterion of what will happen in the future. In view of this we must obtain the basis of our prognostic knowledge by finding out what has happened to these patients after they have been away from the supporting doctor for many months. When work was begun at Swaylands it was arranged that nothing should be published about the state of a patient at the time of discharge; but it was hoped that if a report were obtained every year from every patient who had left the hospital, in time a mass of material would be obtained which would lend itself to statistical treatment, and that thus there might emerge a statistically stated prognosis for the psychoneuroses, always bearing in mind the proviso that it would be a prognosis of these illnesses in patients whose cases had been modified one way or the other by residence at Swaylands. As originally hoped for these aspirations were never realized. A number of factors combined to defeat us.

One of these is the protean nature of the disease, which may seem to show us a patient suffering at one time from duodenal ulcer and at another time from heart disease. This difficulty is not in the least solved by the knowledge that the patient has or had a neurotic tendency; that is no reason why he should not also have an organic lesion. It might have been solved, or at least one would not have been so much in the dark, if personal contact with the patients had been possible after they had left the hospital, but this was rarely possible. Therefore, although the answers to our yearly enquiries were often of great value—for indeed this book is founded on these answers—they were often ambiguous. It is difficult to interpret answers of this sort. "I was well till a month ago, when I caught influenza; since then I have felt very weak, and my strength does not seem to return"; or again, "I was well till six weeks ago when I had a serious heart attack and have not felt well since." Reports like these may mean anything. They may mean on the one hand that the patient has had a physical illness from which he will recover presently, or that some serious organic disease has supervened, or, on the other hand, these reports may indicate that the patient is relapsing into neurosis. The matter may, of course, be cleared up next year, when the patient may write and say he is well. We can then be reasonably sure that the previous report recorded some passing physical illness, or nothing more than some very trivial psychological relapse. Such must occur as passing events to all the patients. They do in most people who are called normal. If, however, the next year's report is not favourable the interpretation of what has happened may be pure guess-work. If the patient says that his nerves are all right, but that his heart is still troubling him, that may obviously indicate either organic disease or functional relapse. There are certain conditions where one can of course be quite sure that the named disease is merely a cloak for functional relapse: thus if the patient complains of feeling not well, of exhaustion, of headaches and so forth, but adds that now luckily a doctor has at last found the cause of her repeated ill-health which will therefore soon disappear, and goes on to say that she is suffering from a displaced kidney or womb, one can be sure that she has relapsed into neurosis; but there are many conditions, which are reported, which may or may not be causal of widespread symptoms: suppurating sinuses, dental conditions and the like may certainly in certain people be causative of general symptoms, and in others may be merely the pegs on which neurotic symptoms can be hung. The reports then must sometimes have to be interpreted. It may be urged that the doctor in attendance would soon settle the difficulty: there are, however, certain factors which make his opinion not so valuable as might seem obvious. One man will call a state physical in origin, especially if there be a question of associated mild suppuration as in chronic sinusitis or apex abscess in teeth, which another certainly would not. This is an example of the difficulty of the various observers referred to at the beginning of this book, and of the difficulty of the specialist seeing always his own speciality. The doctor moreover may have got out of his own difficulties with a patient when psychotherapy has failed by saying that the heart is weak or the womb displaced. In saying this I am not criticizing him. He has heard the psychological explanation, and in the case of this particular patient he has found it barren. The theories that widespread symptoms can arise from suppuration, however mild, or reflexly from a displaced uterus are not inherently absurd nor impossible. At the moment they may seem less so to him than those of this psychopathology which has accomplished nothing.

Not only is neurosis capable of appearing in diverse forms, but the word probably covers a large number of conditions which differ in kind. It is as if we were trying to assess a prognosis for, say, all fevers, without being able to distinguish between typhoid and coryza, except to say that one seemed milder than the other. True, there are clinical classifications of the neuroses, but except that they differentiate the obsessive-compulsive neurosis clearly from the others, they are not very helpful or very sound. There is an analytical aetiological classification, but for non-analysts it is a sealed book. But it seems certain that at present we are lumping together a number of conditions which should be in separate categories.

Another kind of difficulty in obtaining facts from after histories is that the patients are sometimes made worse if they are asked about their health. Sometimes the wife or the husband of a patient has written begging us to send no more letters of enquiry. "My husband", wrote one, "is always perfectly well except for about a month after he receives your annual letter of enquiry." Another patient wrote about herself: "Trying to tell a person how you are, often means introspection and reviewing symptoms which is a very evil process in cases like mine." It may be granted that these two patients were not completely well, that their tendency to neurosis was still present, and that we can be quite sure that they will probably relapse under strain, so that in a sense we do know the prognosis in them, viz. that it is precarious. But that is not quite the whole truth. The man of whom the first letter was written was very much better; his wife was very pleased with what had been done for him; he was quite well and easy to live with when he was left alone, and he had not been that before he came under care. There are a number of physical illnesses where recovery is not absolutely complete, but where the patient becomes well except under some special adverse condition, and to know this is an important part of our knowledge of prognosis.

Here, however, we touch on another difficulty in the study of prognosis. Disease processes may result in complete recovery, in partial recovery where the patient is usually nearly well, in chronic disease or in death; it is particularly difficult to assess the value of partial recovery; and yet we must always try to do so. For the moment we must content ourselves by noting that recovery to the extent indicated above may take place, and that it is an important thing to achieve. In the case of this particular patient he had passed through a strain. He had had a love affair with someone and his wife had been severe about it. The thing was over but they had needed someone outside the household to help to readjust matters. It is easy to see how my annual letter might stir up ill-feeling, and that perhaps the husband was upset because the wife was reminded of the past.

There are other reasons why these enquiries should sometimes do harm in patients who have been patched rather than cured. Every patient with neurosis has sought to be supported by somebody. This is true of any patient with any illness, but the desire for support in nervous patients is altogether beyond what is found in physical illness, is indeed, in part at least, the cause of there being an illness at all. In physical disease this desire accompanies the illness, in neurosis it precedes it; part of the cure must always consist in teaching the patient to stand on his own feet. Though he may have learnt to do this, the desire for support has not necessarily been abolished, and the interested enquiry on the part of the doctor, his late supporter, may well whet the patient's appetite for further support, all the more that he has in a sense been starved of it by having kept well. It will be understood that no suggestion is being made that he says consciously: "Let me be a little ill to get further support."

That interest of this kind may often prolong or cause a return of symptoms has been shown to a further extent in patients who have relapsed soon after they were written to, who soon afterwards sought readmission because of the prolongation of this relapse and who did not get well till they were told plainly to stand on their own feet. For example, a woman was admitted to the hospital in a state of physical and mental collapse. For years she had been terrorized by religion, and had been the servant of a committee who had also frightened her a great deal. The religious terror was due to a conflict between religion and sex. It was two years before she recovered confidence sufficiently to face the world again. She did so, however, and obtained a post. She kept in touch with the hospital, and paid regular visits and always had a large number of complaints. She seemed to be slowly losing ground and was re-admitted for a month three years after her discharge. This time she felt no better when she went away. She left because she would have lost her post if she had not. For a few months she continued to come regularly as an out-patient, and then it was inconvenient for me to continue seeing her. She made violent protests, but it was thought that in all probability her symptoms were being sustained by the desire to be supported, and the refusal to see her was continued. Since then she has kept decidedly better and gone on with her work. She was, I believe, unable to drop the support so long as it was offered. But she knew enough and was better enough not to need it. Symptoms had to be provided again, unconsciously of course; so long as she was coming to be seen, the visits had to be justified. I think that there is no doubt that over attention can vitiate the prognosis.

Of course this patient's case was only patched up, and many critics will think that there should be no merely patched up cases, that anything less than complete cure is failure: but, as in other branches of medicine, we shall often have to be content with partial recovery, and recognize that people with partial recovery cannot be treated with the indifference that can be meted out to the completely recovered.

In this matter of the dangers attendant on a follow-up in nervous patients I am not alone in my views. Professor Adolf Meyer in the course of conversation expressed to me exactly the same opinion. At one time he made it a rule to see patients a year after they had left his care; he was informed so often that this visit had been unhelpful that he gave it up altogether.

There is a criticism of Janet's on this subject about which a word must be said, viz. Whose report are we going to take, the patient's or someone else's? For example, the patient may write in a pessimistic mood and some relative may report that things are much better. This may represent one of these temporary fallings back, which have been spoken of already. If, however, a discrepancy of this sort is reported year after year we shall probably decide that the patient knows more about it than the relative; we cannot, however, be sure, for, as hinted above, this patient may be one of those who immediately feels ill if asked how he is, and who yet feels well at all other times. The relatives on the other hand may have taken up the attitude that the patient has got to be better at all costs, and they may be refusing him the right to be ill.

We have also to consider the opposite state of affairs—the patient may maintain he is well while the relatives may think he is not. This is, of course, common enough in the psychoses but it is not psychotic patients who are being discussed at present. It is common enough too in the untreated or uncured patients with anorexia nervosa. In examples of this disease we shall decide easily against the patient's view. But here is something quite different. For instance, a lady with chronic exhaustion of severe type of long standing was admitted to the hospital in 1921. She has not been exhausted since but has always reported herself well. She has been seen by the writer several times since then, not on account of her health, and to him she has appeared as a woman who has remained quite well. Her husband, however, complains bitterly that there is now no peace in the house, and he is, or rather was, sure that she was doing far too much, so much too much that soon she would break down again. As thirteen years have gone by without her doing so he is now not so sure, but still he says that the amount she does is as unhealthy as was her former lethargy. He himself is a not very energetic person, and does not like the house to be always having a committee meeting in it. But who is to say who is right?

It seems that the safest rule is to take the patient's word. Dubois pointed out long ago that no one but the patient was in any position to say whether a neurosis was better or not. Many relatives will insist that there is nothing wrong; many doctors also. They will urge the patient to pull himself together. But in the end it is only the patient who can decide. The fact that there was an illness at all depended wholly on his saying that there was one. There were in an overwhelming majority of these cases no objective signs of illness at any period: it is, therefore, absurd for anyone else to say at any subsequent time that the patient is now well unless he himself agrees. This does not invalidate the worth of the letter from the lady who said that her husband was ill only when we wrote; for she was professing to report him. When we wrote he complained of illness to her; when we did not he was cheerful. It is, of course, possible that the enquiry made her ill too, as has been suggested above.

It might be thought from all these considerations that the only conclusion to be drawn was that a report of any kind was either so fallacious or so undesirable to obtain that we might as well give up the attempt to get them at all. Apart from the conclusions to be obtained in pure mathematics, fallacies of this kind will be met in every human enquiry. We have to be aware that these fallacies are present, and come to our conclusions cautiously and intelligently. If we do so we shall usually obtain useful information and get many reports which will enable us to form some views about prognosis in these disorders.

At the Cassel Hospital, however, the consideration of these fallacies made us alter our plans. It was felt that as the years went on the chances of error became greater and greater, and it was decided to put a period to the number of years during which an enquiry was addressed to any individual; after five years that particular patient was not to be written to any more.[1] This, however, did not prevent a considerable number of former patients from writing spontaneously, and of course their reports were recorded. On the whole these were patients who had done well, and who usually about Christmas time wished once more to signify their gratitude. It was recognized that these letters were of no statistical value, for usually those who have not done well do not write spontaneously unless they have some grievance of a paranoid kind, when they may write very often indeed. But patients of that kind have been few. The number of letters received then which record success is much greater than the number recording failure. But as I read these letters year after year it seemed that though of no statistical value they were shedding light on an aspect of our problems which will be stated in a moment. This light seemed so clear

[1] It is now a matter of regret that this was done. When we dropped some patients and tried to pick them up many years later we got no replies. It seems probable that if we had continued to write each year, we should not have lost as many as we did, as appears on the table on p. 79. Changes of address would have been more frequently notified, and fewer would have felt that we had lost interest in them, which might, of course, make them uninterested in us.

that I determined to depart from our second plan and revert to our first, and circularize all the patients once more. There were excluded from this enquiry the definitely psychotic patients, and also those who had asked that no more enquiries should be made. I wished to see whether the idea which had been impressed on me by the spontaneous writers would be borne out by those who had stopped writing to us when we stopped writing to them.

IV

FEASIBILITY OF TREATMENT

Some of the patients who had written year after year claimed to be "absolutely cured", that is they claimed to be free from symptoms, and to be able to deal with the difficulties of life by the method of trying to overcome them, and not by any method of retreat into illness. Their claim seemed to throw light on an important series of questions, viz.

(i) Whether a permanent beneficial mental change can be brought about in anyone as regards what may be called the neurotic tendency.

(ii) Whether this may be—if it does happen—the result of psychotherapy or is merely spontaneous and incapable of regulation.

(iii) Whether, if it can be the result of treatment, that treatment must partake of the nature of a deep analysis or whether conversations conducted at the conscious levels are ever sufficient to cause permanent change of the kind desired.

There are those who maintain that we cannot by any form of therapy induce a permanent character change in anyone. It is admitted that apparently such changes do occur from time to time, but that they are spontaneous; that all we can do is to ward off adverse influences which might impede the development of such changes. It is understood that I am talking of neuroses and not of psychoses. In the functional psychoses it is, of course, a matter of everyday observation that patients recover spontaneously, and probably in no other way, though of course no one suggests that these changes are permanent; they may be, but there is no feeling that anything fundamental has changed, only that there has been a change of phase in an individual who has not really changed his temperament. No one claims to have done anything in particular to bring about such a change. It is true that indirectly one can help: one can prevent a mild melancholic from being psychoanalysed, a procedure which if attempted usually does harm; in other ways it is likely that we can prevent patients from being made worse or from having their cases prolonged. But it is not of these matters that I am speaking, but of character changes which may be brought about in neurotics, though here again there are psychiatrists who maintain that there is no fundamental difference between psychotics and neurotics. I have detailed many such differences elsewhere and shall not do so again here. The question, however, whether in like fashion large changes take place spontaneously in neurotics is not easily answered. My own view is that they never take place unless there has been either some fundamental change brought about artificially in the environment, or some equally fundamental change brought about also artificially in the patient's way of thinking. There are some instances where it would seem at first sight that the doctor had done little more than he does in the case of the psychotic, viz. protect him till he is better, but closer examination will reveal a profound difference. For example, a man of forty-four came under care in 1925. He was an apparent homosexual, and was very distressed at the emergence into consciousness of some very crude ideas during the last few years. He had been told by those from whom he had sought help, that he had a filthy mind; this had made him contemplate suicide, which, however, had remained no more than an intention. His illness was a depression of neurotic character dependent on his scruples about abnormal sex, and about entertaining sexual phantasies even unwillingly. At that time I thought he was a true constitutional homosexual, and I sympathized with him sincerely in his affliction. I listened to him while he poured out his grievances, which were directed against God and his fellow men, the former for making him as he was, the latter for their brutal lack of sympathy. In eight or nine weeks his homosexuality had disappeared and he had become heterosexual. At the same time he became well and cheerful. He has remained normally heterosexual ever since. I made at no time any suggestions that he would become different sexually; of that I am sure for I thought he would not lose his homosexuality. I did nothing but take care of him. Now in what way is this not as spontaneous as the recovery of a manic-depressive? There was in this case a complete change in mental environment. Instead of living in an atmosphere of blame he lived in one of approval, for he had done nothing for which the most puritanical could find reason for censure, and he was told that every day. The symptoms had been wholly mental; no incontinent act had been attempted. He had been simply horrified at the whole train of homosexual thinking to which he had been subjected apparently against his wishes or will. To him it had seemed like demoniac possession. When he was no longer bullied his personality could develop. I do not think he would have become more adult sexually in a hostile atmosphere—one feels that the manic-depressive will get better in time in any atmosphere. Because of the change which had been created in the environment he allowed his thoughts free expression, and by doing so achieved a change in his ways of thinking, so that there occurred in him a very large change of values with regard to many things. There occurred therefore two things to bring about cure, change of environment and change of mind. This case was described at length in the *Journal of Neurology and Psychopathology*, 1927, p. 313.

Another patient may be quoted who seemed to show spontaneous recovery. He was admitted to the hospital in the summer of 1922 (Group I, Table I, Case No. 7, p. 114). He was apparently cured so easily that no one thought for one moment that the treatment he had received at the hospital had anything to do with it, and viewed superficially it seemed as spontaneous a cure as that of a manic-depressive. Such apparently meaningless cures were from time to time reported in the yellow press for some years after the war. A man would be cured of dumbness on hearing some one sing "Home Sweet Home". It is probable that some factor of the kind to be described presently, unknown to the journalist, was at the bottom of such cures. The patient in question had suffered from pains in the back and paraplegia for eighteen months. He was unable to walk or stand. Many doctors during this period had explained to him that the condition was functional, and some at least of these explanations had been made very kindly. None had had the slightest effect. It is usual that if a purely persuasional treatment has failed once or twice it will fail always in that individual case. The resistances of the patient soon become absolutely proof against any further explanations or suggestions. Yet after a single talk of the same kind at Swaylands this man was walking about quite easily, and in a week he was playing cricket. Since then he has reported every year that he kept quite well till 1929—as is shown in the tables. After 1929 he was not written to till this year, when he reported that he had kept well all the time. Here then is a man who showed gross hysterical symptoms for eighteen months, who became and has remained well for thirteen years after half an hour's conversation of the same kind as had been given fruitlessly many times before. No doctor, however enthusiastic about his own powers of persuasion, could think that he had effected so gigantic a mental change of a lasting nature in so short a space of time in the case of so unpromising a patient. No doubt many can claim to have cured hysterics of their gross disabilities at a single sitting. But I do not think that they would find that such patients would keep well for the next thirteen years from such brief treatment unless something else had happened. In truth no change whatever had been made in this patient's mentality; a few weeks later there was a threatened relapse which was averted, but not by making a mental change. What had produced the change in this man was that his environment was altered totally. He was a workman who had "strained" his back in a garage, and for eighteen months he was engaged in trying to get the maximum of compensation. The case was settled the day he came into Swaylands—hence his easy persuadability there. What happened some weeks later was the discovery that he had been black-listed by the local employers; he knew that therefore he would never get a job again; he knew also that his compensation money would not last for ever. However, just as he was settling into a state of depression it was suggested that he might acquire a small business of his own. He was apparently a clever workman, and a small wayside garage for running repairs was suggested. This fitted in with his abilities and he has managed this place successfully ever since, and has kept his health. It is clear how different this is from the spontaneous recovery of the manic-depressive. Here recovery followed at once when the illness was no longer useful, when the circumstances were better for him. There was nothing spontaneous about this recovery when one examined closely what had happened.

In the manic-depressive it is of no avail to change anything. In the typical cases the patient gets better when the attack comes to an end. In the really typical cases one never gets the impression that one has done anything. I have chosen two cases where the diagnosis is plain, but there are others where it is less simple; it is these examples which give colour to the statement of some psychiatrists that there is no real difference between the psychotic and the neurotic. For example, a patient of forty-five was admitted to hospital in 1930 with symptoms of depression, insomnia and retardation, all of which had followed a phase which was perhaps too hopeful and optimistic, in which he had lost money. It was thought that he was suffering from a manic-depressive psychosis, and no very active therapy was undertaken. He was tired and therefore was kept in bed. After about ten days when visiting him I found he was solving a crossword puzzle, and I judged that this was a sign of improvement and said so. To my surprise he said he had been doing them all the time, which did not seem to me to be compatible with the amount of retardation he showed. I revised my diagnosis, and began to give strong therapeutic conversations. He improved almost at once, and in ten days or so was well. For a time I believed I had been mistaken in my original diagnosis, and thought that I had, in fact, helped a person suffering from an anxiety neurosis. But a few months later he relapsed into a very depressed retarded state from which he did not emerge for months. I did not see this phase but I believe now that his recovery when I saw him was spontaneous, that he was, in fact, a sufferer from psychosis.

These matters have been dwelt on because, if what has been said above is true, we shall treat these disorders in different fashion from what we should if we believed that there was no fundamental difference between neurosis and psychosis. Physicians who hold the view that the conditions are the same might say that as we never see a patient suffering from psychosis without treating him somehow, if we are going to claim successful therapeutic intervention in the one case, we ought not to be so shy of doing so in the other.

At the risk of being tedious it may be useful to review this problem as it occurs in physical illness. Both syphilis and pulmonary tuberculosis, for example, are amenable to treatment, but the principles on which the two are treated are very different. The syphilologist throughout a long course of treatment tends to be consciously active; some indeed hold that he is excessively so, but even those who think that treatment may be overdone are active. They feel that they are attacking the disease. It is otherwise as a rule with him who treats the phthisic. The treatment will also take a long time, but at no time will the doctor feel that he is attacking the disease. He exploits rest to its utmost limit even when he is so very active that he induces a pneumothorax; he does this for the purpose of increasing rest, and perhaps to limit the absorption of toxins. When he allows exercise, it is only after he has satisfied himself that the patient can afford the expenditure of so much more energy. The principle of treatment is not in the least to attack the disease, but everywhere to save the patient so that he may have strength enough to overcome the disease. There are some who use tuberculin, but I omit them from consideration here without prejudice, for it is the others who illustrate the principle. Now it is certain that the tuberculosis specialist is treating his patient as much as the syphilologist is his, but he is looking for spontaneous recovery for which the syphilologist is not looking. Without aid and guidance the phthisic would probably go down hill.

This forms a real parallel to our problem. The psychotic needs care; if badly cared for he may get worse, as may the patient with tubercle or typhoid; and therefore in a sense he is capable of receiving treatment and does indeed receive it, but it is rather in a negative sense. The *nil nocere* principle is important in this kind of treatment. But in those illnesses where active treatment can be given, and where the only hope of lasting recovery lies in activity, we can hear and have heard too much about *nil nocere*.

It is clear also that progressive medicine must always be striving to get illnesses out of the passive into the active list. The successful pulmonectomies are an example of this. Perhaps in some years all that has just been said about tubercle will be obsolete, and indeed this is quite likely.

It is obvious then that the man who believes that neurosis and psychosis are much the same thing will not make a vigorous attack on either illness, and that he will be prone to criticize treatment which sometimes makes people worse. In distinction to the surgeon the physician is prone to condemn treatment which carries with it an element of risk; but in truth every system of treatment which is of the active sort carries risk: it is only purely expectant treatment which is devoid of risk to the doctor's reputation, though even it may be risky for the patient.

It has been said that all talk of what does or does not produce recovery in the neuroses is vitiated by the fact that we have no controls. This charge is laid against many kinds of treatment in many diseases. In acute disease it is not easy for a physician who believes he has a remedy to withhold it from half of his patients in an epidemic; and yet by doing so he could probably settle the question whether his remedy was a potent one or not, for if he had enough cases he would get an average and the characteristics of one epidemic are fairly constant. In chronic disorder, as we have seen, the matter is more difficult. We are not dealing with similars as we are in the single epidemic. There are natural remissions which may occur just when the remedy has been given and so on.

Notwithstanding all these difficulties I hope to show presently that in the neuroses if a sufficiently long history is taken, especially if this history is pursued forwards as well as backwards, we shall be able to collect a mass of evidence which will afford almost complete proof that a particular remedy did bring about recovery in certain patients.

V

THE KINDS OF TREATMENT NECESSARY

I do not propose to offer further proof that patients suffering from neurosis are capable of having their disabilities removed by treatment, or that that treatment must be mental. The question whether a permanent mental change can be induced will be deferred, and we shall now proceed to investigate the important question, viz. whether deep analysis is necessary to effect lasting change for the better or whether there are cases where something much less heroic is sufficient. I am afraid we cannot escape considering the question at some length of what kind of treatment is necessary if it is true that prognosis does in these illnesses depend almost wholly on treatment. No one doubts that patients derive benefit, apparent complete cure indeed, from all sorts of treatments which, whether they are manifestly mental treatments or not, are certainly not analytical. By no stretch of language can treatment by massage or electricity or osteopathy be thought of as analytical, though, of course, it may be and probably is mental. The patients themselves will confirm the idea that the treatment has been beneficial, and say that they know that it has done them good. But it is held in certain quarters that such improvement will almost certainly be evanescent, that, as it depends wholly on a rapport which has been established between the doctor and the patient, the latter will surely relapse when the former disappears. The improvement according to this school of thought depends only on the patient's desire to please the doctor because of a dependent love situation which has arisen between them, resembling that between children and parents, not necessarily of course a conscious dependent love situation. A short treatment, therefore, is apt to be disastrous because it usually takes some months at least for this hypothetical love situation to be resolved satisfactorily. A recent authoritative view on the unsatisfactory nature of non-analytical treatment may be quoted:

> An obsession proved to be a superficial indication of an unconscious problem which had kept a man from doing efficient work and realizing

his professional potentialities. If these fundamental problems were relieved, the presenting symptoms automatically disappeared; if only the symptom was helped, what importance was that to the total life of the patient? Less, the psychoanalyst's experience taught, than the value of an ice-cap to abdominal pain when an etiological process in the appendix is neglected. It is for this reason that the interest of modern psychoanalysts in the presenting symptom is chiefly that it indicates the presence of an unconscious mental problem. Though they concede that hypnosis and other suggestive methods of psychotherapy are often the best expedients for quick and temporary effects, they prefer this laborious and time consuming method of psychoanalysis for obtaining a lasting amelioration of the neurosis itself. (*Facts and Theories of Psychoanalysis*, by Ives Hendrick, M.D., 1934.)

It is also said that in any event it is only in extremely trivial cases that benefit of any kind will be observed by non-analytical treatments. This last sentence, which is one that I have heard often, does sound as if it had meaning, but as may come out later, it is doubtful whether in truth it has much. It is easy to call any case trivial if the treatment which was associated with recovery was simple. It might be a better criterion of triviality to know the amount and especially duration of suffering which that particular illness caused, and what would have happened had that treatment not been given. A whitlow is a trivial thing if a knife is inserted into the proper spot early enough, and that is a simple operation: the failure to do it may turn the condition into a very grave one.

The matter has, however, often been put to me thus: you must make up your mind whether you are going to have a short treatment, mostly on the conscious level, or with only slight scratching beneath it, with temporary benefit, or a longer course in which you will delve deeply into the unconscious with lasting benefit. This is a statement which has been made to me by several analysts, and always in the tone of one who is enunciating a self-evident proposition. I believe that enormous numbers of analysts believe it to be true, and the ground they base it on will be dealt with later. It is connected with their unanimous belief that all neurosis depends on repression into an unconscious, that there can be no neurosis without repression. I had myself hoped that this doctrine is wrong, and that it might be possible by comparatively short courses of psychotherapy to effect permanent beneficial change in a certain number of patients, that long analytical treatments would not be necessary for every patient suffering from even severe neurosis. For if prolonged treatment is necessary for more than a few patients, the outlook for psychotherapy as a practical proposition is black indeed. It is admitted that the neuroses are widespread. If the remedy is complete psychoanalysis, relief can be afforded to a tiny fraction only of the sufferers. In the interests of patients and of psychology as a thing of any use as a medical instrument and not as a mere subdivision of the game of philosophy, we must see if we can find a short therapy, and not reject it on purely theoretical grounds before we have tried it.

In point of fact I think that most of our patients had some analysis: there were always some things which had not been conscious before treatment, which were brought into consciousness. Although our debt to Freud is great for making us more aware of this than we were, this is not Freudian analysis. I have been told too often quite pleasantly by my Freudian friends, of whom I have many, that I know nothing about analysis, not to know that these scratchings of mine below consciousness are not Freudian analysis. The sort of analysis we practised did not take up much time.

For some years now I have felt that I held the proofs which would justify my hope. It has seemed to me, from what the letters of certain patients already referred to have contained, that it is eminently possible to effect a radical change in the mental outlook of certain people by a comparatively short and simple therapy, and that the changes which have been brought about in this way are accompanied by what appears to be a permanent improvement in their health. These letters then have told us not only of the possibility of lasting cure, but also of this being accomplished in a short time.

No one would assert because an individual patient had lost his symptoms and had remained well for a number of years, for any number of years indeed, that his recovery had necessarily any relation to his treatment. We have just admitted that all sorts of treatment will be followed by recovery, and though we have no information to speak of about the probable duration of many of these recoveries, it is possible that it might be quite long in a considerable number of examples. It is likely that, in a number of people, neurosis of so grave a kind as to drive a patient to the doctor is only episodic. There are, of course, many neurotics who spend their lives having one treatment after another; but there are many grades, and there are also some patients in whom neurosis occurs only rarely, only during periods of excessive stress. There is a kind of person where every difficulty in life is met by the flight into illness, and there are those who will stand up to nearly everything, for whom it may require about four years of warfare before they will break down. Thus a soldier, who came under my care in November 1918, had been in the old regular army, had gone out to France in 1914, had never been ill or wounded, and had therefore been on active front line service all the time. He broke down in September 1918, and was greatly ashamed of himself for doing so. It is safe to say of such a man as of many others that it required gigantic and prolonged emotional stress before he gave way. Now if a patient belonging to this tough type acquires neurosis because of some extraordinary strain, the disorder may not disappear as soon as the strain has been relieved. It may persist because the patient has come to believe that his condition is a serious one, because he has lost hope about it. Any treatment which is novel, and which is administered by a doctor who inspires hope, may cure such a person, and cure him permanently. I have assumed that such a one needs a large quantity of stress for neurosis to be evoked, and if the stress were caused by warfare, he may easily finish his life without encountering another great war, and therefore never again be thrown into neurosis. We want then some criterion to enable us to judge whether a given treatment has really been curative, i.e. will enable the patient to stand against future stress, or has acted only by giving a moment of faith and hope to a despairing man. Such a cure may be obviously as permanent as if the treatment had been in itself an efficacious agent, and there are some who say that it does not matter how these people are got well so long as they are got well. But it does matter that we should know whether the thing was merely a piece of luck or not. For if it was just good luck we shall not be able to repeat it at will. We shall be able to do so only in very favourable circumstances. In early days, while I was yet groping for an understanding of these illnesses, some one told me that a patient with insomnia could be sent to sleep if the nurse would sponge his spine with very hot water at the time when he should go to sleep. This was accordingly done, and on nearly every patient on which it was tried it acted, as they say, like a charm, which indeed it was, for it was not rational but pure magic. On the third night it was seldom followed by sleep, and in all cases where it failed once it never produced sleep again. It was therefore an accidental thing. Temporarily hope had been given, but it depended on nothing save the word of the doctor. Now it mattered very much that we should drop this so-called remedy and never use it on anybody, because when it failed it threw the patient into a greater despair than if it had never been used. He felt that what had happened was what had happened to every remedy that he had tried; after a little they no longer acted. This is indeed one of the main objections to irrational faith curing. If it fails the patient is much worse off than if he had never tried it. The same objection does not apply to an open faith cure, where there is no concealment of the aim of restoring the patient's confidence in himself. However, notwithstanding all the pitfalls of *post* and *propter hoc* with which this subject is riddled, it is, I think, possible to demonstrate that there is a therapy which is directly curative, which is capable of repetition and which is simple.

If we take a group, each member of which came under care at the same period of time, each of which was subjected to the same principle of treatment, each of which had the same doctor, and if we find that a considerable proportion maintain year after year that their whole outlook on life was changed, and their health altered for the better exactly coincidently in time with the administration of the treatment, and the mental alteration, it is difficult to ascribe the recovery of the whole number who did change in this way to spontaneous happenings or to lucky coincidences, and to deny the efficacy of the treatment, though, of course, one cannot say for certain that it was not all due to one or the other. If, moreover, we can repeat this series year after year with other patients, the likelihood that it is a real therapy is increased.

Before we come to conclusions, however, there are certain precautions to be taken. As has already been foreshadowed, we have to bear in mind that it is easy, unless one is on guard, to include in the series which is being examined patients suffering from one of the manifold forms of the manic-depressive psychosis, but it is hoped that with respect to the cases which are about to be reported they are sufficiently clear cut to make it certain that we are not dealing with anything but neurosis. We have to bear in mind also that there are those who maintain that there is no real distinction between neurosis and psychosis; and indeed the fact that both conditions may be present simultaneously or successively in the same individual makes such a view possible. In the reports of the Cassel Hospital there have been published examples where the removal of gross hysterical symptoms had been followed by depression so profound as to make us watch the patient on account of the danger of suicide. Some of these are described on p. 102 *et seq.* But while such examples are to be met, it also happens that there is a large number, indeed a majority of patients, in whom there is no real difficulty in assigning their cases on purely clinical grounds to one category or the other, and in whom there is no tendency to pass subsequently into the other category, as has been borne out by our follow-up; see the tables in the latter half of the book.

VI

REPORTS FROM PATIENTS

With all these precautionary points we are now prepared to consider the replies to the letters of enquiry which were sent during the year 1934 to nearly all old patients, with the exceptions stated on p. 23, so far as we could trace them. Of these replies I am selecting half a dozen for special examination. These were all from patients who were admitted at the same period, June, July or August 1921. They are all patients who did absolutely well; and when that is said, what is meant is that each of them has maintained that he has kept perfectly well during these thirteen years. He has not been allowed to have any intercurrent illness if he were to come into this category, because in the last resort it is, as has been suggested, quite impossible to distinguish for certain between physical and mental illness, when one is dealing with a report only. Not to have been ill for thirteen years is a hard test; some might say it was impossible. I think myself that it is likely that some of them had at least a cold in the head, but they did not report any illness though they were asked specifically about their health. If they had illnesses they must have been so trifling that they had forgotten them altogether, and as a rule neurotic patients do not minimize their intercurrent ailments. They were therefore no longer seeking the excuse of an illness to account for any failures in overcoming difficulties.

This high standard has not been followed absolutely in all subsequent cases. It has been maintained for these six because it was necessary to demonstrate what can be done. They are by no means the only examples in which it has happened. In other instances, as will be seen from the tables, patients may have sent one or two less good reports, but if they have recovered themselves again they are allowed to be classified as "well", if they report steadily that they feel well. But no one has been called well in any one year unless he himself said that he was well in that year. A glance at the tables at the end will make clear what is meant.

These letters and reports must be given verbally unaltered if they are to carry conviction. There are some sentences in them, the publication of which might seem to argue a great want of modesty on my part. Certain things in the way of praise have been said which any decent person would wish to keep to himself. Yet if this were attended to, there would be such weakening of the reports that their value would be diminished, and I shall therefore quote them without further apology. I do not wish it to be said that these letters have been tinkered with in any way. Here then are certain reports from patients who were in the hospital during the summer of 1921, and who have remained well since. The letters are not necessarily complete. Irrelevant news has been omitted, but where the letter reports about the patient's health no jot or tittle has been altered.

1921, *Table I, Case No.* 4*.

A lady of forty-eight was admitted in June 1921 complaining of exhaustion, the fear that she might kill her mother or herself, terrors of all sorts, dyspepsia and neuralgic pains which came on when anyone looked at her. These symptoms had been present for four years; she had had three rest cures in nursing homes and other treatments. Each rest cure had benefited her greatly, but after each relapse had been speedy. She was sure that her symptoms were due to nervous exhaustion, as was proved to her own satisfaction at least by the invariable improvement which rest had brought about in the past. She was equally sure that she had never rested long enough to accumulate enough energy for ordinary purposes. Each doctor, she believed, had made her get up and take exercise before her reserves of energy had been filled up, and had stopped the treatment when she had acquired only enough energy to live as it were from hand to mouth, with nothing to fall back on. At the last rest cure before she came to Swaylands she had felt extremely well, and the day before she came away the doctor had unwisely induced her to walk about five miles, with the consequence that she must have emptied her reserve, and therefore next day in the train going home she became utterly exhausted. She regarded herself exactly as a storage battery. No one had let her

* This and similar references are to the tables at the end of the book.

stay long enough on the charger, and everybody had allowed a larger discharge to be drawn off than her battery could stand. This view is a very common one among patients. This lady determined that the same mistake should not be repeated, and she proposed to stay in bed for eighteen months or thereabouts, by which time she thought that she would have acquired enough energy to last her for some years at least. In actual fact she was not kept in bed at Swaylands at all. She stayed in the hospital for five weeks only, during the last three of which she was engaged in very vigorous exercise indeed, walking on one occasion twenty miles in one day without any undue sense of fatigue. During this period she had interviews which totalled about twelve hours. The treatment consisted first in taking her history, which included, of course, an enquiry into her home environment. She was then told that the analogy of the storage battery, though commonly repeated, was entirely unproved and was probably false, that there was no exhaustion in her case, but that, for certain reasons, she herself was unwittingly withholding her energy, and thus acquiring the sensation of fatigue. From her history she was told that it was obvious that her symptoms were caused by a desire to escape from her mother, whom she disliked, and it was pointed out how admirably these symptoms had achieved their purpose. It was, of course, made perfectly plain that she had been totally unaware of what she had been doing. A discussion was then entered on with her as to how she could get on better with that mother; the present plan of running away was obviously no solution of anything. She must either go back and face the situation, or say plainly that she could not or would not. The mother was in a state of senility, had often given way to furious outbursts of temper, and had even made some physical assaults on the patient. There would have been no disgrace if she had made up her mind that she could not go on with the case; the mother was probably certifiable, and certainly required the care of mental nurses. Our patient on due consideration decided to go home and take care of her mother, and as she went back with her eyes open she succeeded. She lived with her successfully till the mother died four years later, and it gave her immense satisfaction that she had done her duty. She has remained quite well since she left Swaylands. She had written only in answer to letters of enquiry, and I had not heard from her for six years till she was written to this year. In these earlier letters she had always described herself as well. This year she wrote:

> I am very happy and well and am a most fortunate woman in my surroundings. This does not mean that I never have qualms as I don't suppose that would be possible. Since my mother's death in 1925 I have not been tested in any way, but I think I should prove myself a worthy patient of Swaylands. It was a most lucky chance that brought me under your influence and which led to my cure. I hope you may be receiving many letters of gratitude from those of my day and since. It does not seem like thirteen years ago.

Commenting on this letter it does look as if a change had been brought about. First a change was effected when she herself recognized, after explanation, that ill-health had been brought about deliberately even if unconsciously because it had enabled her to escape from an extremely disagreeable old woman. It may be said that this was an explanation by means of the unconscious, a thing which I have tried to show was not always necessary. It was not, however, an exploration of the unconscious in the Freudian sense: it was didactic and according to the analysts you cannot get at the unconscious by teaching; it must well up from below; it did not get at the Freudian unconscious; at best it was a mere scratch of the surface. As soon as the patient had been instructed that symptoms could arise as a reaction to depressing thoughts she saw without difficulty what she had been doing.

Secondly, I think we may describe this change for the better as permanent. It is as permanent as anything we shall find in any department of medicine, reckoning merely by the time that has elapsed; but the tone of the letter manifests something which makes for permanency of recovery in the future. The patient obviously has not forgotten what the condition was on which her recovery depended. She says that she has not been tried since her mother's death. Clearly she has remembered that her nerve health depends on whether she stands up to trial or not, and we must remember that she was well tried for four long years till her mother died, and that she stood up to that.

Thirdly, it cannot be suggested that this change, this improvement depended at any time on the patient continuing to receive support from the doctor, for doctor and patient have been wholly out of touch for the last six years, during which the patient has been well. True, during all the time she was living with her trying mother, doctor and patient were in touch; i.e. once a year the doctor wrote a typewritten letter dictated to a secretary asking the patient how she was and she replied that she was well. This, I think, could hardly have satisfied the needs of any love affair or any state of dependence, however unconscious. I think, indeed, that the improvement never did depend on any transference, on any rapport between the two, but that it depended on the fact that here was an intelligent woman having the emotional reaction of the sense of fatigue whenever she was confronted with difficulty because it helped her to evade difficulty. She reacted strongly, and, like most people who have not considered the nature of emotional bodily reactions, she thought that the feeling of fatigue must mean the fact of fatigue. Like everybody else she believed that the proper treatment of fatigue is rest. Of course it suited her to believe these views, but although there must have been this strong desire to believe them, there was not the smallest difficulty in getting her to believe the opposite once it was put to her. Her sense of duty, once she envisaged it, was stronger than her desire to run away. Her tendency to believe that she really was exhausted was enhanced by everyone in authority whom she came across. Invariably she was sent to bed to get rid of exhaustion, which is, of course, one way of telling her to be very careful not to overdo things. All these things were altered as soon as intelligible reasons were given.

Indeed it seems likely that the whole doctrine of the rapport, of the transference, has arisen out of prolonged treatment, which therefore causes that very danger which was supposed by theorists to necessitate the long and invalidate the short treatment. The fear that prolonged treatment may cause such a dependence so that breaking off of treatment becomes always a hazardous proceeding is a real one; it has often occurred to me how desirable it would be if possible to end a treatment before this state became established.

Next there is the question whether this case was a trivial one. It was easily remedied. In that sense it was trivial. A whitlow was taken a short time ago as an example of a trivial illness, easily cured if properly treated. This lady's illness had, however, crippled her for four years, and unless it had been properly treated it would have gone on indefinitely. No other treatment could have been followed by a better or more permanent result. That is obvious, and it would be a proper question to ask whether a full analytic treatment would have been followed by as good a one. Even if, which is not certain, analysis would have been followed by as good a result, surely we shall have done much to solve the problem of the neuroses if we recognize that there are cases where a short treatment is as good as a long one, and that we should foster these short treatments and not decry them because they conflict with cherished theories.

Finally, I do not think that anyone could maintain that this lady suffered from a psychosis and that her recovery was spontaneous and unrelated to the treatment. Every time there was a holiday from the disagreeable environment she became well; as soon as return to it became imminent she relapsed. When she saw what it was all about she ceased to relapse. The history bears no resemblance to that of a recurrent psychosis with exhaustion.

The details of technique which were followed in a case of this sort were described fully by me in *The Common Neuroses* and they need not be repeated here.

1921, *Table I, Case No.* 38.

Let us now examine a kind of case where the response to persuasion is usually considered rather hopeless. I should myself have thought such a patient quite hopeless to help by this method until I came in contact with this one, and I should have considered that some analysis would have been necessary. Circumstances arose, however, which precluded any analytical approach, and it was a question of helping by persuasional methods or of doing nothing at all.

The patient was a man of forty with severe claustrophobia and agoraphobia. He was admitted in June 1921. He was a very religious man, who had been unable to attend his place of worship for many years, and it was this disability especially for which he sought aid. Further, he was unable with any comfort to follow the profession of architect for which he had been trained, as he could never be sure whether he could go out on any particular day or not. He was, therefore, unable to make an appointment. Although he had done no regular work for sixteen years, odd jobs had been sent to him by a colleague in the same profession, such as copying plans, a thing he could do at home. His illness had been present more or less all his life. As a child he had been very nervous; he had been subject to fainting attacks for the last sixteen years. Gradually he had become more and more nervous, till now he was a virtual prisoner in his brother's house. The latter wrote that "at times my brother goes through a martyrdom of fear, though he tries to fight down his troubles which he knows are phantoms".

Whatever else can be said of this case no one could say that it was trivial. It had existed to some extent from childhood, say for at least thirty-five years. For sixteen years the patient had been completely deprived of liberty of action. Yet after three months only of treatment he became and has remained well. He has for all these years gone about wherever he wished with ease and comfort. He has practised his profession with success. He has taken his part in religious services with complete freedom and great thankfulness. It is of interest to note that the discussions which were his sole treatment were wholly on the conscious level, about fears connected with health and insanity, about responsibility and the like. Neither religion nor sex was discussed. He said he had quite definite views of his own on these subjects, and that he would not discuss them with anybody; he had no desire whatever to hear my views or to know what they were. His greatest fear was that he had heart disease, and that he, therefore, might make an exhibition of himself in public by dropping down dead—a common fear, and a common associated factor in the production of agoraphobia. In a number of other instances if this fear was removed the agoraphobia was relieved to a considerable extent. In this patient the fear had arisen many years before, when he had fainted in church, at a missionary sermon where a medical missionary appears to have given some gruesome medical details. He was then about eighteen years of age. Whether this fear represented something deeper I do not know. But when he learned that his heart was normal and that he would not drop down dead, and that he was not more liable to become insane than anyone else, he gradually lost his phobias. I have no letters of his to quote because I have seen him sometimes. He lives near Swaylands and has often walked over in the summer to see a cricket match or something of that kind, and in this way I have seen him occasionally. He himself has no doubt that he changed his mental outlook during these three months, and that that change has abolished his symptoms. Now it can be said for certain that this case was not trivial nor a psychosis, that he was better after his mind was relieved of certain fears, that the improvement has not depended on a continuing support, that there was no exploration of any sort of unconscious.

It seems probable that the reassurance about his heart was of great importance, and it might be thought that he must have been reassured about it often. That, however, is not so. He never told anyone that he was afraid of his heart, only that he had terror in the street, and apparently no one had got so far as to enquire even into proximate causes for this terror. It was when this was done, when he realized that it was not proposed to tell him any more that the streets were free from danger, but to try to find out why they were full of it for him, that he allowed this fear about his heart to come out.

Without indicating further these criteria for the opinion that the patients were really suffering from neurosis, and that they were permanently benefited by the treatment which was given, I shall quote some more cases where all these criteria are shown without doubt.

1921, *Table I, Case No.* 7.

A lady of fifty-nine came under care in July 1921, complaining of throbbings, pains all over, giving way of the legs so that she fell, insomnia, failure of concentration and various fears and phobias. Thirty-three years before, her baby had been killed in an accident, and she had been subject to nervous symptoms ever since. There had been periods when she had felt fairly well but never for more than a few months, and she described herself as always anxious and worried. She was in the hospital for seven weeks, and has been well ever since. Her treatment at Swaylands consisted only of conversations about conscious worries and anxieties. She had not been heard of since 1926 till this year. In response to the letter of enquiry she now writes:

I am happy to inform you that I enjoy very much better health and although seventy-two years of age walk two to three miles daily; my present trouble is cataract which I trust will diminish as time goes on. We often speak of Swaylands and you as the first doctor that gave me real good advice and put me on the right road to health and sanity.

Such optimism about a condition like cataract is unusual; even for those hitherto sound in their nerve health it is commonly a depressing word, so much so that young ophthalmologists are often adjured not to use it, but to say that there are some signs of opacity in the lens. It cannot be suggested either that the patient is welcoming the condition, because she intends to exploit it. The whole tone of the letter is different from that.

1921, *Table I, Case No.* 28.

A lady of forty-three was admitted May 1921, complaining of absolute exhaustion, giddiness, faintness and severe headache. She was so exhausted that she had been unable to get up for many weeks. She was unable to raise her head from the pillow because any attempt to do so brought on severe headache. These symptoms had been present in all their severity for eighteen months. She had not been feeling well for some months previously, but eighteen months before admission she had fainted in the street, and since then had lain in this prostrate condition. Superficially it was clear that she dreaded collapsing again. It transpired that the fainting attack had taken place just outside her husband's office. She had regarded this as a curious coincidence, and had consciously attached no importance to it. It also came out that she was displeased with him at the time. He was not being successful in his business, and she had had to resume her former employment in ladies' tailoring to keep the home going. Rightly or wrongly she had come to the conclusion that he might have done better if he had wished to, and that she was suffering from an intolerable injustice. Naturally she had felt very tired for some time, and when her complaints met with less sympathy than she expected this faint occurred just where it did. No direct statement was made that this had been done on purpose consciously, but it was pointed out that these things were apt to happen when a demonstration might be useful in making other people do something. The same arguments were used as have already been described in the case of the lady who did not wish to go back to her insane mother. No further investigation into the unconscious was undertaken, and in six weeks she left the hospital feeling quite well. We heard each year up to 1928 that this state of affairs had continued. This year (1934) she was written to and replied as follows:

> I am glad to say I've been keeping very well indeed since I wrote to you last, which is a long time ago, and I often felt I should like you to know this. I manage my home affairs for three of us single-handed, which is very marvellous considering what a terrible wreck of humanity I was when I came to you. I shall ever feel grateful for the many kindnesses during my stay at Swaylands and the help you gave me.

There certainly was the making conscious of something that had been unconscious, viz. that she was demonstrating to her husband how badly he had treated her. But again to have elicited this is merely to have scratched the surface.

1921, *Table I, Case No.* 5.

A lady of forty-eight with extreme exhaustion was admitted June 21, 1921. Her illness had begun twenty-two years before. During this period she had undergone seven formal rest cures, many of which had been followed by benefit for a few weeks or months. Then in some way she always over-did things and relapsed. When well, if she ever did so great a thing as to dust the drawing room, she would usually have to go to bed for three weeks or thereabouts. She was in Swaylands for six weeks, and what was discussed was a number of anxieties which had been on her mind all these years in complete consciousness, i.e. they were continually cropping up. There were the usual fears of what would happen if she over-did things. There was an intense fear of influenza. She believed that her exhaustion dated from an attack of influenza twenty-two years before. She had caught it since then whenever there was an epidemic, and she often had it entirely by herself when no one else had it, and she was always exhausted for weeks after it. It is probable that she never had it even once. The first was one of these a-febrile influenzas: there was an epidemic at the time, but there was another reason why she might well be ill then. Her father had committed suicide, and at the same time she was trying to make up her mind whether she should become engaged to be married or not. She became engaged and married, but was never happy about it. There was a feeling of guilt in having married with this in her family history, and the still worse feeling that her punishment would be that her children would become insane. She became well in a few days after admission to Swaylands, and has remained well since. It seemed to the writer that the really important point in her treatment was giving her a proper understanding about exhaustion. As soon as she had grasped it she was up and about, and it was after this miraculous transformation had occurred that she began to tell the story of her doubts and scruples. It is perhaps an easy road into a patient's confidences to have been able by words alone to get fatigue abolished when the fatigue no longer served any purpose; to a person of intelligence such a demonstration affords striking proof of the necessity to get a comfortable mind. Her mind had been most uncomfortable on the subject of just how much she could do. When it had been made comfortable on this point she spontaneously brought forward all these old bogies which had troubled her for so long. I think that for her permanent recovery it was necessary that her scruples and her fears for her children should be discussed; but the ease with which all this was accomplished was due to her receiving a striking demonstration about exhaustion. This patient has been heard of often because ever since she was in the hospital she has been recommending people to come to Swaylands. She has not needed help for herself. Her case has been described in greater detail in *The Common Neuroses*, p. 43 *et seq.*

1921, *Table I, Case No.* 10.

A lady of twenty-one was admitted in May 1921, complaining of tachycardia which had necessitated absolute rest in bed, insomnia, headache and various phobias. She had felt vaguely unwell for many years, but these symptoms had been present for four or five years and were getting steadily worse. The home conditions were unsatisfactory. The father had deserted his family, which was struggling to live in genteel poverty. The mother was an inefficient, depressed, flabby woman. A rich aunt helped very ungraciously. The patient was in hospital for eight weeks and no exploration of the unconscious was made. The chief therapy was an explanation of how a heart could palpitate when there was no disease, and an evaluation of the importance of that. Since then she has been well and happy. She has earned a precarious living at music. She seems to be frequently short of food and always short of money, but every Christmas she has written spontaneously an amusing account of the year's doings. From being a morose, nervous child she has changed into a woman of gay courage; and she always herself takes care to say that that change occurred during those eight weeks at Swaylands, which is, I think, true.

These six cases seem to carry weight and to go far to establish the views which have been suggested, and which will be more particularly emphasized in a moment. It is, I think, of importance that these patients were all treated at the same time; every one of them was in the hospital in July 1921. That seems to me to lessen the likelihood of the lucky accident. To get six lucky accidents all at the same period is unlikely. Every year we have had similar examples, as may be seen from a glance at the tables at the end of the book, but these six have been chosen for comment because they came simultaneously, and because they have stood the test of time longer than the others. They seem to establish the truth of the following propositions:

1. By a comparatively short course of treatment it is possible in certain instances to bring about a drastic and lasting change in the outlook on life of some patients, so that they cease to regard the world in a way which leads to invalidism. This change must be as great as any that could be brought about by psychoanalysis, granting that that procedure aims at character change. It does not follow, but I believe it to be true, that these successful short treatments might be much commoner than they are, were it not for the general air of pessimism which has been allowed to surround the whole subject of the neuroses. It has been assumed in many quarters that patients with long standing neuroses must of necessity expect that it will be a long time before they get well. This is held not only in analytical

circles. Many who do not practise analysis seem to tell their patients not to expect recovery for a long time. It is quite certain that if a patient is told this, it will be a long time before he is well. We know that many patients are not in a hurry to get well, and the absence of imminence of cure suits them perfectly; we know that others have almost lost hope about getting well, that many of them have been told "once a neurotic always a neurotic", and it is to my mind a certainty that these postponements of cure to a remote future fill up the cup of their despair. The non-analytic physicians who do this might remember that Weir Mitchell, who certainly cured people, did not spend more than a couple of months over any one of them; but he did not say pessimistic, or cautious things, and probably he was not afraid to be wrong sometimes, which is probably one of the reasons why the lengthy prognosis is given. There are, of course, other reasons why patients cannot be cured quickly, but this is a common one.

2. These examples teach that it is not essential that we should treat only early cases. The shortest of these histories was eighteen months. The other patients had histories of thirty-three, twenty-two, sixteen, five and four years of intense symptoms, during which they had had from time to time courses of active treatment; some of them had had symptoms of milder degree very much longer. We need not therefore be discouraged at length of history. The perpetual cry for early cases may indeed be prompted from the unconscious of the physician, who wishes to provide excuses for not getting patients as well as he would like to. It has indeed sometimes seemed to me that some patients have presented great difficulty because they have not been ill long enough. No person likes to hear that he has been ill because of some mental difficulty. Everybody has had it rubbed in so much throughout childhood that where there is a will there is a way, that will and success in life seem to have become synonymous; it is ingrained in everybody that if he exercises his will enough he need never be nervous nor have nervous symptoms, and therefore if he has them it is his own fault. And though the therapist may gild the pill he cannot help showing the patient that there was in fact a defect in morale—difficulties had at least not been met intelligently. If a patient has been ill a short time only, it may be difficult to get him

to listen to propositions of so distasteful a kind, and if he does not want to listen he will not. But when he has tried all sorts of treatment for years with only temporary benefit, and if he is sufficiently weary of his illness, he may be in a better mood to listen to psychological explanations of it, however disagreeable.

The faculty of not taking in what one does not wish to hear is well developed in most of us, but in these people it is excessively so. They seem to listen and to understand, and very soon, in the same interview perhaps, will tell you that you have said the exact opposite of what you did say: they totally forget all explanations which they had apparently found interesting and satisfactory, unless the information was really desired. Further, at the outset most of these illnesses have a value. The lady whose brother had committed suicide might have been prevented from marrying by her illness. Part of her felt she ought not to marry, and the illness was on the side of that part. The illness did in fact delay the marriage. The illness at that time, therefore, had value; when I saw her it had none, and had not had any for many years, and therefore she was cured easily. Obviously it is more in the cases of long standing than in those of recent origin that one will meet with patients who are only too ready to leave off being ill if they can be taught how to do it.

3. Similarly age does not seem to be of so much importance as is often alleged. All these patients except one were at least middle-aged and most of them are now decidedly elderly.

4. None of these patients suffered from a subsequent crippling dependence on the doctor. The stage of the transference neurosis on which so much stress is laid in psychoanalytic literature does not seem to have been realized. This has been described as follows:

> A patient who at first was eager for health, entirely absorbed by the treatment of his problems, intelligent, mature and adult in many ways, no longer shows these qualities consistently during the hour (of analysis). So far as his efforts show, he is no longer co-operating, is indifferent to what the necessities of treatment are, forgets and disregards all that he has learned in the introductory period, and makes little obvious progress. On the other hand, he feels distinctly that he is battling with the analyst, attempting to trick him into doing what he does not intend to do, disregarding all his advice. Gradually it becomes apparent that his most compelling reason for coming to analysis is no longer to get well, but is

entirely to win some type of emotional satisfaction from the analyst. He will not close a door for himself, it must be closed for him. He will wear no coat and risk pneumonia unless the analyst orders it. In innumerable ways the same effort to secure one thing or another from the analyst may be manifested. (*Facts and Theories of Psycho-Analysis*, by Ives Hendrick, p. 208, 1934).

Surely if by a short treatment we can avoid this stage without harm it would be a good thing. The Freudians say we cannot; that this stage, which is a return to mental childhood, must be lived through, so that the repressed emotions of childhood can be worked off on the analyst. It is of interest to note that Freud recognized this transference neurosis in 1904, some time after he had already been curing neurotic patients without encountering it. He was convinced of its truth after failure with a long case the treatment of which lasted over four years. This, oddly enough, was then described as a universal phenomenon, if cure were to be obtained, but I think the cases quoted above show that it need not be; indeed his own earlier successes might have proved as much.

5. I think that these histories show that in no one of the examples was spontaneous recovery likely to have been the explanation of the change. As has already been mentioned, it may be argued there are no control cases, and that other doctors employing totally different methods, manipulative methods, drug methods, or even by merely holding watching briefs, could apparently show a number of cases showing equally striking results. It is quite possible that those who use these other methods could show a series treated all at the same time in which the patients had remained well for thirteen years. I have not come across such a record, but even if it exists it does not minimize the importance of these. They certainly show that deep analysis is not always necessary for prolonged cure. They also show that changing certain conscious ideas which the patient held is not to be neglected. It is likely that the purely physical methods referred to sometimes do this also, though it is theoretically possible that osteopathy, for example, may cure without reference to suggestion. If it does, then we do not understand in the least why it does, whereas the methods used in this series do fall into place with other knowledge which nobody doubts,

into the knowledge of the emotional reaction and the conditioned reflex. And it seems better in many ways to adopt a treatment whose rationale can be understood by everybody in the light of general knowledge than one which can be understood only by an esoteric few in the light of a knowledge which is denied by everyone who has studied science. The first method is more capable of repetition and of being extended than the second; and there is some chance of finding out where it is defective and so improving it. The other physical methods act probably by giving hope to a patient who was in despair; they must therefore be in the fashion of the moment, as osteopathy is. Whether, if his treatment has been apparently physical, he will stand up to subsequent strain as well as if he had been taught something about his mind I do not know. I have suggested in the case of the man with the strained back described on p. 26 that he will not stand up so well.

6. There is the question of whether these cases were trivial or not. It was mentioned before that a whitlow was a trivial disease provided a knife was inserted into it at the proper moment, and that failure to do so might convert it into a grave one. Not only could it be turned into a grave one by such an omission, a too extensive operation might also be disastrous. If we knew as little about physical pathology as we do of psychopathology, one could imagine a highly intelligent and bold surgeon in such a case finding enlarged glands, and saying that not only must he open the whitlow, that these glands are also diseased; therefore he must immediately incise or excise them also—and the result might be fatal. I am inclined to think that some of these so-called trivial cases have occasionally been made grave ones by too extensive mental surgery.

There is yet another point about triviality. Most of the patients at Swaylands came from consultants. To one of these I once said: "Will you not send some easy cases? All those you send are very difficult." He replied that he kept the easy ones, and that indeed it was not necessary to send them into hospital, and that he would continue to send the hard ones away. It is fairly true that we got no easy cases at Swaylands. As I write these words it is a year since I left Swaylands, and during that year I have had some easy cases. Quite a number of these later patients do not need as long as two months, though, of course, the after histories may show this to be wrong.

All these six then are enthusiastic, and all know that they have been changed from walking in fear and dread, from being afraid of everything to being afraid of nothing, to being careless of, because uninterested in, their health, not merely because they had lost symptoms such as fatigue and dyspepsia, but because cure of health was no longer the supreme affair of life. They know that they have acquired a fund of energy to be used for the purposes of living and the solution of real problems, a fund which was formerly employed and employed unavailingly in taking care of their health. Whereas formerly they had to spend much time wondering whether it were wise to do this or to eat that, now such ideas never enter their heads. They have, therefore, now the satisfaction of knowing that they are not merely troublesome passengers on the ship, but have become among those who are worth while.

The Freudians have thought that they alone had the idea that this was desirable; they have considered that any therapy which did not deal with the unconscious at length, and according to their tenets, was at the best mere symptom-removing which left the patient a prey to all sorts of disagreeable feelings. Thus:

> symptoms are not primary neurotic problems, but merely indicate the existence of a problem. It is not primarily the symptoms but the total adjustment, the incapacity of the patient who has such symptoms to find a reasonable place in life without psychically conditioned suffering, that should interest us most as therapists.

With these sentiments everyone would agree, but, as has been shown, a complete or even extensive psychoanalysis is not always necessary to attain such an end.

These facts were all known to those whom I may call the old masters, to Dubois, to Weir Mitchell, to Dejerine. None of them concerned himself merely with the removal of symptoms; all sought by altering the morale of their patients to alter their health. Possibly one of the reasons why the psychoanalysts have not understood these writers is because the early analysts had for the most part been practising hypnotism; that was their chief therapeutic weapon before the discovery of analysis. Now hypnotism connotes two things: (1) it explores a kind of subconscious or unconscious, (2) it has to do mainly with the removal of symptoms. While it may be used to cure symptoms or to check a bad habit like alcoholism, it is not a good instrument for investigating the problems of a patient's life. Psychoanalysis lends itself easily to that, and in so far as it does so it is a superior instrument, and was recognized as such at once. But from their hypnotic experiences there therapists had learned to depend so much on subconscious phenomena that they were unable to work with those of consciousness. Hence their profound belief only in processes out of consciousness. Hence their thought that no one but themselves saw the necessity for doing more than relieve symptoms, for they had not known that others were doing this already. The later analysts have hardly been free agents. They have been brought up like the priests of a religion, using their intellects only for the purpose of learning the true faith, knowing that other knowledge is dangerous.

The phenomena described are indeed difficult to reconcile with the doctrine of the unconscious as it is usually set forth, not against it as it might be set forth. It is usually taught by analysts that repression is an essential factor in neurosis, that there can be no neurosis in the absence of repression; and by repression it is not meant merely that a patient has not cognized something, has been, to use Rivers' phrase, "unwitting" about something which he can see on being shown. Had the doctrine been that repression was sometimes the cause of neurosis and sometimes not, that repression could sometimes be dealt with by instruction and sometimes not, and if it had been recognized more explicitly that we must treat what is conscious also, these cases would have had less significance than they have. There is no doubt whatever that repression is frequently causal of neurosis, but as the doctrine has been that repression is always causally present and that that cannot be altered by direct teaching, I think that these cases are important for they show that such a view is untenable. It is necessary to add that no statement has been made that these patients had not repressed anything, for obviously everybody has repressed much. The statement is only that their repressions in the Freudian sense do not seem to have been as important as their defective medical knowledge; that repressions were not so causal as their conscious ideas.[1]

[1] There has been a tendency lately among certain writers on medical psychology to indulge in some quasi-philosophical-mathematical quibbling about causation, which apparently some physicists have considered an old-fashioned idea because of some difficulties with the quantum theory. It may be mentioned that Einstein and Planck do not agree with this ultra-modern view, but hold that when the quantum theory is better understood the idea of causation will return. Even if causation were held to be discredited however by all physicists, we are not living in their conceptual world of whirling atoms and empty spaces, but in a phenomenal world. We are, in Eddington's phrase, within another frame of reference. In our world if I knock a man down I have caused him to fall. If something can be changed without a particular condition being changed, then that condition was not causal. If I can make a miserable man happy without discovering in him the Oedipus complex, or, supposing it to be present, without altering it or his views about it in any way, then the Oedipus complex was not causal of his unhappiness. That is not to say it might not have been so in other people. Nor is it to say that he has not got that complex, only that it is not causal of symptoms even if present. But it will be said that when I took an interest in the man I had altered his Oedipus complex, and who knows that by merely taking an interest in him I may have done enough. Perhaps, but if I recommended that as a good method of dealing with the complex in question I think I would be laughed at by the very people who said I had altered it.

VII

POSITIVE INDICATIONS FOR SHORT TREATMENTS

In describing these patients it has been said that neither age nor duration of symptoms was against the success of a simple course of treatment. It might be well to attempt to discover some positive qualities which might make the recognition of favourable cases easier. One of these patients had certainly a strong motive for getting well, viz. the man with agora-claustrophobia (p. 42). This man's religious faith was passionate and with a very little encouragement he was prepared to face anything if only he could get to church and stay there for the length of the service. He had not succeeded for a long time in doing so before he came under care, because he had come to the conclusion that it was impossible. At the hospital even, there were several occasions when he would have given up if he had been left to himself. Most people, however, have discovered that it is easier to carry a difficult thing through if some one else is backing them up either by giving orders or by displaying companionship than if they are trying alone. To have some one to give encouragement, to be assured that nothing disastrous will happen from trying, may make the difference between success and failure. These factors would not in my view have sufficed to bring about cure had there not also been the enthusiasm. Mere reassurance in the absence of something else would not, I think, have been enough for so bad a case.

In none of the other five examples was there this flaming enthusiasm. In the case of the lady with the difficult mother there was a good substitute for enthusiasm, a sense of duty, and contempt for the idea of shirking that duty by means of an illness which existed for that purpose alone. In the other four there was a strong degree of common sense and, what is most important, no great objection to getting well. Each of them required to have something pointed out, and when this had been done the case disappeared. The lady who fainted outside her husband's office had no notion,

I think, that she was doing this to teach him a lesson; but when she grasped this idea, as she did immediately on the whole story being pieced together, she saw that nobody was going to gain anything by conduct of this sort, and she had enough sense of fairness to see that he could not really help himself as much as she had assumed, that it was not his fault that business was bad, that he certainly was not as blameworthy as she had considered. Even if he were a rather feeble person it was the more necessary that she should be strong and help him.

The lady who had been exhausted for twenty-two years was ill for most of that time because she was in a fog. She believed what she had been told over and over again that if she overdid things she would have to pay for it, that she had no reserve of energy, that she had only a supply sufficient for a very small expenditure. Consequently she lived in perpetual fear of using up this reserve. She had apparently proved again and again, to her own satisfaction at least, that this belief was well founded. It is of course well known that fear of bringing on a particular symptom is a sure way to have it often. If I dread the effects of fatigue, the best way to prevent me exhausting myself in fact is to feel fatigued on slight exertion. I am then automatically stopped from overdoing things. In passing it may be said that this theory, of a reserve of energy which we must be careful not to exhaust, is very common indeed, and is more productive of the symptom of exhaustion than any other theory I have come across. How could it be otherwise? The sensation of exhaustion is one of the commonest bodily reactions to anxiety, worry, preoccupation and the like, and if it is to be treated as physical, as a warning that the battery has run down, and that great care must be taken not to overdo things lest some nameless disaster should ensue, then, if this warning is believed, it follows that every time a patient attempts to do anything requiring exertion, he must do it in a state of anxiety, and therefore the more he tries to do, i.e. the braver he is, the more tired he will feel. The matter is complicated further by the fact that a sense of exhaustion is often the first symptom of many physical ills, and therefore it is difficult for a doctor to avoid being the agent who increases the symptom. It is natural that he should warn the patient, but it would be well if he were not dogmatic about it in the early stages of illness before he is sure. If he has been dogmatic and has said that fatigue indicates always the need of rest or other physical treatment, he cannot change his mind and be believed by that patient; but if he says at the outset that he is not sure but must wait for more data, no harm will have been brought about by putting the patient to rest in bed until time has shown what is the matter.

To return for a moment to these patients, this lady lost her fatigue as soon as she understood that it depended mainly on her belief that it was physical.

The two others became well similarly when they understood. The younger woman realized that though her illness had in fact got her away from home this time, it was not likely to do so again. She had enough foresight to perceive that financial stringency would not permit of a second escape; and she also was able to see that permanent escape would be obtained only through health. She was therefore eager to listen to a view which showed that all her previous invalidisms were not necessary and that she need take none of the precautions which had been laid upon her.

Apart from similar indications from the patient's character which may be difficult to assess at an early stage, what other points are there which might enable us to recognize beforehand which are the patients whose illnesses are likely to yield to this simple treatment? The majority of patients whom I see have believed when they came to hospital that they were suffering from some physical disability, from nervous exhaustion, or auto-intoxication, from an essentially weak digestion, from incipient insanity and so on. I was told of these things at the outset of treatment, and it has been my habit then to take a preliminary superficial history and make a physical examination. Very soon I have taken the opportunity, if this examination revealed no organic disease, to explain how physical symptoms may be an expression of mental distress of some kind, that the history has shown—as it usually has—that there was some such distress at the beginning of the illness; I have also been able to show very often that the illness has been kept up, long after the original distress which started it has sunk into unimportance, because of misunderstanding of the nature of these emotional bodily or mental reactions. The patient has treated them as if they were factual, whereas they were only sensational. The endeavour is made to show, for example, that the sensation of fatigue is not the same thing as actual exhaustion; that discomfort after food does not necessarily mean that there is anything wrong either with the stomach or the food which has been put into it; that the fact that the brain seems to work uncomfortably, that concentration and therefore memory are poor, are not signs of impending insanity. Very soon after this I shall be able to tell in many instances whether the treatment will have to be long or not.

If the patient understands this explanation of his case readily, and especially if he can reproduce in writing the ideas which have been put before him, and if he obviously welcomes these ideas, there is a strong probability that a short course of treatment may be embarked on with some hope of success. On the other hand, if he seems an ordinarily intelligent person, and yet can make neither head nor tail of the explanations, and seems to get more and more stupid, puzzled and confused if the explanations are continued; if he cannot reproduce them; if he tells you that you have said the opposite of what you did say, or if he tells you that all that you say is obvious, and it is manifest that he does understand, but if he adds that he does not see what difference it makes to his case, then it is likely that there is great resistance to the acceptance of the ideas, and success with a short treatment is not so probable. By this time too it will often have been discovered whether the illness has value at present or not. If it is enabling him to get away and keep away from an abominable environment, if there is money to be made out of keeping ill, if in short it has positive value, then a short treatment is not likely to succeed. All this can usually be discovered within the first week.

It is not true that if he shows these signs of resistance once, if, for example, he has been puzzled after one explanation and gives it back all wrong, that the short explanatory course need be abandoned. Most people show resistance to any new idea which in the end they may adopt. It is indeed the usual way to meet new ideas, but then most people are not hoping for a changed outlook. The neurotic should be if he is to be easily cured.

It will be seen that in trying to find what are the suitable patients I have spoken of those with somatic disorders only, and have suggested not only at this moment but elsewhere in this book that physical symptoms are comparatively easy to deal with, and that the dealing with them frequently opens the door to further discussion about other difficulties. The majority of the patients whom I see have believed that they were suffering because of some physical condition, and therefore there is no lack of those on whom this may be tried. Nothing in making such an attempt prejudices deeper investigation. No promise has been made that understanding this explanation will effect a cure; nothing has been said which is not certainly and indeed obviously true. The details of technique of such treatment have been given in *The Common Neuroses* and need not be repeated here. Even when the symptoms are more mental than physical, e.g. failure of concentration with concomitant fear of insanity, the patients whom I see as a rule consider this a physical illness. It is seldom that they have achieved any conceptual distinction between mind and brain. It is their brains that they are worrying about just as the dyspeptics are anxious about their stomachs or diets. Many of them do not know that the brain is an organ which lends itself to physical diagnostic enquiry—how could it be, shut up as it is in a hard box? Even educated people are agreeably surprised to hear that it is as easily examined as the heart.

There have also been a number of patients, still dealing with those who have had a short course of treatment only, in whom, though there was great improvement, the mental change has not been so complete as it was in those whose cases have been detailed above. Such patients have on the whole kept well, but certain things have happened which make one not so sure about them. They may and probably will relapse in the face of stress.

For example, a young naval lieutenant, aged nineteen years, was admitted in June 1921 (1921, Table I, Case No. 3) complaining of fears in the dark, of crowds, of headaches and of terrifying dreams. He had recently had several epileptiform fits, and had become subject to somnambulism. These symptoms had been present for four months only and had come on after a concussion of the brain, caused by tripping over something on a dark deck when he had fallen down the companion. He was in Swaylands for four weeks, and became apparently well; he then returned to duty. The fear of the dark was a regression towards an infantile fear of the dark, and was associated with the thought of burglars, and of his mother calling him a coward because of this fear, when he was a very small boy. This association and memory had been repressed. To this extent there was the revival by treatment of a repressed memory. There was, however, no Freudian analysis. When this unjust scolding by his mother was brought to the surface the fear disappeared. He had done enough actual fighting in one of the little wars, which went on in the Middle East after the Great War was supposed to be over, to know that he was not a coward, and he had apparently long ago grown out of caring very much what his mother thought of him. When this fear disappeared all his other symptoms vanished, for they were dependent on it. But while it was present and it was possible that he was a coward, he had better be out of the Navy, and there was little doubt that the other symptoms existed for the purpose of getting him out of the Navy. If he were not a coward he could stay in. The fear of the dark was a land fear; it was absent when he was at sea. He had been at sea all the time he was in the Navy and had not experienced any fear till the night of the accident. The ship—a destroyer—was then tied up in port where burglars were a possibility. He was on deck alone in the dark when apparently causeless terror seized him, and he ran and stumbled and fell down the ladder. The infantile fear was quite specifically of burglars and you cannot have burglars at sea. As it was certain he was not a coward he could and did go back apparently happy.

It is probable that none of this was conscious until we had talked. He had had an accident followed by fits and could not stay in the Navy if, as looked probable, he was an epileptic. That was the manifest explanation of events. Now, if these explanations were true, why had this fear of the dark not been operative before? Why should the idea of being a coward come up only when it did? There was indeed another reason why he wanted to get out of the Navy, but I did not discover it till he had gone back. He wanted to marry, and the Navy and marriage, if the officer is very young, as in this instance, do not go well together. It is wonderful that he should, so to speak, have consented to get rid of his symptoms seeing that he intended, unconsciously I believe, to use them. Probably he was so pleased at getting rid of fear of the dark that neurosis as a means to an end no longer seemed so attractive. The fear of the dark when ashore had been a nuisance for years though it had never caused panic till now; it was, however, enough of a nuisance to make its disappearance very welcome.

He went into the submarine service and seemed quite happy. He married two years later. He showed me over his submarine with great pride and pleasure a year after that. Suddenly in 1927 he wrote to me that he had been troubled with his eyes, informed me that he was to be boarded on account of them, and that he feared that he might be invalided out of the service. He wished to see me before the board sat, to talk the matter over and hear if I had any suggestions to make. He was invalided out, after which his eyesight recovered very soon; he took up a civilian occupation and he has remained well ever since. He was heard from in 1934. It is, of course, just possible that he had some temporary failing of eyesight of physical origin which recovered, but it is extremely unlikely. It is much more likely that it was a nervous asthenopia associated with a desire to leave the Navy. He professed, of course, to be heartbroken at the board's decision, but he seemed to get over it very quickly. A civilian ophthalmologist, he informed me, had told him that the asthenopia was due to his general health; as that is always excellent the statement more than smacks of neurosis. What clinches the diagnosis is the letter which he wrote to me asking my advice as to what he should do at the board, whether he should put in some certificate from me as to the likelihood of his recovery or not. He posted this letter so that I got it after the matter was settled. That, of course, might also be accidental, but there are too many unfortunate accidents in this story for that to be likely. Had he wanted my help the letter would have come early; the symptoms had been running for weeks. He wanted to get out of the Navy, but he did not want it to be a voluntary act, but one forced on him. I had returned him to the Navy once, when he was certainly minded to leave it. I was therefore a dangerous person, to be avoided when he wanted to get out next time. There is also the feeling which most people have who see much of the neuroses, viz. that the traumatic neuroses do occur only when there is something to be gained from them, much more obviously than in non-traumatic cases. One feels, therefore, that here is a person who will probably solve some of his difficulties by an attack of neurosis and who therefore cannot be put in a first class.

It might seem that a lot of fuss is being made about nothing in this case. Here is a young man who had such severe symptoms that the question of operation had been considered before he came into hospital. He became well and except for a slight relapse remained so for thirteen years at least. The case is really a creditable one to have had. He keeps well over the minor things in life. The result has been a good one as things go in this world, but it might have been better. It is possible that this person is more affected by what his mother or mother surrogate thinks of him than I had thought. His attempt to blunder out of the Navy by a post-concussional neurosis the first time had to be done in that way, because in actual fact he could not have told his mother at that time that he wanted to leave. She was too spartan for him to have faced her on that point. Even six years later he probably could not have told her.

It is therefore probable that this course of treatment was in fact too short, and that it should have been longer, and that here the analysis should have been deeper. He had not got over the fear of his seniors as much as I had hoped. That deeper analysis may be necessary in the apparently cured will be demonstrated later. In the tables at the end he is marked throughout as Well, with one Relapse. See p. 110.

In contrast with him we might glance at the record of another post-concussion neurosis (1927, Group I, Table I, Case No. 24). This patient, an officer in the Indian Cavalry, was thrown from his horse in India in May 1925. He was seen by a neurologist in 1926 on account of severe headaches, and was sent to Swaylands to see if we could help to solve a problem, viz. whether he was suffering from contusion of the brain and should undergo an operation, or whether the condition was due to neurosis. He was treated by reassurance and a discussion of his difficulties, and in his case it was discovered definitely that he did not wish to return to duty in India. At home there was a profligate brother who was sponging on his parents. Partly from disinterested affection and partly because he disliked that his inheritance should be frittered away, he knew that he could look after things more easily if he were at home. He had been home once since the accident and had recovered, only to relapse when he went out again, since when the theory that patients with head symptoms, especially post-concussional symptoms, cannot stand hot weather had been called in to keep him at home. Now that he was threatened with an operation if he stayed at home he was ready to see whether other means to guard his parents could not be taken. He succeeded in this and returned to India and has kept well ever since. A much deeper analysis was undertaken in his case. He was in hospital for eleven weeks.

There are other patients also whom one must not put into the first class because it is impossible to be sure whether certain residual symptoms are organic or neurotic. A lady of fifty with mitral disease suffered from palpitation, headache, insomnia, depression and dyspnoea. Certain cardiologists had regarded these symptoms as signals of a failing heart, but others had thought that there was an overlay of emotional origin. She came to the hospital in 1921 (Table I, Case No. 25). She would hardly walk across the room for fear of straining the damaged heart, and as usual the violent increase of palpitation, which such an attempt brought on, made her sure that she was right to be careful. She was in hospital for three months; her treatment involved no exploration of the unconscious. When she left she could walk some miles without discomfort and had regained her courage. She has written frequently to say how much better she is and says that her friends call her a resurrection. But she takes more care than a healthy person does and she is not wholly without symptoms; it does not seem possible to know how much this depends on cardiac disability and how much on remnants of unnecessary fear. However pleased both doctor and patient may be with this result it cannot be quoted for certain as one in the first class.

There are not in the 1921 tables any patients who were in for long periods to compare with these, but there are some who were admitted at the same time, and who because they were in longer were not discharged till 1922. One of these who did equally well was of the same period; a male patient, aged forty-one (reported 1922, Group I, Table I, Case No. 1), admitted in August 1921. He complained of depression, dyspepsia, insomnia, phobias and inability to work. The dyspepsia had come on at the age of sixteen and had been present oftener than not during all these years. In the seven months he was under care he lost all these symptoms and he has been quite well ever since. A detailed history was obtained in which it became clear that he had been a mother's darling, and that the onset of symptoms coincided with having to leave her. At first they had been so severe that he got back to her, and when he was better and went away from home again he fell ill once more. After that his life was a more or less ineffectual struggle against neurosis. In the discussions at Swaylands nothing resembling the idea of the Oedipus complex was envisaged. What was envisaged was that his mother had spoilt him, and that he did not like facing a cold, unsympathetic world. He saw this and became well. Certain other worries were explained. He thought his hands had a peculiar smell. This on investigation meant that he thought he had syphilis. This fear was dissipated quite easily by direct discussion of the symptomatology of that disease. There was no suggestion that he was suffering for self-punishment or other obscure reason. It was a straightforward fear of syphilis because he had put himself in the way of acquiring it on one or two occasions. The point is that the fear and the belief that he had an odour did disappear with straightforward common-sense explanations. It is necessary to insist on this because it is being constantly instilled that straightforward explanation cannot get rid of such ideas for their roots are in the unconscious. Now this patient took much longer than the six originally described: the result has been equally good, but there are one or two possible reasons for his slower result. It took a long time before he could bring himself to tell about the fear of syphilis; it took a long time after he was well symptomatically before he could brace himself to face the world. He has done so to the extent that he has married happily and successfully, after being a bachelor for about forty-six years. This is probably strong proof that he has not only altered his outlook, but successfully adapted himself. There is a third reason for his delay in getting well. He was at first under the care of a very junior doctor who left about a month after treatment was started. He had not succeeded in acquiring confidence in this doctor, and for this kind of treatment what happens at the first interviews is very important. If a bad start has been made and a new doctor has to take up the case, he does not start from zero, but from a minus position.

In subsequent years we meet with similar examples. In the year 1922 there are eight who were in for periods of three months or less who have kept quite well, who write in the same fashion. One of these (Group I, Table I, Case No. 7) has already been discussed on p. 26. He was the patient with pain in the back and hysterical paraplegia, the compensation case where the symptoms cleared up as soon as the case was settled by the Court. Now nothing was done to this man's mentality to make it less likely that he will break down if there is anything to be gained by breaking down. He was not a pleasant person; he was fond of boasting how he had swindled people in a mild way, by pretending that their cars needed things done to them when there was no such necessity, and how he had picked up a good many unjustified pounds by doing so. But probably the prognosis in his case is good in actual fact. He will not become the subject of neurosis from the sense of sin nor even from hardship. He will be liable to become it if there is anything to be made out of it, and, I believe, if he does he will be quite unaware of what is happening. He never had any insight into his case; when he became better originally after his compensation was settled, he was naïvely happy, and it never crossed his mind that he had to perhaps defend himself against a suspicion of malingering. But the opportunities of neurosis becoming a paying concern for him in the future are less than they were in the past. For now he is his own master, and though some years he has written about trade difficulties and the great effort which is needed to make both ends meet, he has not shown the slightest tendency to neurosis. Anxiety will not make him ill, only the unconscious hope of gain.

Another patient in this next year (1922, Group I, Table I, Case No. 15) had attacks of depression, suicidal thoughts, pains in the neck, fatigue and dyspepsia. She had also shown odd traits of conduct such as, so it was stated, trying to set the house on fire. She was in the hospital for nine weeks. She had been ill for some years, more or less at intervals so long as she could remember. The father was a domineering, terrifying person who ordered his wife and the children about. He was attached to the patient, who, however, did not like him because he bullied the rest of the family, especially a brother whose life was in consequence very unhappy. She herself was afraid that she might have inherited some of her father's objectionable qualities. Her treatment consisted in talking over these home difficulties. At no time did we get near any question about her relation to her father being sexual, in any sense of that word. There may have been such a bond but if it were causal of her illness she became well without any necessity having arisen of discussing it. She went home and remained well. A few years later she married and has kept well. Her case is mentioned as being yet another where one would have expected that a very long and deep treatment would have been necessary, where I believe most modern psychopathologists would have considered analysis was essential. This sort of person showing schizoid traits is not usually thought to be amenable to reasoning.

A glance at the tables will show a number who were in hospital for a short time only and who have been well since.

Sufficient has been said to make it certain that short courses of treatment, in which there was no exploration of the infantile unconscious and no formation of a transference which had to be resolved, may be sufficient to bring about character changes of a kind which are accompanied by durable improvements in health in patients whose cases did not seem slight or trivial. It is equally certain, and in consideration of all that has been said, this must be emphasized very strongly, that short courses will not do this always; but the occasions on which they are sufficient are by no means uncommon, and the tacit assumption, which is very widespread, that anything short of complete Freudian analysis is useless, is not true. There has been much talk about the shortening of analysis and much feeling that, however desirable this may be, it is not easy to know how to do it. It is unlikely that formal analysis can be shortened. If there is to be shortening it can be accomplished only by substituting teaching for analysis, a thing which all analysts are unwilling to do.

VIII

SOME CASES WHERE A LONGER COURSE WAS ESSENTIAL

A number of cases have just been described of patients who have kept well after a short course of treatment. We must now state with equal emphasis that there are others who have become well apparently, who went away with great hope and who relapsed quickly. Some of these returned, and a deeper investigation was instituted with good results. For example, a school teacher aged thirty was admitted in 1927 on account of phobias connected with buildings and crowds, and a sensation of being strangled (1928, Group I, Table I (*a*), Case No. 61). These symptoms had been present for eight years. She had struggled to do her work all the time with increasing difficulty. She had many anxious worries which were discussed. For the most part these concerned her father. She and he had quarrelled a great deal as far back as she could remember. She had been devoted to her mother. After she had left home to go to the training college she had been back very little, and after her mother's death, which occurred when she was twenty-one, still less. Her father had married again, and her present grievance was that he had retained certain of her property, chiefly books. At least that was how she looked at it. In truth he had said she could fetch her things, but she wanted them to be sent to her. She would not go to get them. After some time she perceived that all this was very silly; she even saw that she was jealous of the new wife, and that there was an erotic element in her hate of her father. Her symptoms disappeared, and in four months she was discharged apparently well. She returned to hospital in six months, complaining once more of all her symptoms, and saying that the sensation of being strangled was much worse. It was as if a cord were tied tightly round her neck. She began to remember acts of carelessness towards her mother especially when the latter had been ill, all of which had been repressed. It emerged that she had repressed thoughts that these acts had been contributory to the death, and also that she had repressed death wishes directed against her mother. The strangling sensation was a symbol of the hanging which she deserved, and by which alone her matricidal designs and unfilial conduct could be expiated. During this second course of treatment, which lasted seven months, no infantile fixations or fantasies were discovered. These repressions with regard to her mother, which were certainly post infantile, were the only ones to emerge. She has now been well about six years and has written letters of the enthusiastic type. It is interesting to note that at the end of her second treatment she hated her father and stepmother just as much as ever, so that it looks as if that had not had a great deal to do with the genesis of the case. It was not till she had brought into consciousness what she had failed to do for her mother, and evaluated it rationally, that she got comfort. So long as this neglect could not be envisaged it was active and producing symptoms. When it was faced up to it could be viewed in proper proportion and then it disappeared.

It is arguable of course that the neglect of the mother and the death wishes towards her were because of her frustrated incestuous desires towards the father. It is also, however, possible that a young girl with an ailing mother may go out and play tennis instead of sitting with her mother, and reproach herself afterwards; and if other people upbraided her while her mother was ill she might wish the mother's case was over. That was the sort of thing she said, and it seems to me to be as complete a story as the Electra one. Anyhow she became and kept well without having to correlate the death wishes with incestuous desire.

Sometimes too the short treatment fails because the patient did not tell the whole story which was in consciousness even during the first time. A case in point is found in the tables of 1927, Group I, Table I (*a*), Case No. 20. The patient suffered from exhaustion, headaches, claustrophobia, poor concentration and epileptiform fits. She was in hospital two months. The claustrophobia was worse in church, and the fits occurred usually just before going to church or in church. She went to please an elder sister who dominated her. The epileptiform fits were clearly intended—unconsciously—to provide an illness excuse for not going. She had been told that they were truly epileptic. Her treatment at Swaylands was largely of a reassuring nature, that she had not epilepsy, and that she must come to an understanding with her sister of whom she was very fond and whom she admired greatly. She left greatly improved, and on the whole was much better than she had been, but still was subject to headaches and on two occasions she had a fit. She came back to the hospital in 1930, and then said that she neither loved nor respected her sister; she acknowledged that she had deceived me on this point because she was ashamed of it, but she said that she could not now live with her. She did not return home and has kept well since. It may be said that this is failure. If it is meant that there is no kind of situation that should not be faced then it is failure; and if it is meant also that a proper therapy will cure everyone so that no one need fail in any situation I would reply that that may be true in theory, but that it is not true in fact; some situations are intolerable for certain people.

This however is not a book on treatment but on prognosis, and the fact is that for five years now this patient has been well and happy. During the time she has earned her living, a thing she was not doing when she lived with her sister.

There was one patient (1924, Group I, Table I, Case No. 70) who was in on four periods over nine years. When she came first she was complaining of fantastic pictures mostly of a masochistic nature. She thought but was not sure that they represented incidents which had actually occurred in her life. They were so vivid and intolerable that she was unable to lead an ordinary life. She was married, but because of the intervention of these images was unable to have sexual intercourse. Before she came to the hospital she had been hypnotized often, and while this treatment had helped her temporarily she was unable to stand on her own feet when the attempt was made to get her to do so. At times the images were hallucinatory. She would, for example, see a naked man sitting on a chair in the corridor. She preserved her judgment and knew that these sights were unreal. During her last stay at Swaylands the plan was formed that she was not to be allowed to go into an hypnotic state during any interview. She had become so suggestible that she could hardly talk to any doctor about her case for more than a few minutes without going into a trance state. Ordinary talk in the open with her very wide awake brought to light a number of infantile fantasies such as the psychoanalysts have described. Since then she has been able to manage her home and live a much more normal life. She is not put forward as a well person, but only as one very much improved, by prolonged treatment.

Because of cases like these we are presented with a real difficulty in deciding whether a patient should be encouraged to leave soon if the symptoms disappear early. If they are to leave soon the doctor must not hedge, he must not try to protect himself. He must not suggest that leaving is anything but the very best thing to be done. If he casts doubt on it he may reckon on failure, and it is extraordinary how little is needed in the way of an unguarded remark to change the future of a patient for years. In 1927 a lady came to the hospital complaining *inter alia* of severe asthenopia; for thirty years she had been unable to read for more than ten minutes without pain. If she persevered she might get a headache which was capable of lasting for three days. She had, therefore, given up any attempt to fight her troubles. There seemed little doubt on investigation that this originated in a casual remark made by an eminent ophthalmologist whom she had consulted thirty years before. He gave her glasses, and as she left the room said to her, "Don't strain your eyes", in the tone in which one might say, "Well, good luck". With the help of the pain she had carried this instruction out very faithfully all these years. She was told, and she believed it, that this was all nonsense, that she could not strain her eyes in the ways she thought and in a couple of days she was reading in comfort all day. No better example of how prognosis depends on treatment could be imagined.

Some years ago when the local anaesthetic injections began to be used in dentistry, I had occasion to have a tooth extracted. The anaesthetic worked beautifully and I spoke well of it to my patients, who also reported to me that it had been given to them with success. Suddenly I began to hear of patients who had severe pain on the day following the operation. On investigation it was discovered that the dentist was telling everyone that it was quite likely that this would happen, and I confess that I was astonished that there were so many suggestible people in the world. On being asked what grudge he had against these people he said that he had none, but that one person had come to him and complained bitterly about pain on the day following the injection and had told him that he ought to tell people that this after-pain was much worse than the pain of having a tooth out without an anaesthetic at all. He had not gone so far as to say this, but he had warned them that they would probably have pain. He owned that he was protecting himself by telling them what he did tell them. I suggested that his reputation need not be treated so delicately, and that it might be better that he stopped saying things which might get a valuable method into ill-repute. After that I heard no more of this symptom. But the lesson is obvious. People are easily persuaded into illness, and therefore if we wish that our treatment by persuasion should succeed we must be careful not to damn it by doubting. Doctors are on the whole too prone to caution. A little enthusiasm is essential in psychotherapy, the kind of psychotherapy which cured these patients. We shall alter the prognosis for good in many patients only by enthusiastic use of the method. The doctor must, therefore, be prepared to be told sometimes that his treatment has not succeeded, and that he is not always right in his prognosis.

From the point of view of the patient there is a risk from the short course of treatment which is of importance. There must be a number of patients, like the school teacher with the sensation of strangulation, who left apparently well, but who relapsed and did not come back. A proportion of those who got apparently well, and who never reported in subsequent years, may be in this group, for it is certain that some patients will have nothing to do with the person who failed to cure them or who nearly cured them. The naval lieutenant is a case in point. Another is a woman of forty-nine (1926, Group I, Table IV, Case No. 9) with spasmodic torticollis, which in this particular instance was almost certainly hysterical, and which was exploited in more directions than one. She had been under many doctors without avail, and then came under the influence of a Christian Scientist. After some weeks the torticollis movement stopped, and they were wholly absent for three days, after which they returned. She immediately sent for a doctor, not the Christian Science healer. Seeing that the latter was the only person, out of many, whose ministrations had been followed by anything resembling success, this seemed odd. When asked why she did not send for the healer she replied, "But the treatment had failed", nor could she see that the doctors and indeed the very one she sent for had never done anything else but fail in the past. Like the lieutenant, she would have nothing to do with someone who nearly cured her, for her illness had a money value. By trying then to make short cures, a curable patient may be lost for ever, and yet the existence of these short cases makes it a grave thing to start any patient on a treatment which may last for years, a treatment which in itself is not free from the suspicion that it sometimes prolongs a case.

It might be thought that a patient who did not want to be cured as much as all that would not be cured however long he was kept. But if we can keep patients long enough there is a number whose desire not to be cured may be changed into a desire to be cured. It is also true, as was mentioned on p. 11, that it is often difficult for a patient to break off treatment. The patient may want to leave, but leaving is a thing which requires more effort than staying and therefore many will stay. But once they have, so to speak, escaped it is equally difficult to come back—that, too, requires effort.

There are, of course, also those who want to be cured but who might resent being sent away uncured, who might lose faith altogether in someone who had been inept enough not to see that they were at best half cured. They may, indeed, account for a number of the "lost" patients, for it is quite certain that they would not write if their mood were of this kind.

On the whole I am inclined to think that we are justified in trying the short course. I am inclined to think that the number who do relapse after feeling quite well is not great.

I do not think we shall be able to decide very much from the type of symptoms presented. Agoraphobia and claustrophobia are usually symptoms hard to get rid of, and yet in the half dozen examples from 1921 there was included quite as severe a case apparently as I have ever seen. Nay more, one of the speediest recoveries I have observed was a phobic case. This patient, a man of forty, was admitted in 1930. He came on a Monday. He complained of inability to travel in a railway train unless he were accompanied, and he had found it impossible to stand on any height. He could not remain on the flat roof of a bungalow; even to stand on a hillock gave great discomfort. In two days he travelled alone in a train for a couple of hours and on the following day he stood on a parapet sixty feet above the ground. He then felt perfectly well and remained so for a year at least. He was then lost sight of.

This man illustrates that even in a short course one may often release a repression which is active in producing symptoms. This man's phobia depended in consciousness on the fear of committing suicide. He did not know why he had this fear. His mother was insane; he had been compelled to have her certified, and had been roundly abused for doing so. He felt guilty about it. He himself might go insane, and on talking it over he became aware of feeling that he would have deserved it; he had not felt this before he began to talk. After talking it out, he saw that there was nothing in it, and the symptom dissolved.

An even better example was shown by a patient in the first year of the hospital (1921, Table I, Case, No. 35). This patient had one complaint, the belief that he had tabes. He was depressed. During the war he had been guilty of a serious cowardly act. There can be no question that the offence was serious, all the more as he was a regular officer. As soon as he got into safety he went to a prostitute, and almost at once acquired the fear of syphilis, which soon became the fear of tabes. This so overwhelmed his consciousness that it seems to be true that the act of cowardice disappeared from his mind. On talking carefully over the period at which the fear arose, the recollection of the act came back to his mind with terrible force. For some days his depression was intense, but with care he was induced to look at the affair as done with. He became well and remained so till 1928, when he had a return of nervousness: he managed, however, to get rid of this by himself, and when written to in 1934 was well and said that he had been so for some years. Here again, though an unconscious factor was released, no shadow of the Freudian unconscious was revealed.

Once the fashion of long treatments gets into an institution the number of patients who can be cured in a short time diminishes considerably. The impression derived from a few failures that short treatments are uncertain gets more and more fixed on both doctor and patients, and, as has been already stated, such beliefs are probably one reason why patients do in fact take a long time to get well.

At the Cassel Hospital the average duration of stay got longer and longer, and I am told that at another place where similar patients are treated they are finding the same thing. And, as we shall see presently, the average results were no better than when the average stay of patients was shorter.

In actual practice this question of the long or short treatment is settled by the patient rather than by the doctor. Fortunately there is a considerable number of patients who are sufficiently desirous to get on with the proper business of their lives, so that they will learn easily, go off and commonly succeed; but the doctor can do a good deal to influence their decision one way or the other.

Even if it should ultimately turn out that prolonged and deep analysis is the best method of improving the prognosis in the neuroses, and if it were conceivably possible to provide a sufficient number of trained analysts to take the cases, the question of the treatment of these disorders would not in the least be settled. The Cassel Hospital has always been comprehensive; the psychoanalysts have always been exclusive. Patients who go to a professed analyst go because they wish to be analysed. Such patients are already in a very specialized group of neurotics; in fact a classification of patients could be made on this basis, which would in many ways be more profitable than by grouping them either on the ordinary clinical basis (into psychotics and neurotics and the latter into obsessives, conversion hysterics and so on) or aetiologically as the analysts themselves have tried to do. They might well be divided into those who really wish to be cured and those who do not. No doubt soon after the treatment has started a large number will apparently drift into the second category, but the fact that they did not start in it is vital; for those originally in this second category obviously never or hardly ever get into the analyst's consulting room. The analyst is, in truth, familiar with a very limited class of clinical material. Most of our patients arrive with the belief that they have organic disease, a large proportion are actively hostile to being treated at all and have come only to please some relative whom they do not wish or do not dare to offend. After they have been persuaded that their illness is psychogenic, large numbers do not wish to go deeply into their feelings, and refuse to tell everything they think of. The religious man on p. 42 with agoraphobia is a case in point. Many of them too are bedridden, and it may not be possible to get them out of bed for some weeks. These obviously cannot go either to an analyst or, as has been already stated, to an out-patient clinic. Certain psychotherapists, with consulting room practice only, say sometimes that no patient with neurosis need be in bed for more than a few days. The secondary results of neurosis may however necessitate a longer period. Not only may there be the results of failure of nutrition, but such factors as excessive drugging may make it essential to have bed treatment while drugs are being removed.

In physical illness, refusal on the part of the patient to co-operate may result in the doctor being compelled to give up the case. With nervous patients to do so has seemed to us to indicate some degree of incompetence on the part of the doctor. The desire to exploit illness, not to get well, not at least soon, is a common factor in these cases, and this must often be exhibited as a dislike of co-operation. Non-co-operation is therefore merely a symptom of the disorder to be treated as such. Hostility therefore should never be a reason for the doctor giving up the patient though it may end in the patient giving up the doctor: but it is seldom that this happens.

How very different is this kind of patient from the only kind whom Freud says that he will treat. He has laid down that he will not treat any patient unless the latter promises to make no reservations, unless he promises to tell him everything that comes into his mind. Once Freud broke this rule; the patient was an official and said he would be unable to tell anything connected with his office, and later Freud felt that he was using this reservation to cover other things; indeed he could hardly have avoided doing so, for one's private life and one's official work must in all sorts of places be intertwined. But this ideal patient who is going to co-operate to the extent that Freud demands is already half-cured. This rule of Freud's is followed by the other analysts, who therefore see only one kind of case. About half the patients I see would refuse to make any promise of the kind. It is an odd thing that for the Freudians this very common symptom of neurosis—hostility to the doctor—should be picked out, and made different from all their other symptoms, and be a bar to treatment. If the hostility can be overcome, its presence to start with is no bar to success. For example, in 1923 (Group I, Table I, Case No. 12) a lady of thirty-six was admitted suffering from contractures of both feet in the position of talipes varus so that she could not stand. She was also in a condition of terror, so that she had almost the facies and eyes of a patient with exophthalmic goitre. She could not even sit down when she arrived until she had a definite promise that we would not keep her against her will, and she constantly implored a friend who had brought her to take her away at once. Yet she was quite well in a month and remained so for ten years.

IX

TABLE OF RESULTS

Up to this point patients have been spoken of as becoming well, and the illustrations given have been nearly all of patients who have been quite well since their treatment, or whose illnesses, whether of an intercurrent physical nature or relapses of neurosis, have been short-lived, so that later they were well again and remained so. There is, however, also a large class where the patients say that they derived great benefit, but that some of their symptoms have remained, and they therefore cannot report that they are well. For example, a patient who had been prostrated with illness, confined to bed with exhaustion, prone to dyspepsia and insomnia, will report that he is working and usually well, but that sometimes he has a few nights of insomnia or a period of dyspepsia, or that from time to time he gets a headache—a new symptom in these partly benefited patients is common. Such patients are not called well, but as they are quite certain that they are very different, and that they can now do their work and usually enjoy life, they are called improved. We have not made more than one category of these patients. We might have had an "improved" and a "much improved" category, but it would have been difficult to assess this, unless the opportunity had been given to see all the patients personally and not to trust mainly to written reports. We have therefore three classes only—the well, the improved and the ill. The latter fall under two heads. There are those who never improved at all, and those who relapsed after being well or improved.

The following table shows what has happened to all the patients with psychoneuroses who have passed through the Cassel Hospital between the years 1921 and the end of 1933. The final reports were collected in the year 1934. This is not the total number of patients who passed through the hospital. That was 2270. The remainder suffered from psychoses, from organic diseases, from being psychopathic personalities, from drug addiction or from alcoholism. Some figures will be given separately about the alcoholic patients. The

Year	No. of patients	Av. stay months	Reports one year after discharge: Well	%	Improved	%	No benefit	%	Lost sight of	Reports after three years: Well	%	Improved	%	Lost sight of	Reports after five years: Well	%	Improved	%	Lost sight of	Reports in 1934: Well	%	Improved	%	Lost sight of	Known to have relapsed in the whole period
1921	58	2·3	24	41	21	36	13	22	0	24	41	10	18	24	22	38	8	14	28	12	20	3	5	43	7
1922	98	3·2	40	40	40	40	18	18	0	36	36	16	16	46	32	32	8	8	58	20	20	4	4	74	19
1923	98	3·9	31	31	34	34	22	22	11	36	36	15	15	47	30	30	5	5	63	16	16	3	3	79	18
1924	118	3·6	49	41	38	33	27	22	4	41	34	13	11	64	37	31	5	4	76	30	25	5	4	83	15
1925	85	2·8	43	51	17	20	23	27	2	37	42	11	13	37	32	37	5	6	48	13	15	5	6	67	9
1926	103	4·1	52	50	17	16	18	17	16	44	43	13	12	46	35	34	7	6	61	33	32	4	4	66	8
1927	101	3·8	50	50	24	24	18	18	9	34	34	8	8	59	24	24	8	8	69	30	30	3	3	68	15
1928	94	4·2	54	57	16	17	16	8	8	41	43	5	6	48	38	40	3	4	53	30	32	6	7	58	13
1929	95	4·6	40	42	24	25	18	19	13	44	48	4	5	47	40	42	9	9	46	40	42	9	9	46	5
															After this there is no five-year after history										
1930	100	4·4	63	63	17	17	14	14	6	49	49	6	6	45						47	47	5	5	48	12
1931	93	6·2	41	44	23	25	17	18	12	35	37	11	12	47						35	37	11	12	47	9
										After this there is no three-year after history															
1932	75	4·4	33	44	18	23	11	14	13											36	48	11	14	28	4
1933	68	7·2	27	40	17	25	21	30	3											27	40	17	25	24	
TOTAL	1186	4·1	547	45	306	25	236	19	97	421 out of 1043 patients	40	112	10	510	290 out of 850 patients	34	58	6	502	369	31	86	7	731	134

The percentages are calculated to the nearest integer. Decimals have been omitted.

drug addicts were too few to make them worth a report. The psychopathic personalities comprised the sort of persons who stole money, passed worthless cheques, were pathological liars and so forth, but who were not complaining of illness. These patients, though they are certainly suffering from mental disorder, should not be mixed up with any statistical enquiry into the progress of the neuroses.

With these remarks the first table (p. 79) gives the results so far as we know them one year after treatment, three years after treatment, five years after treatment and in 1934.

A few comments on this table are necessary. The figure 1186 is approximate. It is believed that it is possible to differentiate between psychoneurotic and psychotic patients. If we can show that there is no great tendency for those who were placed in the neurotic category to pass into the psychotic category this claim will be so far strengthened. But the figure is only approximate, because no one could be sure of determining between these two categories in every example. The borderline cases are difficult to place: those in the centre of the picture are clear. The important point is that we should be able to make this diagnosis when we can, for the purpose not only of treatment, but of making a prognosis. If we can be sure that few of the patients whom we have diagnosed on clinical grounds as neurotic become psychotic, we shall have assisted greatly in clearing up one important point in prognosis. This subject will be returned to later.

At the end of a year out of these patients 547 had reported themselves well and 306 as improved, 45 per cent. and 25 per cent. respectively. Seventy per cent. therefore had remained well or improved one year after discharge. It has not been our habit to attach much importance to the state of a patient on leaving the hospital, because one of two opposite things sometimes happened. The patient might go away feeling very brave and well and collapse soon; or he might go away apparently ill with all his symptoms back, and write in a week or two that he was quite well, and ever after that he was well. The first patient had achieved one of those pseudo-cures to which reference has frequently been made; the second was more wisely perhaps frightened by the thought of going away, though when he tried the world he found that he could manage it. The first were rather commoner than the second, and seeing that many kinds of treatment can be followed by temporary improvement which disappears with the disappearance of the supporting healer, it did not seem that the state of any patient on discharge was of much interest. During the same period 236, or 20 per cent., declared that they had not benefited at all from the hospital, while 97, or 8 per cent., had been lost sight of. The average stay was 4·1 months.

If we look at the different years, some curious facts emerge. The column for average duration of stay is interesting. It will be seen that there is a slow increase of duration of stay rising suddenly in the last year: but on the whole the duration has increased regularly; not so the numbers of the "well" expressed either as actual figures or as percentages. There is an improvement in results up to 1930, which is fairly regular, with two relapses, one in 1923, and the other in 1929. After 1930, which was the best year, there is steady worsening of results. If duration of stay has anything to do with this, it would seem that the optimum duration was round about four months. If the columns for the subsequent years are studied, these middle years retain their supremacy in a remarkable way.

It will be noted also that in all years after the year after discharge, the number who report themselves well is better maintained than those who report themselves improved. The explanation is due partly to the fact that more of the improved get lost than the well; they get more easily tired of us and our letters, and more easily do not wish to have anything more to do with us. But this is by no means the whole explanation. For the year 1923, thirty-one patients reported well a year after discharge; but three years after discharge thirty-six reported themselves as well. For the year 1929, forty reported well a year after discharge, forty-four at the three-year period. The explanation of this is, as may be seen in many examples in the tables at the end, that certain patients who reported themselves as improved in the earlier years after leaving the hospital, reported themselves later as well. The significance of this is great. So far from patients collapsing as soon as the supporting hand of the therapist is withdrawn, there are many instances where the patients have gone on improving themselves in the art of living, the first lessons in which had been given at Swaylands. In this connection there occurs to me a little story.

About ten years ago I met two former patients about the same time but on different occasions; but they both asked me much the same question. They had been patients before the war. The question was in this wise: "Do you still teach your patients something on a Monday and expect them to be well by the Tuesday?" My reply does not matter, but they went on to tell me that what I did was to sow a seed, which in favourable soil produced a plant which went on growing for a long time, much longer than I had probably ever conceived. It seems that these figures confirm this doctrine, which has, of course, been put forward by many others, somewhat notably by Count Keyserling, and given by him the striking title of the Logos Spermatikos.

It is also to be noted that as the years go by the number who are "lost," i.e. do not report themselves, increases. One must not infer from this that all these relapsed. Some did; but it has been common for us not to hear for some years and then to get a report saying that the patients had been well all the time.

It will be seen that about 40 per cent. of the patients have reported themselves well at the end of three years, 34 per cent. at the end of five. The final statement that in 1934 this figure had fallen to 31 per cent. is not quite fair to our results, because the number lost in the earlier years had become very high; and this probably has reference to the fact that they had been left alone and not written to in some instances for as long as seven years. By reference to the tables of the individual cases at the end it will be seen also that no claim is made that all these patients who are called well were well all the time.

X

SPECIAL GROUPS

1. *Anorexia Nervosa*

The table which has been exhibited on p. 79 is a general survey. Every person who manifested symptoms of the kind of illnesses which are usually called psychoneurosis is in it. But it is worth while to make some subdivisions, as every kind of neurosis, even on clinical grounds alone, does not carry the same risk. We shall therefore now proceed to analyse the figures of certain clinical groups. The first of these is the group anorexia nervosa. This condition is one which is quite definite, though in the literature the term has unfortunately often been used to cover a multitude of totally different clinical conditions. Any nervous or psychotic person who is not eating well is apt to be included in it. It is most important that whatever name is used we should be very clear not to confuse this group with patients suffering from psychosis; in psychotics who are refusing their food for delusional reasons, nothing but forcible feeding is of the slightest avail; for the group we are now considering such a proceeding would be an unjustifiable outrage. In neurotics who take their food badly because of anxiety there is usually no difficulty in getting food taken as soon as the anxieties have been relieved; but in the patients we are now considering there are no conscious anxieties of any kind, none at least that the patient will talk about until she has been seen on several occasions. In view of the extreme importance of these cases, and of the fact that the patients are frequently given inadequate treatment for months or years, it may be well to recapitulate certain characteristics which mark them out from every other kind of patient. They are extremely easy to diagnose, and with proper treatment the cures should be 100 per cent. This figure I regret to say we did not quite attain.

The characteristics are:

1. The patient is an unmarried girl or young woman.
2. There is anorexia of extreme degree.

3. There is loss of weight, which is progressive and proceeds to a degree seen only in the late stages of cancer or chronic phthisis; any organic wasting disease should be easily excluded after a short time.
4. Amenorrhoea is always present.
5. No matter how near to death the patient may be, she never owns up to being tired, or indeed ill in any way.

I have never seen a case in a male, though they have been described. Several young men were sent to the hospital alleged to be suffering from this condition, but all had manifest delusions such as that food would rot their brains, or that they could not eat because they had a stoppage in the bowels.

I have seen one example of the illness in a married woman, but it is probably significant that she had no children. I did not attend her, but only met her socially and therefore can supply no real facts.

These patients do not complain of anything. They have no dyspepsia, which contrasts very strongly with certain other thin girls, who do not eat because of the subsequent discomfort. These do not eat, solely because they are not hungry. In very advanced cases it may be obvious to everybody that the patient feels ill and weak, but as a rule, even if they are carried to hospital in an ambulance, they will not own that this was necessary. There are a few other characteristics of the very advanced cases; when the patient is emaciated, she commonly has a blue nose and blue finger tips, and the skin is harsh and dry and has lost its elasticity all over the body, so that it cannot be pinched up.

We have records of nineteen patients which are given below in tabular form. Sixteen out of these nineteen did absolutely well. One died from relapse, two have been lost sight of. One patient kept well for five years and then died suddenly of septicaemia. I have ascertained that this was really septicaemia, and that the word is not an euphemism for a relapse of anorexia nervosa. It will be observed that the patient who died relapsed as soon as she left the hospital (Case No. 16). It will be seen also that five others relapsed, but all did well on a second course of treatment. Those who were lost sight of are not ill so far as I know.

These patients who relapsed, although they were fat when they left the hospital, had not made any real mental change, and I suppose they had not been kept long enough. They accomplished a sufficient mental change in their second visit. It is possible that they had got tired of the regime of rest in bed with full feeding and were more willing to listen on the second course of treatment.

Résumé of the Patients with Anorexia Nervosa.

	Year of treatment	Duration of treatment	Age	Gain in weight	Subsequent history	Known period of keeping well
1	1922	6 weeks	22	16 lb.	Well up to 1931	9 years
2	1923	8 ,,	18	20 ,,	A food faddist but well. Lost sight of in 1928	4 ,,
3	1925	8 ,,	14	21 ,,	Relapsed and readmitted same year. Well since	9 ,,
4	1925	10 months	23	28 ,,	Well to 1930. Died of septicaemia	5 ,,
5	1926	6 weeks	16	28 ,,	Relapsed in 1927. Re-admitted. Gained 20 lb. Well since	8 ,,
6	1926	16 ,,	17	34 ,,	Well to date	8 ,,
7	1926	6 ,,	19	10 ,,	Lost sight of	
8	1926	7 ,,	17	17 ,,	Well to 1934	8 ,,
9	1927	5 ,,	20	14 ,,	Relapsed but got well later	2 ,,
10	1929	11 months	19	22 ,,	Well to date	5 ,,
11	1930	16 weeks	17	14 ,,	Well to date	4 ,,
12	1930	12 ,,	19	23 ,,	Well to date	4 ,,
13	1931	7 months	19	28 ,,	Well to date	3 ,,
14	1931	2½ ,,	18	7 ,,	Well to date	3 ,,
15	1931	3 ,,	22	25 ,,	Well to date	3 ,,
16	1931	5 ,,	14	28 ,,	Relapsed and died in 6 months	
17	1932	10 weeks	23	14 ,,	Well to date	2 ,,
18	1932	4 months	19	19 ,,	Relapsed at once, but cured elsewhere	
19	1932	2 ,,	25	19 ,,	Relapse. Re-admitted. Gained 10 lb. Well since	2 ,,

The treatment which was adopted was practically that laid down by Weir Mitchell for the conduct of the rest cure: rest, isolation, full feeding and the discussion of difficulties. These discussions were, on the whole, not very deep. In one or two there was some enquiry on a deeper plane, but these patients did no better than the others; in fact one of those who relapsed was one who was investigated more deeply. With a regime of this sort, carried out away from the relatives, nothing is easier than to fatten a patient, nothing more difficult than to try to do it outside an institution; but if a mental change has not been effected at the same time, relapse is very likely. I think it can be said that if relapse is going to occur it will do so quickly.

I have seen one other death from relapse of this illness many years ago. But it cannot be said that every patient who relapses will die. In the nineties, for example, a young woman saw her brother killed, and soon went into a condition of anorexia nervosa. I treated her in 1902; she gained 28 lb. in weight and relapsed immediately. After that she lived on next to nothing, and in a state of great emaciation for about thirty years more, during which time I met her socially on many occasions. She had the typical appearance during all that period, emaciated with cyanosed extremities. She died ultimately of cerebral arterial disease. I am unable to give a death-rate for patients who relapse and are not again or finally cured, but from the grave way that certain doctors, who should know, talk of this condition, I imagine it is high. I know personally only of the two about whom I have spoken.

2. *Traumatic Neuroses and Compensation Neuroses.*

The next group to be specially studied is that of the traumatic neuroses. Along with them are taken compensation neuroses.

It has been held that the prognosis in these conditions is dependent on whether the patient is deriving benefit from the illness or not. In a sense this might be said of most other neuroses, but in these particular examples, the pressure put on the patient to retain his neurosis is often peculiarly strong. Many of these patients are in the hands of a lawyer who urges them on no account to come to terms so long as any symptoms are present, because, he will say, no one can foresee the end, nor tell what expensive treatment may not be necessary before cure is reached. It is natural that a legal adviser should take this view and that he should press it on his client, but everyone with an elementary knowledge of average human psychology is aware that suggestion of this sort is accepted very readily, and that its acceptance is sure to be accompanied by increase and prolongation of symptoms. There is certainly no other neurosis where the patient is so free from receiving advice from his friends to pull himself together and get on with his business, which is a curious reflection on the attitude of the family towards these disorders. Dr Lewy of New York, who is chief medical examiner for the Compensation Commission of the State of New York, says that he has "never known of a single case from my very large material, which was ever disposed of, unless the individual received a monetary remuneration to his own satisfaction" (*Bulletin of New York Academy of Medicine*, January 1930, p. 3. Foster Kennedy). This is probably true for the mass of patients and it is probably easier to settle these cases by legal means than to treat the patient, though if time enough for treatment is given some of the patients get better without bribery.

We have had only eight cases of traumatic neuroses since the hospital opened, but though the numbers are small a close study of them may be worth while.

Compensation neurosis is not identical with traumatic neurosis, as far as the starting-point is concerned, though their aim or intention is the same. Compensation neurosis may occur without trauma as in that almost comic condition of miner's nystagmus without movement of the eyes, or as in soldiers who joined up but acquired neurosis before they went to France—sufferers from "khaki shock" as their fellows, who had been blown up or buried, rather unkindly called it. I do not think traumatic neurosis ever occurs unless there is a compensation element. Trauma in itself does not cause neurosis: but in all the cases dealt with in this section, though the history of trauma occurred, the neurosis depended on the exploitation of that trauma. I have had experience elsewhere of a large number of patients belonging to a particular class of compensation neuroses, most of which started with trauma, though not all. For eighteen months after the close of the war I was attached to a hospital which cared for "neurasthenic pensioners", i.e. for patients with war neuroses, who had not been discharged when the war ended. During these months I had fifteen beds under my care and the superintendence of about thirty or forty others. During the last two years of the war, I had had 130 beds for patients with war neuroses under my care, most of which were traumatic. I shall deal with these two sets of patients presently.

Three Swaylands patients have been already referred to, the man who strained his back in the garage and who was cured when the Court gave the final award (see p. 26); the naval lieutenant and the cavalry officer who were persuaded out of their neuroses (see p. 60 *et seq.*).

A fourth (1923, Group I, Table IV, Case No. 3) was a sea captain. In 1915 he had stood on the bridge for many hours in bitterly cold, freezing weather. His legs felt numb, and he did no further duty from then onwards. He came under care in 1923. The symptoms came on while he was on active service in an auxiliary vessel, and because his disability had come on during active service he was receiving a war pension. His complaints were pain in the back, anaesthesia of both legs and an odd gait. There were no signs of organic disease. I think it has been found generally that the subjects of war neurosis, if they were not cured during the war itself, were the unlikeliest patients of all the compensation neuroses to get well. During the war there was the immense bribe that one might get out of the army if recovery occurred and in consequence there were many recoveries among the occupants of the 130 beds under my care during the war. I am aware that it has been alleged by some psychotherapists that some of their patients even returned to duty at the front. There are, however, no available statistics about the duration of recovery, and my impression is that none stood the return to duty for long without relapsing. I heard at the time many stories of speedy breakdowns in those who had returned to duty, and in the early summer of 1918 a medical general called at the hospital in which I served and informed us quite unofficially but distinctly that we would do well to recommend our cured patients for discharge, and not for return to duty. The depots, he said, were cluttered with men who had had shellshock and who were really of no use to the army. On the other hand, I heard from many who had been returned to civil life that they were doing well. When the war ended a very different story was told. These men who were discharged as "well" from the army during the war had no difficulty in finding lucrative employment: the factories were all short of men; the heaven of civilian life, after the hell of the trenches and the purgatory of sergeant-majors, provided exactly the right atmosphere for cure. After the peace, to exchange neurosis for civil life meant exchanging an income for semi-starvation; for unemployment soon showed itself after the end of the war, and to be well meant exchanging the comfort of a well-run hospital for the discomfort of a home where food and fuel were difficult to get. Therefore the prognosis of the pensioner was absolutely bad.

While the man was an inmate of a hospital he was fed, lodged and clothed, and his wife and family received a full separation allowance as if he were on active service. If he were discharged from hospital, the separation allowance ceased, for now he was supposed to be in a position to support his dependants. He himself would be assessed at say 20 per cent. disability, and get perhaps 10*s*. a week altogether. What happened was that the man became fairly well in hospital. Then one day the doctor asked him if he thought he were well enough to go home. He usually said that he was. A few days later something happened which brought all his illness back. Either a motor-car had backfired near him, or he saw an aeroplane, or something occurred which brought back the war to his mind, and all his symptoms returned. After that he never became properly well again. So that if he were discharged the disability had to be assessed very highly. The sea captain was therefore in this hopeless class. His disability was officially 100 per cent. He could live if he remained ill; it was improbable that he could do so if he became well. There was no question but that his pension would be drastically reduced if he did become well; the fact that he had suffered for years, and had become on that account alone unemployable, would have been given no weight. It was quite certain that after ten years no one would give him another ship.

I have no figures, but my impression is that patients who have suffered from a compensation neurosis of this sort for any length of time never get well. In Dr Lewy's report he says that they do not get well till they receive a satisfactory payment, but he says also that some never get well, even though they have received payment.

The next patient was a man of thirty-nine (1922, Group I, Table I, Case No. 11). Fifteen months before admission he fractured the base of his skull in a motor accident. He became well enough to resume duty in the Navy but soon began to have attacks of giddiness for which he was discharged. He took a cottage in the country and kept fowls. At first his health improved, but soon the attacks of giddiness became much worse and were apt to lead to loss of consciousness. They were, of course, attributed to the accident. By ordinary history taking it was discovered that he was getting on badly with his wife, the idea of living with her in a cottage had attracted him while he was in the Navy, but he had seen very little of her, and they quarrelled very frequently when they tried to live together. The wife had even gone so far as to make a suicidal demonstration, and it was then that he relapsed. Both husband and wife were seen on several occasions, and both fortunately saw that they must behave differently. A year after discharge he was still quite well, but was then lost sight of. It is probable that he remained well. Here then was a person whose neurosis was used twice, once to get out of the Navy, and once to get away from his wife.

The next patient became well. She was a lady of forty-four, admitted early in 1926 (Group I, Table I, Case No. 24). She suffered from foot drop, insomnia, constipation and fears of a vague character. These symptoms had been present for eighteen months. Before that time she had been well, though she was a woman rather disappointed with life, who for years had been apt to grumble. Eighteen months before admission she was working as matron in a school, which she hated. She disliked the headmistress. She slipped on a parquet floor on to her spine; soon after that the foot drop appeared. She had gone through much painful treatment including the extraction of twenty-seven teeth, most of which were healthy. Throughout she was greatly encouraged by a solicitor to make no compromise of any kind. She was treated by direct explanation of what she was doing, that she was revenging herself on the school and on the headmistress, and even on the world generally; she was told that so long as she went on getting money for this illness, even though it was a pittance, so long would she remain ill. There was a considerable resistance, as was natural, for such a view is unpleasant; there were indignant proposals that I should write to the insurance company and say that she was a malingerer; in the end, however, she accepted my view, stopped the receipt of the money herself, and became well. The result of the whole thing has been that she has adjusted herself to the world much better than before she had treatment. She was four months under treatment. It is known that she kept well for over four years; since then she has been lost sight of.

The next patient was a workman who had received a slight blow on the back. He was admitted to hospital in 1928 (Table I, Group I (*b*), Case No. 10). He was complaining of paraplegia, with coarse tremor of the limbs, agoraphobia and nightmares. The sense of grievance in him was very strong; it had been aggravated by a doctor having given evidence in court that his symptoms were probably due to masturbation. This had drawn some strong remarks from the judge, who had stated that the defendants ought to treat the man till he was well. He himself hoped that he would get seven hundred pounds, with which he intended to start a dairy farm. Hitherto he had worked in an engineering shop. He was in hospital seven months and became quite well though he never received any lump sum. The insurance company paid for his treatment, but that was all.

The last patient should have been cured. He lost his symptoms but relapsed (1931, Group I, Table IV, Case No. 12). He had been burnt in a chemical works on an occasion when he had displayed great courage. The case had drifted on into neurosis. There was no ill-feeling against his employers, but everyone had discouraged him when he wanted to return to work. His symptoms were nervousness, weakness of the left leg which had been badly burnt and insomnia. He was, of course, receiving financial compensation.

These symptoms disappeared entirely, and he was advised to go home and to start work immediately. His doctor was written to about the importance of this, for the man had already been out of work for eighteen months. Incredible though it sounds, some doctor advised him when he went home not to resume work for a month, and naturally when that month was up he had reacquired many symptoms. He believed, of course, that if he were not yet fit to return to work after all these months, there must be something very serious indeed. It is eminently possible that if there had been no money bribe for keeping ill, the doctor at home would not have been listened to. The re-formation of symptoms was greatly assisted by the fact that three teeth had to be extracted, about which much fuss could be and was made.

Commenting on these examples it may be said that the prognosis in traumatic neurosis is not so hopeless as Dr Lewy suggested, even where the patient is being paid so long as he keeps ill. The post-war cases were probably all hopeless, for there the patient had nothing to look forward to if he became well. Of our eight patients only two did absolutely badly, and one of these—the man burnt in the chemical works—was almost invited to become ill again after he had been cured. Only two of the others were actually receiving money so long as they were ill, but the others were trying to get benefit by being ill. For the particular patient who was quarrelling with his wife it was easy to get him to see that that could lead to nothing, that he was not in fact getting sympathy or anything else from her by neurosis. But though there were two patients receiving money, who were cured without any satisfactory money settlement, the time spent over them would make it rather an undertaking to treat in this way the large numbers with which the insurance companies have to deal. If the legal profession, bench, bar and solicitors, could grasp the conception of neurosis, and if it were possible that legislators could become capable of being educated to see that not trauma, but advantage to be gained by a history of trauma, was what made these people ill, this form of illness would disappear. There is not, of course, the slightest hope that this will happen—the trend is the other way, and miner's nystagmus without oscillation should warn us that probably more and more people will be able to enjoy incomes merely by stating that they are not feeling well.

XI

PROGNOSIS IN THE OBSESSIONAL-COMPULSIVE NEUROSIS

Nearly every patient has compulsions and obsessions, nay more, nearly every human being has them. This class can therefore be as large or as small as you like. It is accordingly easy enough to produce good results if only the class is kept large enough.

In our reports the term has been kept narrowly to those patients whose symptomatology was confined entirely to these troubles. Further, the patients afflicted with these disorders had no time in their lives for any activities except to attend to their symptoms. The condition to be reported on is one of degree, of the amount of symptom. In every other respect the patients were quite well; they made no complaints at all of any other kind except the mental distress which their symptoms gave them.

For example, a married woman of forty was obsessed with the thought that she might have put poison somewhere where it would harm people. If she went out for a walk she might have bought some, though she could not remember doing so, and the fact that she had not got it with her might have been because she had left it under a hedge. She might therefore have to go over the whole ground again and again to be sure that it was not lying about somewhere. Consequently it gradually came to pass that she never went out. She cooked the meals of the house, but had to destroy a great deal in case she had put poison in it, and all this took endless time. She knew intellectually that the whole of this was nonsense, but that made no difference. This patient did not get well.

Or, again, another woman of thirty was compelled to put everything straight. She would spend the whole day doing this. It took her hours to dress, because she might not have put her dress on straight, or she might have put on the upper part of one dress and the skirt of another. She had to reassure herself over and over again that this was not true before she could leave her bedroom.

And the endless straightening of things in the house was then continued throughout the day. This patient improved very much.

The commonest of these unfortunates are the washers. They spend hours washing, and may scrub sores in their skins, and nothing can make them clean. Or the compulsion may be purely mental. Certain words are heard and the patient must stand stock still to get them right. A young girl had to react in this way to certain words like "silly", "blood" and several others. If she heard any of these words to which she was sensitized, she had to stop whatever she was doing and perform some indescribable mental exercise to get the thing right. This might take half an hour, and as the harmful words were all common, she spent a good deal of the day doing this.

The disease is usually chronic, but I have met one which was acute and which seemed to be a form of the manic-depressive psychosis (1926, Group I, Table IV, Case No. 14). This was a man aged fifty in whom the compulsion to put things straight was so great that he found it nearly impossible to get to bed. Everything in the room had to be right: he had three or four pairs of boots and shoes, and these had to stand with their heels exactly in line, and it took perhaps an hour to be sure that they were: then other things had to be treated in similar fashion. In the morning the room had to be straight before he could leave it, and the day was always far spent before he could go out. The condition had come on suddenly about a month before admission. He remained in this state for about a year and then got well, also rather suddenly. He remained well for about five years, and then wrote to say that all his symptoms had returned. While he was under care he was full of a sense of sin because he had sexual thoughts directed towards his father's second wife. The illness was his own fault and a fitting punishment for evil in his youth. Though the picture was dominated by the furious energy which he displayed in getting things right, which is almost the opposite of the retardation usually found, there is little doubt that this was a variant of the manic-depressive psychosis, especially in view of the complete recovery from this attack which occurred spontaneously, followed long afterwards by relapse. There are other incipient psychoses where obsessions are prodromal symptoms, but that does not invalidate the existence of a chronic obsessive compulsive neurosis.

We have had about thirty-four of these severe cases at Swaylands. Nine have done fairly well. The attempt to analyse was made in nearly all these patients, but sometimes this failed, not in the sense of failing to cure, but in that of failing to be accomplished as a process. Sometimes the patient's compulsions prevented any flow of associations being communicated. Psychoanalysis is not here, however, a *sine qua non* for cure. Some patients do apparently get better when something happens. In 1928 the attempt to analyse a man with severe obsessions was made, but he was rather "sticky" and little was got from him: his sister thought him better at the end of four months when he left, though there seemed little difference to us. A year later he was well and he has remained well since. A choice of explanation of this is offered. The sister wrote to say that the cure had been finally effected after a course of osteopathy: during that course of treatment the patient's father had died, and the sister said that it was marvellous how well the patient had stood this loss. In point of fact the only striking finding which had been obtained in the examination of the patient's mental state was aversion for the father.

In 1933 a woman, already mentioned, who had to put things straight, and who did not seem capable of pursuing the analytical method, derived great benefit from simple argument, that she should constantly keep before herself the thought that it did not matter whether things were straight or not. She was compensating for certain sexual peccadilloes, and also for some sins of disobedience in childhood which came out in her history, and their enormity was considerably reduced by talking these things out so that she saw that putting pictures straight on the wall was not going to expiate her sins.

Many of these patients can be helped considerably by talks of this kind, and the improvements obtained may be more than temporary. I believe that Freud is correct in saying that the regression in these cases is great. If they are not curable they may therefore be responsive to the sense of being supported. This is actually true; but this should be a matter for the general practitioner rather than for the specialist. They will require a supporter in future.

The cases have been kept in the tables separately from the others since 1927, and will be found under the appropriate headings. Before that time they will be found scattered along with the other examples of psychoneurosis. They are included in the general table of results given on p. 79, and it may be pointed out that the average of these results would be better without them.

Sex troubles seemed to predominate in these cases more than in most. Quite conscious anal sexual interest was met with on several occasions. On the whole it may be noted that in what may be called the more general cases of neurosis, there seem to be many factors of causal and therapeutical importance besides sexual, however widely that word may be used. Many of these general patients had sex difficulties. They were people who found many departments of life difficult and therefore the sexual department was so too. In the six patients who were specially studied on p. 38 *et seq.*, sex difficulties seemed of no importance; this is true of many others, and this is said on two grounds: (1) that many of them did not talk about sex troubles at all, (2) and yet they became and remained well. The theorists will say that sex difficulties could certainly have been found if they had been looked for, and though I have no doubt that this is true, the two statements just made show that if they had been found, they would have been of no causal importance for the case in hand. In the obsessional cases, however, sex difficulties were great, quite often of the nature of conscious perversions.

Something must be said about the patients in all the groups who did not derive any benefit from Swaylands, of whom we know that there were at least two hundred and thirty-six. Apart from the obvious criticism that they were not treated well enough or long enough, there were reasons why many of them should not get better. For some of them the outside world was tolerable only if they were ill. If they were well, they were expected to do all sorts of things which they could not do; sometimes this was because their environment was usually harsh, but actually softened by illness; but more often it was because they themselves could not bring themselves to face quite ordinary difficulties. As an example of the first we may cite the case of an elderly man whose wife was a terrible shrew if he were well, but she was quite nice to him if he were ill. As an example of the second we may take an oldish school teacher, very weary of her job, who could retire earlier than the normal age for retiring on her pension only if her health were not good. Her task was really not excessive but she could face it no longer.

It is of interest to know that in the first ten years of the history of the hospital we have heard only of about sixteen patients who became well elsewhere after we had failed. It must be true, of course, that many more have been cured elsewhere, but I think that the number is probably not large. I have not included in these failures those patients who relapsed soon after leaving us, but who came back for a second course of treatment, after which they kept well. These are put along with those who derived benefit from the first. The relapse is noted in the tables.

This closes our analysis of prognosis of particular forms of neuroses. I have not attempted to differentiate the results between hysteria and the anxiety state. For years we have returned patients under these two heads, but the distinction between them seems a little unreal. There is hysterical paralysis on the one hand, and there are patients on the other with, say, a phobia and nothing else, but the categories do on the whole run into one another. I think that in fact we seldom saw the classical hysterical paralytic with the so-called *belle indifférence*. Our patients with paralysis seemed mostly to be very anxious, nervous people. I never understood the Freudian classification of anxiety neurosis, true neurasthenia, anxiety hysteria, and so on, and therefore there is no hint of it here.

There are, however, two subjects of importance which remain to be discussed:

1. What is the chance of neurotic patients committing suicide?

and

2. What is the chance that they may become insane?

XII

PROGNOSIS WITH REGARD TO SUICIDE

The fear of committing suicide is a common symptom among patients suffering from anxiety states; the threat to do so is one frequently made by certain hysterics. It is therefore important to know whether these fears or threats are of any value, do these patients ever commit suicide? This question is closely related to another—do these patients become insane, and in what proportion? In the manic-depressive psychosis the prognosis of any attack is almost identical with the question of whether the patient will commit suicide or not; if he does not, he will almost certainly get better. Is there anything to correspond in the neuroses?

I believe that certain patients who are undoubtedly suffering from neurosis may commit suicide without having first passed into a state of psychosis; though I think also that such an event is very rare.

I have notes of seven patients who seemed to be psychoneurotics, who committed suicide. I am not stating their year in hospital. These will be briefly summarized.

1. F. 50. She was desperately unhappy at home, and suffered also from insomnia and dyspepsia for which she was sent to hospital. The time was near when she would have to return home. She committed suicide in the hospital. Method employed, morphia.

2. F. 39. In twice. Complained of headache, insomnia, loss of weight, poor memory, easily worried. She improved but relapsed. Her husband was a drunkard and not European, and I have little doubt that he was a tyrant of the worst kind. Suicide one year after last discharge.

3. F. 43. A ruminative obsessional, who felt she must have said or done the wrong thing, and had to go over it again and again to get it right. She improved greatly and kept well four years. There was then a slight return of the obsession which she got over easily. She kept well another four years when she relapsed. She committed suicide soon after. It is possible that this was really an example of the manic-depressive psychosis.

4. M. 45. Came with history of a fugue lasting four days with insomnia. Attempt made to clear the fugue up by hypnotism. Came out of the hypnotic sleep, and two days later tried to commit suicide by taking 100 grains of aspirin. A fatal case had been published in the papers. He committed suicide six years later. The details are not known. It was thought that he had been swindling and feared exposure before he came to Swaylands.

5. M. 24. Marked sense of inferiority because of undescended testicles, with diminished virility. Always felt a fool. Committed suicide when he had come to the conclusion that he could not become virile, nor escape from the feeling of inferiority. He was inferior in other ways. He was clumsy; though very musical he could not acquire technique, could not learn games, etc., etc.

6. M. 41. Phobia that he would murder his wife. Insomnia. Committed suicide when it was time to go home. No other symptoms save the phobia and insomnia. His wife was older than he and had ceased to be sexually attractive. Other people had become so.

7. M. 39. In hospital for six months. Had phobias about standing near passing trains, that he would be swept away by one, fears that he would kill his wife and children, that he might fall out of a window. There was probably unconscious homosexuality. Committed suicide, while under treatment, from a train a few days after the death of a man friend. The patient at all times seemed eminently sane.

M. 58. There is also the following, who was not absolutely certainly the subject of neurosis:

He had suffered for a year from severe headaches, shakiness, insomnia, sensitiveness to noise. He had been investigated at a diagnostic clinic, and was assured there that he would get well, and that there was no serious disease. He soon became quite well, and remained so for three months when he relapsed. He looked well when he came to Swaylands but stated that his headache was very severe. He was shown the evidence against organic disease, which he considered he must have. The same day he slashed his scalp and cut his throat.

This has more resemblance to a psychotic hypochondria than to a neurosis, though he seemed very unlike a dangerous psychotic. Patients like this present a difficult problem. With his characteristic lucidity Dubois describes these patients: "One patient who groans and walks up and down his room, a prey to unspeakable agony, will never think of suicide, while another, who with apparent calm tells you of his annoyances, or who complains only of gastric symptoms, will kill himself as he goes out of your house."

In addition to these there are patients who do not succeed in their attempts to commit suicide, and the question arises whether they meant to make a demonstration which would move their friends to pity and increased attention, or whether life had become so intolerable that they were anxious to end it. It is of some interest that one cannot be sure that they meant to do it even when they succeed, and do actually kill themselves.

For instance a woman of thirty-four was admitted with mutism, headache and general unhappiness. She had a bad hare lip, and this had spoilt her life. She was highly sexed, and had felt keenly the neglect she had received from men on account of her deformity, all the more because, viewed from one side, she was decidedly pretty. The mutism disappeared quickly after persuasion, but the headache continued. She became moody, and began to feel that the doctor was neglecting her, just as everybody else had in time. One night the night sister saw her rushing along the corridor, and into a bathroom, not water-closet, but really a bathroom, and slam the door after her. The sister thought it odd, as she had no occasion to go there at that hour, and therefore she followed her; when she opened the door the patient shrieked, threw herself out of the window and disappeared. She fell fully thirty feet on to a stone flagged court, but was not killed. She was unconscious for some hours, but made a complete recovery, and was very frank about the whole business. She remembered events actually up to jumping at the window, which she said was never meant to be more than a demonstration. If she had been rescued with most of her body out, the doctor would probably not have neglected her any more. If, however, she had been killed, the case could have been thought of only as one of a hysteric committing suicide. I am inclined to believe this patient. She was much better after the accident, so much better that she went as a voluntary patient to a mental hospital, because she recognized that she ought to be under care, where suicide was difficult even though she was quite sure she would not do it. She saw that she owed that amount to other people.

There have, of course, been many patients who took insufficient amounts of drugs, and who were probably demonstrating. There have also been others where the diagnosis was difficult. The borderline case may be a dangerous one.

I think then that we may say that the risk of a person committing suicide who is suffering from frank neurosis is very small, and that the old saying that these patients are too fond of themselves for this to be a serious risk is a true one. It is not certain that even all these patients had neurosis. The third patient with the obsessions was possibly a manic-depressive. The fourth with the fugue may have been an untruthful person in that he may never have had any neurotic symptoms. Nothing is more certain than that the story of a fugue is frequently concocted. I have met with other swindlers who said that they had had lapses from consciousness, and it is true that I saved one at least from prosecution because I believed his story: the aggrieved person said that if what I said were possible, he would not prosecute. Years after I was given by the patient himself considerable evidence that his story was a fabrication. It is probable that the patient (No. 4) did make a genuine attempt at suicide; he was exceedingly ill for some days with bloody vomiting and diarrhoea; but it is more likely that he was malingering because he had swindled than that he was neurotic. The fact that he ultimately committed suicide is not specially in favour of either view.

None of these patients threatened suicide, and so far as hysteria is concerned, the threat of committing suicide may be safely disregarded. With depressed psychotic patients this would not, I think, hold good. If they say they are going to kill themselves, they will probably do so, if given the chance.

XIII

PROGNOSIS AS REGARDS BECOMING INSANE

The fear of insanity is one of the commonest symptoms in the neuroses, and this question of its probability or possibility is therefore constantly cropping up. Certain psychiatrists hold that there is no essential difference between the two states, that the one is merely a milder degree of the other and that a patient may pass from one state into the other. As regards the similarity of the two states, that is merely the old difficulty of defining insanity. We all know that there is a difference though we cannot define it, and, I think, while people are neurotic only, they are sane. That patients may pass from the one state into the other is true, but I do not think it is common. This may happen in two ways. The early symptoms of certain insanities may look very like those of neuroses. For example, healthy men of middle life who have hitherto shown no interest in their health may suddenly acquire a nosophobia. This may at first look like a neurosis, but later the patient often becomes delusional. Now the psychoses are not singular in that their beginnings may look like something else. The beginnings of disseminate sclerosis, for example, may look like hysteria. The other way in which neurosis may develop into psychosis is because a patient may find reality too burdensome and need some flight into illness. A flight into hysteria may suffice. In certain instances, by no means common, if this is disturbed, instead of the usual result, which is the return to health, there may be a further flight into psychosis. Thus a lady of fifty complained of dyspepsia and of nothing else. This was diagnosed correctly as a nervous dyspepsia, and it disappeared after an explanatory conversation. A few days later she complained that an old trouble had revived. People were talking about her, saying that she had done a scandalous thing thirty years before, but that it was not true. After a week or two her dyspepsia returned and the ideas of persecution disappeared. No further attempt to treat her was made.

Again, a man of sixty complained of severe indigestion which he feared might be due to cancer; he was disabused of this idea and then thought he had kidney disease, then pernicious anaemia and so on. When he had been driven out of each illness in turn, he became delusional and violent. He remained insane for over two years. This patient was certified.

The following examples may also be quoted:

F. 40. *Hysterical paraplegia.* Paraplegia disappeared after persuasion. Patient at once became delusional about food, said it was poisoned and she had to be certified.

F. 20. *Hysterical paraplegia and mutism.* These were removed by persuasion, and patient soon showed delusions that she had got into an animal's body and must drown herself to free herself. She had to be certified after struggling to throw herself out of the window.

We have had six patients of this kind where psychosis has followed the immediate removal by treatment of hysterical symptoms.

Some examples where an illness resembling neurosis preceded a psychotic illness may be given:

1. A man of twenty-two complained of inability to concentrate, of pains in the eyes, exhaustion, loss of weight and shyness with strangers. He gained weight easily, and lost all his symptoms. In six weeks he was discharged quite well. After a few months he felt less well, and after a year or so was exhibiting well-marked symptoms of schizophrenia. He had to be certified, and four years later was still under certificate.

2. A man of twenty-three complained of faintness, palpitation, flatulence, chilly feelings, and pollakiuria. He improved but never said he was well. Two years later he developed obsessive-compulsive symptoms with insistent rituals. This also improved. Seven years later he showed persecution symptoms and assaulted his father with a knife, wounding him severely. He was then certified.

3. A woman of twenty-nine complained of pressure and tension in the head, poor sleep and panics. She improved, and three years after discharge from hospital reported herself as well. Next year she exhibited ideas of persecution which necessitated certification.

It is no doubt from stories like these that the view has arisen that there is little difference, save that of degree, between neurosis and psychosis. There is, however, good ground for thinking that such histories are uncommon. It has been possible to obtain reliable information about the whole of these 1186 patients whom we have diagnosed as neurotic, so far as subsequent certifiable psychosis is concerned, up to August 1935. From our own follow up it was known that 23 had had sometime or another a definite psychotic attack. With regard to the "lost" patients there was no information one way or the other, but it was realized that that information could perhaps be obtained, if it be accepted that on the whole the number of patients who developed psychosis roughly corresponded to the number who had been certified. They would not correspond absolutely, because by no means is everyone certified who develops psychosis, and conversely not every patient in a mental hospital suffers from a psychosis. A number of hysterics and patients with anxiety states will be found in these institutions. It seemed however that the correspondence would be sufficiently close to make enquiry worth while. The names and addresses, therefore, of our lost patients were sent to the proper authority, and in reply I was given from official sources the number of persons in that list who had been patients in a mental hospital after they had left Swaylands. I was given the number only and not the names, because of the necessity of keeping the information confidential. I wish now to record my thanks for these figures which have made this part of the book far more useful that it would otherwise have been.

Ten out of these lost patients have been certified, sixteen others have been received into mental hospitals as voluntary patients. Although, as has been stated, it is uncertain that all of these suffered from psychosis, it is safer to assume that they did. With my own twenty-three added on, we can say that about 50 patients out of 1186 have become insane, not a very large number. The objection may be raised that the time has been short, and that if I enquired again in a few years I shall find that a larger number had become insane. Still we must look at the figures we have got, and as they stand they suggest that what has been maintained in this book is justified, viz. that the prognosis with regard to becoming insane is good. There seems here also additional ground for believing that psychosis and neurosis are not different degrees of the same thing. Of the 26 patients from official sources, it is of some interest that 9 were patients who had not improved at Swaylands, 17 had improved. This, so far as it goes, means that there was no marked proclivity for the failures to become insane.

XIV

PROGNOSIS OF ALCOHOLISM

Here we are dealing with a vague subject. How much alcohol does one have to take before one should be labelled alcoholic? Also a man may be taking far too much alcohol though he never gets intoxicated; such a one may suffer from gastritis, cirrhosis of the liver and what not. The people we have had to do with have been labelled alcoholic because either steadily or in bouts they were taking enough alcohol for people to say that they were drunk. Of course we had many patients suffering from neurosis who did from time to time get drunk to escape from misery, but unless alcohol was a very prominent thing in their symptomatology they are not included in this list.

Since 1923 there have been about forty patients who were called alcoholic by their relatives, who themselves admitted that they were taking so much alcohol that they were frequently intoxicated.

Thirteen did very well. In twelve of these alcohol was taken because of psychological difficulties, some of which were unconscious. Homosexuality has played a considerable part. Most of the others were lost sight of.

One man was in a position where he could get alcohol very easily; he had gradually slipped into taking too much. He came to the hospital, made a resolution and kept it for five years. He then had a short relapse of three months' duration; then he kept well to date, about three years. His lapse came from thinking that he could take a little.

The other patients are summarized in the following table:

Sex and age	Duration of alcoholic excess	What did alcohol relieve?	Treatment	Duration of sobriety
M. 31	8 years	Morbid blushing	Analysis	8 years
M. 40	15 ,,	Agoraphobia	Analysis	8 ,,
M. 34	2 ,,	Marital difficulties	Separation from wife	7 ,,
M. 40	3 ,,	Obsessional thinking	Analysis	5 ,,
M. 32	1 year	Nosophobias	Analysis	4 ,,
M. 45	1 ,,	Marital difficulties	Adjustment	1 year
M. 40	1 ,,	Anxiety state	Became well after discussion	1 ,,
M. 30	4 years	Homosexual inversion	Analysis, but threats from father seemed more effectual	6 years
M. 35	Many ,,	Anxieties. Homosexual inversion	Analysis	1 year
M. 53	,, ,,	Anxieties	Analysis	1 ,,
M. 23	3 ,,	Anxieties	Analysis	2 years
M. 30	4 ,,	Anxieties	Analysis	2 ,,

It will be noted that we have no very favourable results in women to report: also that when these patients will consent to analysis the results have been good.

TABLES AND CASE HISTORIES

TABLES AND CASE HISTORIES

The following tables are the record of patients suffering from neurosis, who have been heard from for at least two years after discharge.

To save space certain abbreviations are employed:

W means "Well". The patient has reported that he is well.

I means "Improved". These patients are sensible that a considerable change for the better has taken place.

R means that the patient has relapsed from either W or I and that he is now ill.

Re-ad means "Re-admitted" to the hospital.

ISQ explains itself.

The headings need some explanation. A frequent heading is "Patients who are well or improved". That is the statement of the patient one year after discharge. As will be noted, the patient may have relapsed the year after. That would not alter his place in that special table. These tables were brought up to date by year and reprinted every three years, and it was most convenient to leave a patient where he had been even if he had relapsed quickly.

1921. Table I. *Patients who are Better*

Case no.	Sex and age	Duration of stay	Symptoms	Duration of symptoms before admission	Result on discharge	Reports in 1922	1923	1924	1925	1926	1927	1928	1929	1930	1931	1932	1933	1934
1	F. 34	4 weeks	Pains. Exhaustion. Sweats. Tremors. Insomnia	1 year	W	W	—	—	—	—	—	—	—	—	—	—	—	—
2	F. 48	4 ,,	Insomnia. Depression. Headache	—	W	W	—	—	—	—	—	—	—	—	—	—	—	—
3	M. 19	4 ,,	Fear of darkness and crowds. Epileptiform fits. Somnambulism. Headache. Terrifying dreams	4 months	W	W	W	W	W	W	R	W	—	W	—	—	—	W
4	F. 48	5 ,,	Pains. Dyspepsia. Fears that she might become insane and kill her mother. Fatigue	4 years	W	W	W	W	W	W	W	W	—	—	—	—	—	W
5	F. 48	6 ,,	Fatigue (extreme). Indigestion. Depression	22 ,,	W	W	W	W	W	W	W	W	—	—	—	—	—	W
6	M. 56	6 ,,	Insomnia. Shuffling gait	1 year	I	W	—	—	—	—	—	—	—	—	—	—	—	—
7	F. 59	7 ,,	Pains. Inability to stand. Insomnia. Palpitation. Fear of insanity	33 years	W	W	W	—	W	—	—	—	—	—	—	—	—	W
9	F. 48	7 ,,	Depression. Weeping. Worry over everything. Insomnia. Fears of future	18 months	I	I	I	I	I	I	—	W	—	—	—	—	—	R
10	F. 21	8 ,,	Tachycardia, necessitating absolute rest. Insomnia. Fears. Exhaustion	5 years	W	W	W	W	W	W	W	W	—	W	W	W	W	W
11	F. 20	12 ,,	Headaches. Insomnia. Hysterical attacks. Refusal to live at home	1 year	W	W	W	W	W	W	W	W	—	W	—	—	—	W
12	F. 40	10 ,,	Headache. Insomnia. Fear of apoplexy. Severe gastric pain. Fear of insanity. Polyarthritis	2 years	W	W	W	—	W	W	—	—	—	—	—	—	—	—
14	F. 37	2 months	Depression because of marital infidelity	1 year	W	W	W	R	—		—	—	—	—	—	—	—	—
15	M. 60	1 month	Depression. Cloud in head. Hysterical pain in knee	—	ISQ	W	W	W	—	R	R	R	—	Dead				
16	M. 48	4 weeks	Lack of energy. Depression. Headache	—	W	W	R	—	—	—	—	—	—	—	—	—	—	—
17	F. 38	8 ,,	Fatigue. Insomnia. Nervousness	—	I	W	—	—	W	—	—	W	—	—	—	—	—	—

18	M. 47	—	Insomnia. Tempers	—	W	W	—	—	—	—	—	—	—	—	—	—	—	—
19	M. 47	6 weeks	Peculiar feelings in head. Inability to work or concentrate. Impotent. Probably organic, absent knee joints	8 years	W	W	W	W	R	R	—	—	—	—	—	—	—	I
20	M. 38	10 "	Fatigue. Inability to do things. Always quarrelling with superiors	5 "	I	W	W	W	W	W	W	W	Re-ad	W	—	—	—	I
21	F. 48	2 months	Weakness. Feelings of impending death. Difficulty in concentration. Cannot walk out of house	2 "	W	W	W	W	W	W	—	—	Re-ad	—	—	—	—	W
25	F. 50	3 "	Fatigue. Headache. Insomnia. Asthenopia. Cardiac pain and fears. Depression. Has mitral incompetence and been alarmed about it	2 "	I	W	W	I	I	I	I	I	—	—	—	—	W	W
27	M. 70	4 weeks	Insomnia present for 16 years. Never slept without drugs	20 "	I	I	I	I	R	W	I	—	—	Died				
28	F. 43	6 "	Headache. Exhaustion. Giddiness. Palpitation. Faintness. Depression	18 months	W	W	W	W	W	W	—	W	—	—	—	—	—	W
29	M. 69	12 "	Pollakiuria. Palpitation	—	I	I	I	I	I	—	—	—	—	—	—	—	—	—
30	F. 64	5 "	Fatigue. Worried. Insomnia. Fears of insanity, murder and noises	30 years	I	I	I	I	I	I	I	R	—	—	—	—	—	I
31	M. 37	5 "	Exhaustion. Inability to work. Dyspepsia. Failure of concentration	—	I	I	I	I	I	I	—	—	—	—	—	—	—	—
32	M. 32	8 "	Apprehension. Shyness. Weakness	—	I	I	R	R	R	R	—	—	—	—	—	—	—	—
33	F. 53	10 "	Neuralgic pain everywhere	—	I	I	Re-ad	W	W	—	—	—	—	—	—	—	—	—
34	M. 45	4 "	Headache. Pains in right arm. Poor sleep. Loss of temper. Loss of weight	5 years	W	W	W	W	W	W	W	—	—	—	—	—	—	—
35	M. 40	1 month	Fear of tabes	5 "	I	I	W	W	W	W	—	R	—	—	—	—	—	W
36	M. 32	6 weeks	Headache and fears of disease	5 "	I	I	I	I	W	W	W	W	—	—	—	—	—	W
37	F. 45	3 months	Severe headaches. Violent outbursts of temper	40 "	I	I	I	I	I	I	—	—	—	—	—	—	—	I
38	M. 40	3 "	Claustrophobia, especially of churches. Agoraphobia. Inability to keep any engagements or meet strangers	16 "	W	W	W	W	W	W	W	W	—	—	—	—	—	W
40	M. 26	3 "	Abdominal pains	—	W	I	—	—	—	—	—	—	—	—	—	—	—	—
41	M. 26	3 "	Headache. Insomnia. Depression. Lack of concentration	—	W	R	R	W	W	R	R	—	—		—	—	—	—

1921. TABLE I (*continued*)

Case no.	Sex and age	Duration of stay	Symptoms	Duration of symptoms before admission	Result on discharge	Reports in 1922	1923	1924	1925	1926	1927	1928	1929	1930	1931	1932	1933	1934
43	F. 40	5 months	Astasia-abasia, headache and depression	11 years	I	I	I	I	R	R	R	—	—	I	—	—	—	—
44	F. 63	3 ,,	Noises in head. Fainting. Cardiac pain. Inability to leave bedroom or see people	10 ,,	I	I	I	R	I	I	R	—	—	—	—	—	—	—
45	F. 53	5 ,,	Depressed. Headache. Insomnia. Failure of concentration. Fatigue. Very thin	—	I	I	W	W	W	W	—	—	—	—	—	—	—	W
46	F. 23	4 ,,	Weakness. Lethargy. Cannot walk a mile. Headache. Inability to concentrate. Sense of inferiority	3 years	I	R	I	I	W	W	W	—	—	—	—	—	—	R
48	F. 35	7 weeks	Spastic paraplégia. Headache. Insomnia. Tinnitus. Fears	1½ ,,	I	I	I	W	R	W	W	—	—	—	—	—	—	—
49	F. 40	6 months	Fear of insanity. Depression. Insomnia. Dyspepsia. Fatigue	—	I	I	R	W	R	W	—	R	I	—	—	—	—	R
50	M. 55	1 month	Depression. Insomnia. Instability about religion	14 years	W	—	—	W	W	W	—	—	—	—	—	—	—	W
51	F. 38	4 months	Depression. Pain in back. Insomnia. Hysterical weeping	1 year	I	—	—	W	—	W	—	—	—	—	—	—	—	R
54	M. 22	3 ,,	Giddiness. Headache. Fear of sudden death. Always nervous	—	I	I	—	W	W	—	—	—	—	—	—	—	—	—
55	F. 35	5 weeks	Depression. Weakness. Fears and emaciation. Insomnia	—	ISQ Gained 11 lb.	ISQ	ISQ	I	I	I	—	I	—	—	—	—	—	—
56	F. 53	5 months	Headache. Depression. Insomnia. Fatigue	—	I	I	—	—	W	—	—	W	—	—	—	—	—	—
57	F. 54	3 ,,	Depression. Insomnia	—	I	—	W	W	W	R	R	R	—	—	—	—	—	—
58	F. 38	2 ,,	Exhaustion. Insomnia. Nervousness	—	I	W	—	—	W	—	W	W	—	—	—	—	—	—
59	M. 55	2 ,,	Pains in abdomen	—	I	W	W	R	W	—	W	W	—	—	—	—	—	R

1921. Table II. *Patients who did not improve*

Case no.	Sex and age	Duration of stay	Symptoms	Duration of symptoms before admission	Result on discharge	Reports in 1922	1923	1924	1925	1926	1927	1928	1929	1930	1931	1932	1933	1934
2	F. 30	3 weeks	Dyspepsia. Asthenopia. Diarrhoea. Giddiness. Exhaustion	11 months	I	R	W	W	R	R	I	—	—	—	—	—	—	—
4	F. 48	2 months	Giddiness. Phobia of streets, railway platforms and people	—	I	R	R	R	I	R	R	R	—	Died of cancer				
5	M. 38	3 "	Fear of suicide. Depression and insomnia	—	I	I	R	I	I	I	W	—	—	—	—	—	—	—
16	F. 34	10 weeks	Dysphagia. Backache. Loss of weight. Fatigue	—	ISQ	ISQ	ISQ	—	ISQ	ISQ	ISQ	ISQ	—	—	—	—	Not well	—
17	F. 23	3 months	Feelings of stiffness and pains all over body. No objective stiffness. Fears of venereal disease	6 months	ISQ	W	W	W	W	W	W	—	—	—	—	—	—	—
18	F. 34	4 "	Headache. Unable to feel pleasurable emotion	2½ years	ISQ	ISQ	ISQ	ISQ	ISQ	ISQ	ISQ	ISQ	ISQ	ISQ	W	W	W	W
19	M. 45	3 weeks	Loss of vision. Detachment and haemorrhage. Fear of insanity	—	ISQ	—	—	I	W	W	—	—	—	—	—	—	—	—
22	M. 34	6 months	Depression. Feeling of unworthiness. Retardation	—	ISQ	—	—	—	ISQ	ISQ	ISQ	Gradually got better and was well in spring of 1931 but died July 1931, pneumonia						
23	F. 48	4 "	Lack of concentration. Headache. Inability to carry out plans	—	ISQ	—	—	—	R	ISQ	—	—	—	—	—	—	—	—
24	M. 58	3 weeks	Depression and anxiety. Insomnia, due to financial loss	—	ISQ	ISQ	—	R	I	I	—	—	—	—	—	—	—	—
25	M. 39	1 month	Fatigue. Inability to work. Collapsed in pulpit. Fears	—	W	R	R	R	I	—	—	—	—	—	—	—	—	—
26	F. 17	4 months	Obsessions about words	—	ISQ	—	—	—	R	R	—	—	—	—	—	—	—	—

1922. GROUP I, TABLE I. *Psychoneuroses. Patients who are Well or Improved*

Case no.	Sex and age	Duration of stay	Symptoms	Duration of symptoms before admission	Result on discharge	Reports in 1923	1924	1925	1926	1927	1928	1929	1930	1931	1932	1933	1934
1	M. 41	7 months	Depression. Dyspepsia. Insomnia. Phobias. Inability to work	16 years	W	W	W	W	W	W	W	W	W	W	W	W	W
3	F. 54	5 ,,	Dysphagia. Excessive salivation. Depression. Unable to work	6 ,,	I	W	W	W	W	—	—	—	—	—	—	—	—
4	F. 46	2½ ,,	Cardiac pain. Worry. Not worked for three years	2 ,,	W	W	W	W	—	W	W	—	—	—	—	—	—
5	F. 45	7 weeks	Exhaustion. Depression. Constipation. Anaemia	20 ,,	I	W	W	W	W	W	W	W	—	—	—	—	W
6	F. 44	10 months	Depression. Fatigue. Insomnia. Various fears	3 ,,	I	I	W	W	W	R	R	W	Died of cancer				
7	M. 42	8 weeks	Pain in back. Hysterical paraplegia	1½ ,,	W	W	W	W	W	W	W	W	—	—	—	—	W
8	M. 23	8 months	Inability to work. Bad sleep. Hysterical fits. Coma. Fear of sex	3 ,,	W	W	W	W	W	W	W	W	—	—	—	W	R
9	M. 17	3 ,,	Fear of streets, of death. Depressed. Emotional weeping	8 months	W	W	W	W	W	R	W	W	—	—	—	—	W
10	F. 29	2 ,,	Depression. Inability to concentrate. Poor sleep. Fatigue. Epileptiform fits	8 years	I	W	W	W	W	R	W	W	—	—	—	—	W
11	M. 39	4 weeks	Vertigo. Headache. Attacks of unconsciousness. History of trauma	15 months	W	W	W	W	—	—	—	—	—	—	—	—	W
13	F. 40	3 months	Sensitiveness. Feelings of unworthiness. Fits of temper	20 years	I	W	W	R	R	—	W	—	—	—	—	—	—
14	F. 22	5 ,,	Hysterical paraplegia. Vomiting. Depression	11 ,,	I	I	W	W	W	W	W	—	—	W	—	W	W
15	F. 25	9 weeks	Attacks of depression. Suicidal thoughts. Pains in neck. Fatigue. Dyspepsia	2 ,,	W	W	W	W	W	W	—	W	W	—	—	—	W
16	M. 30	10 ,,	Phobia of old men. Depression. Headache. Insomnia. Suicidal thoughts. Inability to work	10 ,,	W	W	—	W	W	W	W	W	—	—	—	—	—
17	M. 31	2 months	Unable to work. Memory bad. Headaches. Loss of weight. Loss of confidence	—	I	W	W	W	W	W	W	W	—	—	—	—	—
22	F. 29	3 ,,	Loss of strength, physical and mental. Headache. Bad sleep. Apprehensive. Loss of weight. Inability to work	2 years	I Gained 2 st.	W	W	W	R	W	W	—	—	—	—	—	—
23	M. 34	5½ ,,	Fear of people. Claustrophobia. Bad dreams. Compulsive thoughts. Hallucination of voices, but aware that they were unreal	1 year	W	W	W	W	W	W	W	—	—	—	—		

25	F. 22	5 months	Headache. Insomnia. Fears of dark. Diarrhoea	3 years	I	W	W	W	W	W	W	W	W	W	W	W	W
26	F. 25	2 „	Nervousness. Dyspepsia. Emaciation. Headache	4 „	I Gained 22 lb.	W	W	W	W	W	W	W	—	—	—	—	W
30	F. 34	5 „	Headache. Depression. Mutism. Not worked for 3 years. Attempted suicide in Hospital	6 „	I	I	I	I	I	I	I	—	—	—	—	—	—
32	M. 21	11 weeks	Depression. Fear away from home. Dyspepsia. Fatigue. Inability to work	8 months	I	I	W	W	W	W	W	W	—	—	—	—	—
35	F. 56	3 months	Exhaustion. Insomnia. Pains in head. Coughs. Constant catarrh and fear of colds	20 years	I	I	R	R	R	—	R	—	—	—	—	—	R
36	M. 43	2 „	Loss of intellectual power. Pains all over body. Fatigue. Indigestion. Nervousness	10 „	I	I	W	W	—	W	W	—	—	—	—	—	W
37	F. 47	3½ „	Prostrating headaches. Photophobia. Lay in dark. Insomnia. In bed for over a year	3 „	I	I	I	I	R	R	R	—	—	—	—	—	I
38	M. 28	10 weeks	Palpitation on going off to sleep, wakens screaming. Head dazed. Fatigue. Inability to work	7 „	I	I	I	I	—	—	W	—	—	—	W	—	W
41	M. 49	6 „	Nervousness. Failure of concentration. Agoraphobia. Indigestion. Off work 9 months	6 „	I	I	I	I	W	W	W	—	—	—	—	—	—
42	F. 40	3 months	Inability to move left arm or hand (contracture). Insomnia. Dyspepsia	5 „	I	R	R	R	R	R	R		—	—	—	—	—
43	F. 52	2½ „	Paraplegia (18 years). Noises in head. Constipation	—	Able to walk	—	—	—	—	—	—	R	—	—	—	—	R
44	M. 59	2 „	Depression. Insomnia. Loss of concentration. Dyspepsia. Inability to work	1 year	I	I	—	R	I	I	W	—	—	—	—	—	—
45	F. 47	3 „	Headache. Dyspepsia. Nervousness. Fatigue. Poor concentration. Visceroptosis. Many operations; at work but finding it very difficult	10 years	I	I	I	—	R	R	R	—	—	—	—	—	—
47	F. 30	10 weeks	Headache. Insomnia. Fatigue. At work, but finding it impossible to continue	1 year	I	I	R	R	I	I	I	W	—	—	—	—	W
48	M. 34	8½ months	Depression, unable to concentrate. Insomnia. Many phobias. Inability to work	18 months	ISQ	I	R	W	W	W	W	—	—	—	—	—	I
49	F. 43	9 weeks	Depression. Indigestion	2 „	I	I	I	W	—	R	R	—	—	—	—	—	—
50	F. 22	7 „	Anorexia. Amenorrhoea. Emaciation. Distension of abdomen	2 years	I Gained 16 lb.	I	I	I	W	W	W	W	—	—	—	—	—
51	F. 43	4 „	Phobias. Insomnia. Inability to work	—	ISQ	I	I	R	R	R	R	—	—	—	—	—	—
52	M. 68	5 „	Headache. Poor sleep	1 year	I	I	I	I	I	W	—	—	—	—	—	—	—
53	M. 60	3 „	Insomnia. Lack of concentration. Lack of interest	2 years	I	I	—	R	—	—	W	—	—	—	—	—	—

1922. GROUP I, TABLE I (*continued*)

Case no.	Sex and age	Duration of stay	Symptoms	Duration of symptoms before admission	Result on discharge	Reports in 1923	1924	1925	1926	1927	1928	1929	1930	1931	1932	1933	1934
54	F. 43	3 months	Loss of confidence. Exhaustion. Shyness. Depression. Aches and pains. Constipation	10 years	I	I	W	W	—	I	—	R	—	—	—	—	—
55	M. 23	6 weeks	Poor sleep. Depression. Fears	6 weeks	I	I	I	—	W	W	W	—	—	—	—	—	—
57	M. 26	3 months	Fears of falling in street. Inability to concentrate. Dyspepsia. Depression	2 years	W	R	W	W	W	W	—	—	—	—	—	—	—
61	F. 35	5 weeks	Weakness. Hysterical attacks. Depression. Poor sleep	—	W	I	I	R	R	R	R	—	—	—	—	—	—
62	F. 40	13 months	Exhaustion. Pains all over body. Violent tempers. Inability to work	15 years	I	I	I	I	R	R	R	—	—	—	—	—	R
63	M. 49	4 weeks	Fits of weakness. Loss of weight. Fear. Depression	2 „	ISQ	I	W	I	W	W	—	—	—	—	—	—	W
64	F. 44	2 months	Dyspepsia. Fatigue. Fears. Insomnia. Depression. Loss of weight. Visceroptosis. Inability to walk 1 mile	—	W	W	W	W	W	W	W	W	—	—	—	—	W
65	F. 25	4 „	Headache. Insomnia. Dislike of people. Worried. Suicidal feelings. Inability to work	5 years	I	I	R	I	R	R	R	W	—	—	W	W	R
68	F. 40	13 „	Insomnia. Fear of being alone and of suicide	All her life	I	I	I	I	I	I	I	—	ISQ	—	—	—	I
69	M. 46	5½ „	Exhaustion. Pain at heart. Diarrhoea. Fear of people	7 years	I	I	I	I	—	W	—	—	—	—	—	—	—
70	M. 29	4 weeks	Attacks of depression	Many years	I	W	R	—	—	I	—	—	—	—	—	—	—
72	F. 41	4 „	Fear of something about to happen to her legs. Nervous sexual fears	2 years	I	I	W	W	R	R	I	—	—	I	I	I	I
73	F. 40	10 „	Headache. Pain on right side. Loss of confidence. Fear of insanity, and of going about	10 „	I	I	I	I	W	W	—	—	—	—	—	—	—
74	F. 39	7 weeks and 3 months	Depression. Exhaustion. No power of thought	All her life	I	I	W	W	W	I	I	—	—	—	—	—	R
75	M. 60	7 weeks	Inability to concentrate. Irritability. Memory poor. Unable to face people	3 years	I	W	W	W	W	W	I	—	—	—	—	—	W
77	F. 59	4 months	Fatigue. Headache. Tinnitus. Poor sleep	—	I	I	—	W	W	W	W	—	—	—	—	—	—
79	F. 40	4 weeks	Giddiness. Insomnia. Agoraphobia	8 years	ISQ	—	ISQ	I	—	—	I	—	—	—	—	—	W
80	F. 31	2 months	Exhaustion. Loss of weight. Hysterical gait. Insomnia	10 „	I	—	I	W	W	W	W	—	—	—	—	—	—
82	F. 30	6 „	Difficulties of expression. Depression	10 „	I	I	—	I	—	—	I	—	—	—	—	—	—
83	M. 41	3 weeks	Pain in tongue. Fear of cancer	—	W	—	W	W	—	—	W	—	W	W	—	W	W

1922. GROUP I, TABLE II. *Patients who state they are not any Better but who are at Work*

Case no.	Sex and age	Duration of stay	Symptoms	Duration of symptoms before admission	Result on discharge	Reports in 1923	1924	1925	1926	1927	1928	1929	1930	1931	1932	1933	1934
1	F. 36	5 months	Fears. Faintness. Headache	2 years	I	I	I	W	W	W	W	—	—	—	—	—	—
2	M. 38	10 weeks	Headache. Fatigue. Dizziness. Insomnia. Fears. Depression	2 "	ISQ	ISQ	ISQ	ISQ	ISQ	—	ISQ	—	—	—	—	—	—

1922. GROUP I, TABLE III. *Patients who are Better, but who do not admit that their Improvement is due to treatment at Swaylands*

Case no.	Sex and age	Duration of stay	Symptoms	Duration of symptoms before admission	Result on discharge	Reports in 1923	1924	1925	1926	1927	1928	1929	1930	1931	1932	1933	1934
1	F. 38	2 months	Intense depression. Many phobias	30 years	ISQ	I	—	R	R	—	—	—	—	—	—	—	—
2	M. 46	8 weeks	Headache. Poor sleep. Lack of vitality. Abdominal pains. Emaciation	5 "	I	W	R	R	I	—	—	Been in a nursing home for years					
3	F. 54	4 months	Profound asthenia. Wasting of muscles. Paraplegia. Knee jerks absent	—	ISQ	W	W	W	W	W	W	W	—	—	—	—	—

1922. Group I, Table IV. *Patients who are no Better*

Case no.	Sex and age	Duration of stay	Symptoms	Duration of symptoms before admission	Result on discharge	1923	1924	1925	1926	1927	1928	1929	1930	1931	1932	1933	1934
						Reports in											
4	F. 43	5½ months	Severe headache. Depression. Inability to work	13 years	ISQ	ISQ	ISQ	W	W	W	W	W	—	—	—	—	—
5	M. 19	8 „	Attacks of dyspnoea. Pains in legs. Inability to concentrate	14 months	ISQ	ISQ	ISQ	W	W	—	—	—	—	—	—	—	—
6	F. 34	4½ „	Pains in neck. Depression. Fatigue	—	ISQ	ISQ	ISQ	ISQ	—	ISQ	—	—	—	—	—	—	—
7	F. 50	2 „	Loss of energy and of concentration. Depression	2 years	I	I	W	W	W	I	I	—	—	—	—	—	—
9	F. 41	—	Pain over left sacro iliac joint. Insomnia. Fear of insanity. Fugue	3 „	I	R	—	I	R	R	R	—	—	—	—	—	I
10	F. 33	—	Heart attacks. Weakness. Tremblings. Asthenopia. Emaciation. (6 st. 8 lb.)	7 „	I Gained 9 lb.	R	—	I	R	R	R	—	—	—	—	—	—
11	F. 20	7 weeks	Nervous attacks in street; has to sit down. Dislike of meeting strangers	5 „	ISQ	ISQ	W	W	W	W	W	W	—	—	—	—	—
13	F. 52	5 months	Band round head. Depression. Poor sleep. Fear of being alone	—	W	R	W	R	—	Dead.	Suicide						
15	F. 27	10 „	Insomnia. Nightmares. Headache. Violent tempers. Loss of weight	5 years	I Gained 17 lb.	R	R	R	R	—	—	—	—	—	—	—	—
16	M. 56	6 weeks	Indigestion. Depression. Fears	1 month	W	R	R	R	I	—	R	—	—	—	—	—	—
17	F. 48	3 weeks and 1 year	Somnambulism	10 years	—	I	—	R	R	—	—	—	—	—	—	—	—
18	F. 27	5 months	Fears. Bad sleep. Loss of weight. Head pains	—	—	—	—	—	—	—	—	—	—	—	—	—	—
19	42	10 „	Weakness. Poor sleep	—	—	—	—	—	—	ISQ	ISQ	I	—	—	—	—	W

1922. Group II. *Drug Addicts*

Case no.	Sex and age	Duration of stay	Symptoms	Duration of symptoms before admission	Result on discharge	1923	1924	1925	1926	1927	1928	1929	1930	1931	1932	1933	1934
						Reports in											
1	M. 44	13 months	Insomnia. Great depression. Tremor. Paraldehyde drinking up to 18 drams a day	—	I	I	W	W	W	W	W	—	—	—	—	—	No drug relapse
3	M. 48	2 „	Hallucinations. Tremors. Insomnia. Paraldehyde, 8 oz. a week	—	I	—	I	R	I	R	R	—	—	—	—	—	—

1923. GROUP I, TABLE I. *Psychoneuroses. Patients who are Well or Improved*

Case no.	Sex and age	Duration of stay	Symptoms	Duration of symptoms before admission	Result on discharge	Reports in 1924	1925	1926	1927	1928	1929	1930	1931	1932	1933	1934
1	F. 38	2 months	Worries over trifles. Depression with weeping. Frightened feelings	8 weeks	W	W	R	R	R	R	—	—	—	—	—	—
2	M. 32	5 „	Easily fatigued body and mind. Worries easily. Loss of weight. (6 ft. 2 in., 9 st. 13½ lb.)	—	I 11 st. 2 lb.	I	W	W	W	W	W	W	—	R	—	—
3	F. 19	1 month	Headache. Sleeplessness. Indigestion. Fatigue	2 months	I	W	W	W	W	W	—	W	—	—	—	—
5	F. 45	3 months	Pains in limbs and body. Palpitation. Insomnia. Giddiness	10 years	I	I	W	W	W	W	—	W	—	—	—	W
6	F. 19	4 „	Restlessness. Loss of feeling. Feels she does everything wrong	4 months	I	W	W	W	—	I	W	—	—	—	—	—
7	F. 40	2 „	Insomnia. Depression. Loss of weight	1 year	I Gained 13 lb.	I	—	R	—	R	—	—	—	—	—	—
8	F. 24	6 „	Attacks of shaking. Fear of being alone, of the dark, of burglars, of losing consciousness. Fatigue	6 years	W	W	W	W	W	W	—	W	—	—	—	R
9	F. 29	7 „	Confusion. Insomnia. Depression	1 year	W	W	W	W	W	W	—	—	—	—	—	—
10	M. 61	2 „	Obsession about bowels. Will not go out till they are moved. Loss of interest. Symptoms arose after encephalitis	3 years	I	W	I	I	—	—	—	W	—	—	—	—
11	F. 54	1 month	Bodily and mental fatigue. Pains in head and joints. Emotional. Fears of draughts	13 „	I	W	W	W	W	R	W	W	—	—	—	—
12	F. 36	1 „	Insomnia. Perpetual worry. Headache. Fear of insanity. Double talipes equinus	7 „	W	W	W	W	W	W	—	W	W	W	W	R
13	F. 40	13 months	Headaches. Want of concentration. Fatigue. Insomnia. Outbursts of temper. Has had three years of analysis	30 „	I	I	W	W	W	W	W	W	—	—	—	W
14	F. 61	2 „	Lack of will-power and interest. Loss of caring for her family. Fear of insanity	6 „	W	W	W	W	W	W	W	—	—	—	—	—
15	M. 58	2	Depression. Insomnia. Constantly calling his wife's name. Self-depreciation. Fatigue. Unjustified financial fears	1 year	I	W	W	W	W	W	—	W	—	—	—	W

1923. Group I, Table I (*continued*)

Case no.	Sex and age	Duration of stay	Symptoms	Duration of symptoms before admission	Result on discharge	Reports in 1924	1925	1926	1927	1928	1929	1930	1931	1932	1933	1934
16	F. 34	5 months	Poor sleep. Headaches. Poor appetite. Worry. Diarrhoea. Abdominal pains	2 years	I	W	I	I	W	W		W	—	—	—	—
17	F. 25	3 "	Terror. Emotion. Some confusion. Sleeplessness. Menorrhagia	6 months	W	W	W	W	W	W	W	W	—	—	—	—
18	F. 21	4 "	Burning feelings in head. Insomnia. Somnambulism. "Fainting"	6 years	I	W	W	W	W	W	W	—	—	—	—	—
19	F. 24	2 "	Fear of suicide. Depression. Fear of having children	2 "	I	W	W	W	W	W	W	W	—	—	—	W
20	M. 42	2 "	Trembling on right side. Headache. Loss of sense of environment. Poor sleep. Fatigue. Fear of impotence	17 "	I	I	I	I	I	I	I	I	I	I	I	Dead
21	F. 24	3 "	Severe pain in head. Tinglings of skin. Fears of insanity and of paralysis	2 "	W	W	W	W	W		W	—	—	—	W	—
22	M. 36	2 "	Headaches. Broken sleep. Depression. He has twice "disappeared" and been lost for months	1 year	W	W	W	W	W	—	—	—	—	—	—	—
23	F. 40	3 "	Difficulty in walking. Feels as if she could not control her legs	3 years	I	I	W	W	W	R	W	W	—	R	—	I
25	F. 61	4 "	Constipation. Insomnia. Difficulty in swallowing. Poor appetite. Agoraphobia	1 year	I	W	W	W	W	W	—	W	—	—	—	W
27	F. 18	2 "	Great loss of weight. (6 st. 4 lb.) Amenorrhoea	—	I Gained 20 lb.	R	W	W	W	W	W	W	—	W	—	W
28	F. 36	10 "	"Strung up." Very weak. Bad sleep. Diarrhoea frequent. Loss of concentration	All her life	W	W	W	W	W	—	—	—	—	—	—	—
29	F. 33	1 month	Loss of weight. Fatigue. Rheumatism	1 year	I	W	W	—	—	—	—	—	—	—	—	—
30	F. 31	3 months	Mental and physical fatigue. Insomnia. Loss of weight. Self-depreciation	5 years	I Gained 10 lb.	W	W	W	W	W	—	—	—	—	—	W
31	F. 42	5 "	Discomfort and flatulence after food. Vomiting. Depression. Nervousness. Has had four abdominal operations	20 years	I	I	I	R Organic	R	I	—	—	—	—	—	—

32	M. 29	9 months	Full feeling in stomach. Headaches. Insomnia. Attacks of despair. Had had gastro-enterostomy, and subsequent operation for adhesions	—	I		R	R	—	—	—	—	—			
33	F. 55	1 month	Fatigue, bodily and mentally. Visceroptosis	5 years	I	I	I	I	I	W	W	W	—	—	—	W
34	M. 47	4 months	Insomnia. Lack of concentration. Unable to go 200 yards away from a doctor. Has been psycho-analyzed for years before admission	15 „	I	I	I	R	W	R	—	—	—	—	—	—
35	F. 40	2 „	Pains in legs. Tremblings. Faintness. Fatigue	—	I	I	I	—	—	R	—	—	—	—	—	—
36	F. 45	2 „	Pressure on head. Insomnia. Pricklings of body. Dazed feelings. Fear of insanity. Fear of suicide	2 years	I	I	W	W	W	W	W	—	—	—	—	W
37	M. 61	6 weeks	Depression. Insomnia. Inability to concentrate. Nervousness. Fatigue	1 year	I	I	I	I	W	W	—	W	—	—	—	—
39	F. 69	3 months	Depression. Agitation and calling out in morning. Apprehension	3 years	I	I	I	—	—	—	—	—	—	—	—	—
40	M. 61	2 „	Lack of initiative. Pains in back	2 „	W	W	W	W	W	W	—	W	—	—	—	—
41	M. 42	7 „	Fear of doing something to his detriment, that he may shoot someone, that he may write a cheque wrongly	All his life	I	I	W	W	W	W	W	—	—	—	—	—
43	F. 48	11 „	Headaches. Panics in street. Agoraphobia. Bad sleep. Indigestion. Obsessions concerning sex	—	I	I	I	I	W	W	—	—	—	—	—	—
44	M. 36	2 „	Inability to do anything. Bad memory. Bad tempers directed against wife. Fatigue	4 years	I	R	W	W	W	W	—	—	—	—	—	—
45	M. 42	2 „	Pains in head and back. Bad sleep. Loss of weight	1 year	I	I	W	W	W	W	W	W	—	—	—	W
46	F. 45	1 month	Depression. Poor sleep. Nervousness. Indigestion	20 years	ISQ	W	ISQ	ISQ	ISQ	ISQ	Uncertain health all these years					
47	F. 50	2 months	Trembling. Headache. Insomnia. Suspicious of people. Unwilling to tell about herself	10 „	I	I	R	I	—	—	—	—	—	—	—	—
48	F. 25	2 „	Headaches. Insomnia. Fatigue. Phobias. Anxiety	1 year	I	I	W	W	W	W	W	—	—	—		W
49	F. 38	2 „	Pain in back. Inability to stand or walk. Headache. Insomnia	5 months	I	I	I	W	Well as regards nerves. Having heart attacks							
50	F. 55	11 „	Pains in the head. Weakness. Insomnia. Failure of concentration	7 years	I	I	W	W	W	W	—	W	—	—	—	W
51	F. 52	9 „	Aphonia. Weakness. Dyspnoea. Indigestion. Poor sleep	6 „	I	I	W	W	W	R	—	—	—	—	—	I

1923. Group I, Table I (*continued*)

Case no.	Sex and age	Duration of stay	Symptoms	Duration of symptoms before admission	Result on discharge	Reports in 1924	1925	1926	1927	1928	1929	1930	1931	1932	1933	1934
52	F. 30	4 months	Insomnia. Fatigue. Irritability	6 years	I	I	W	W	—	W	—	—	—	—	—	—
53	F. 36	3 ,,	Headaches. Depression. Uncertain sleep. Bad dreams	2 ,,	I	W	W	W	W	Died of cancer						
54	M. 19	3 ,,	Exhaustion. Indigestion. Constipation. Poor concentration. Pain in back	—	I	W	W	—	—	W	—	—	—	—	—	—
55	F. 30	3 ,,	Depression. Fatigue. Twitching of limbs, face and body. Coldness up and down spine. Pregnant	4 years	I	I	I	—	R	—	—	—	—	—	—	—
56	F. 39	9 ,,	Talipes varus. Insomnia. Hideous dreams	—	I	I	I	I	—	I	Died					
57	F. 23	3 ,,	Headache. Palpitation. Bad sleep. Depression. Fixation of right knee, left ankle, right elbow (organic)	4 years	I	I	I	—	—	R	W	—	—	R	I	—
58	F. 24	2 ,,	Tiredness. Attacks of loss of power in legs. Fears of doing things alone	—	I	I	R	R	I	R	—	—	—	—	—	—
59	F. 39	7 ,,	Indigestion. Vomiting. Fatigue. Bad sleep. Panics. Sweatings	All her life	I	I	I	I	—	I	W	W	—	—	—	—
60	F. 24	2 ,,	Fatigue. Palpitation. Headache. Indigestion. Constipation. Loss of weight. 5st. 4 lb. Amenorrhoea	10 years	I Gained 6 lb.	I	R	R Gastric ulcer (op.)	R	R	—	—	—	—	—	—
61	F. 41	9 ,,	Pains in back and head. Apprehensive. Loss of concentration. Terrifying dreams	10 ,,	I	I	W	W	W	W	W	W	—	—	W	W
64	F. 26	6 weeks	Headache. Weakness. Exhaustion Vomiting. Loss of weight	6 months	I	—	I	W	W	—	—	—	—	—	—	—
65	M. 26	4 months	Attacks with fear of death. Feels heart has stopped. Fear of traffic	5 years	I	—	I	W	—	—	—	—	—	—	—	—
66	F. 35	3 ,,	Pains in back and limbs. Exhaustion. Indigestion	12 ,,	I	—	I	I	—	—	—	—	—	—	—	

1923. Group I, Table II. *Patients who state they are not any Better but who are at Work*

Case no.	Sex and age	Duration of stay	Symptoms	Duration of symptoms before admission	Result on discharge	Reports in 1924	1925	1926	1927	1928	1929	1930	1931	1932	1933	1934
1	M. 39	1 month	Fatigue. Pains in head. Uncertain sleep. Irritable. Cannot do his work. Idea that he emits an odour	All his life	ISQ	ISQ	ISQ	ISQ	ISQ	ISQ	—	Ill	—	—	—	—
2	M. 54	3 months	Catarrh of nostrils. Feelings of stuffiness. Tension. Loss of concentration. Insomnia	20 years	I	R	R	R	R	R	—	Ill	—	—	—	—

1923. Group I, Table III. *Patients who are Better, but who do not admit that their Improvement is due to treatment at Swaylands*

Case no.	Sex and age	Duration of stay	Symptoms	Duration of symptoms before admission	Result on discharge	Reports in 1924	1925	1926	1927	1928	1929	1930	1931	1932	1933	1934
1	F. 48	14 weeks	Headache. Feeling of unreality. Phobias of closed spaces. Fear of murdering husband and daughter	20 years	I	I	R	W	W	R	R	R	—	—	—	R
2	F. 40	3 months	Headache. Poor sleep. Depression	4 months	ISQ	I	R	R	—	R	—	—	—		—	R

1923. Group I, Table IV. *Patients who are no Better*

Case no.	Sex and age	Duration of stay	Symptoms	Duration of symptoms before admission	Result on discharge	Reports in 1924	1925	1926	1927	1928	1929	1930	1931	1932	1933	1934
1	M. 39	3 months	Poor mentation. Bad memory. Indigestion. Fatigue	6 years	ISQ	—	ISQ	—	—	—	I	—	—	—	—	—
2	F. 54	6 weeks	Insomnia. Poor concentration	—	I	I	Operation	R	—	R	—	—	—	—	—	—
3	M. 40	3 months	Anaesthesia of legs. Pain in back. Peculiar gait	8 years	ISQ	ISQ	ISQ	ISQ	ISQ	ISQ	—	—	—	—	—	—
4	F. 35	4 ,,	Tired. Indigestion. Flatulence. Headache	—	I	R	R	R	—	—	—	R	—	—	—	W
5	F. 30	6 ,,	Indigestion. Bad sleep. Exhaustion. Dysmenorrhoea	15 years	I	R	R	R	R	R	—	—	R	R	—	R
6	F. 46	2 ,,	Attacks of intense depression with intervals when she is well. Masochistic masturbation during depressed attacks	20 ,,	I	R	I	I	—	I	—	I	—	—	—	I
7	F. 39	3 ,,	Insomnia. Depression. Exhaustion	4 ,,	ISQ	ISQ	ISQ	I	I	I	—	—	—	—	—	—
8	F. 51	2 ,,	Insomnia. Poor concentration	1 year	I	R	R	—	—	—	—	—	—	—	—	—
10	F. 26	2 ,,	Vomiting. Astasia-abasia. Sleep poor	2 years	I	R	I	—	—	—	—	—	—	—	—	—
11	M. 22	6 ,,	Attacks of unconsciousness with epileptiform convulsions. Tongue bitten; occurring about once in two weeks. Inability to work	—	I	R	R Failed in exam.	R	W No attacks	W	—	—	—	—	—	W No attacks
12	M. 40	9 ,,	Lack of concentration. Insomnia. Fear of marriage	10 years	ISQ	ISQ	ISQ	I	I	W	W	W	—	—	—	W
14	F. 57	5 ,,	Uncomfortable feelings in head. Feeling of nerves giving way in head. These present for many years	12 ,,	I	I	W	I	I	I	—	—	—	—	—	—
15	F. 38	3 ,,	Paraplegia. Headaches. Dyspepsia. Pains in back; later intense depression	8 ,,	W	R	—	W	—	—	—	—	—	—	—	—
16	F. 15	9 ,,	Inability to walk any distance because of hysterical contracture	7 ,,	ISQ	ISQ	ISQ	ISQ	—	—	—	—	—	—	—	ISQ
17	M. 25	5 ,,	Tired and weak. Inability to concentrate. Headaches. Fear of meeting people, of being alone in dark. Inability to work	—	I	R	I	I	I	R	—	—	—	—		

1923. GROUP II. *Drug Addicts*

Case no.	Sex and age	Duration of stay	Symptoms	Duration of symptoms before admission	Result on discharge	Reports in 1924	1925	1926	1927	1928	1929	1930	1931	1932	1933	1934
3	M. 54	2 months	Insomnia. Inability to concentrate. Odd feelings in head. Depression. Morphia in bouts	—	I	R	R	—	W	W	—	—	—	—	Died of angina	
4	F. 44	2 ,,	Great fatigue. Difficulty in concentration. Loss of weight. Morphia addiction	—	I	R	R	ISQ	—	Dead						
5	F. 41	2 ,,	Noises in the head. Depression. Deafness. Bouts of alcohol	—	I	R	R	I	—	Dead						
6	M. 30	11 ,,	Dipsomania. Homosexuality	—	ISQ	I	W	R	W	R	W	—	—	—	—	R
8	M. 24	7 ,,	Alcoholism since the war	—	—	W	R		I	I	—	Fair	—	—	Rather better	—

1924. Group I, Table I. *Psychoneuroses. Patients who are Well or Improved*

Case no.	Sex and age	Duration of stay	Symptoms	Duration of symptoms before admission	Result on discharge	Reports in 1925	1926	1927	1928	1929	1930	1931	1932	1933	1934
1	M. 43	6 months	Depression. Nervous attacks. Loss of appetite. Headaches. Poor sleep. Phobias	—	I	W	W	W	W	W	W	W	W	W	W
2	F. 18	7 "	Terrors of different sorts	—	W	W	Died of poliomyelitis								
3	F. 35	6 "	Pains all over. Feeling of inability to work	—	W	W	R	R	R	ISQ	ISQ	—	—	—	—
4	M. 19	2 "	No energy. Tires easily. Indigestion. History of convulsive attacks	—	W	W	W	R	W	W	W	—	—	—	W
5	M. 39	2 "	Peculiar feelings in head. Depressed. Emotional attacks, weeping. Odd sensations in body and limbs	—	I	W	W	W	W	W	W	—	—	—	W
6	F. 26	5 weeks	Miserable. Head feels in a muddle. Tired. Cannot say certain words, such as "death", "funeral"	—	W	W	W	W	W	I	W	—	—	—	—
7	F. 34	2 months	Depression. Brooding. Inability to work. Excessive day dreaming	—		W	W	R	W	W	W	W	—	—	W
8	M. 26	5 "	Feels very weak. Headache. Fear of certain diseases	—	I	W	W	W	W	W	W	—	—	—	—
9	F. 40	2 "	Exhaustion, bodily and mental. Insomnia. Headaches. Indigestion	—	W	W	W	W	W	—	—	—	—	—	W
10	M. 58	3 "	Miserable. Restless. No interest in life. Defective memory. Constipation	—	W	W	W	W	—	—	—	—	—	—	—
11	F. 38	2 "	Obsessional ideas about husband. Alcoholism	—	W	W	W	W	W	—	—	—	—	—	—
12	F. 37	3 "	Headache. Backache. Poor sleep. Exhaustion	—	W	W	W	—	—	—	—	—	—	—	—
13	F. 47	2 "	Worries easily. Headache. Insomnia. Bad dreams. Depression. Fears about her work	—	W	W	W	—	—	—	—	—	—	—	—
14	F. 58	3 "	Anxiety. Fear of insanity. Pain in head. Uncertain sleep. Lack of concentration. Easily tired	—	W	W	W	W	W	W	W	—	—	—	W
15	M. 29	1 month	Exhaustion. Depression. Inability to make up his mind about marriage	1	W	W	W	W	W	W	W	—	—	W	—
16	M. 22	2 months	Feeling of faintness. Tremblings, fear of insanity. Unable to concentrate	—	I	W	W	R	R	—	—	—	—	—	R
17	F. 19	5 "	Depression. Loss of weight. Headache. Indigestion. Constipation. Irregular menstruation	—	I Gained 2 st.	W	—	R	W	W	—	—	—	—	—
18	F. 34	4 "	Indecision. Insomnia. Obsession that she may have said or done the wrong thing	—	I	W	W	W	R	—	—	—	—	—	W

19	M. 33	7 months	Insomnia. Poor concentration and memory. Fear of doing criminal acts. Fear of gas taps	—	I	W	W	W	W	W	—	—	—	—	—
20	M. 46	2 "	Mental prostration and exhaustion. Bad dreams. Trembling of hands	—	W	W	W	W	W	—	—	—	—	—	W
21	M. 26	1 month	Lethargy. Always ready to fall asleep. Sexual thoughts	—	I	W	W	—	I	W	W	Dead.	Accident		
22	F. 29	1 "	Feeling that she cannot do her work, that she skims over her difficulties, and never comes to grips with them	—	—	W	—	—	—	—	—	W	—	—	—
23	F. 41	2 months	Intense headaches so that she has to lie flat. Hiccough	—	I	W	W	W	W	W	W	—	—	—	W
24	F. 26	6 "	Fears. Exhaustion. Depression. Inability to meet people. Self-consciousness	10 years	I	W	W	W	W	W	W	—	—	—	W
25	F. 44	2 "	Insomnia. Restlessness. Palpitation. Depression. Fear that something will happen	1 year	I	W	W	W	R	—	W	—	—	—	—
26	M. 49	1 month	Severe indigestion. Extreme limitation of food. Insomnia. Terrifying dreams. Tremblings. Fits of horror	12 years	I	W	W	W	W	R	R	—	—	I	—
27	M. 33	5 months	Inability to mix with people. Loss of confidence. Tends to lie in bed all day and sit up at night	All his life	I	I	I	I	W	W	W	R	R	—	—
28	F. 29	13 months	Depression. Exhaustion. Obsession, fear of cancer	12 years	I	W	W	W	W	W	W	—	W	—	I
29	F. 36	7 "	Poor sleep. Depression. Hallucinations of the Devil. Compulsive acts. Insight good	1 year	I	W	W	W	W	R	—	W	—	—	—
30	M. 32	5 weeks	Sensations of blankness of mind. Dejection. Difficulty in grasping a situation. Fear of brain deterioration	3 years	I	W	W	W	W	W	—	—	—	—	—
31	F. 22	2 months	Over-conscientious. Sexual fears. Mind strain due to introspection	8 "	I	W	W	—	W	R	—	Re-ad	—	W	W
32	F. 19	2 "	Insomnia. Fears. Religious ideas of depressed nature	5 "	I	W	W	—	R	R	R	—	—	—	W
33	M. 31	6 weeks	Nervousness. Moody, shy, will not mix with people. Palpitation	4 "	I	W	R	I	W	W	W	—	—	W	W
34	F. 23	4 months	Loss of confidence. Terror. Fear of insanity and suicide	5 "	W	W	W	—	—	W	W	W	W	W	W
35	M. 28	9 weeks	Attacks like coming out of gas. Fears that something is going to happen. Off work two years	10 "	W	W	W	W	W	W	R	—	—	W	R
36	F. 21	1 month	Depression. Exhaustion. Loss of weight	6 months	I	W	—	—	—	—	—	—	—	—	—
37	F. 33	6 weeks	Indigestion. Dyspareunia. Loss of weight	—	I	W	W	W	W	W	W	—	—	—	W
38	F. 25	2 months	Cannot adapt herself to married life. Inability to manage her home. Longing for old freedom	—	ISQ	W	W	W	W	W	W	—	—	—	W

1924. GROUP I, TABLE I (*continued*)

Case no.	Sex and age	Duration of stay	Symptoms	Duration of symptoms before admission	Result on discharge	Reports n 1925	1926	1927	1928	1929	1930	1931	1932	1933	1934
39	F. 30	4 months	Exhaustion. Headache. Anorexia. Constipation. Loss of weight	—	I Gained 1 st.	W	W	W	W	—	—	—	—	—	—
40	F. 54	5 ,,	Exhaustion, chiefly physical. Sleep uncertain. Palpitation. Depression	1 year	I	W	W	W	W	—	—	—	—	—	R Organic
41	M. 26	2 ,,	Dullness. Retardation. Depression. No interest. Bestiality	6 months	I	W	W	W	W	—	—	—	—	—	W
42	M. 59	1 month	Insomnia. Depression. Fears of many things. Poor concentration	—	ISQ	W	—	—	—	—	—	—	—	—	—
43	M. 47	3 months	Unhappiness. Unable to concentrate	10 years	I	W	W	W	W	—	?	—	—	R	—
44	F. 41	8 ,,	Insomnia. Worries over work. Obsession that she had done the wrong thing	—	I	W	W	R	—	W	I	—	—	—	—
45	M. 23	6 weeks	Insomnia. Headache. Dizziness. Depression	—	I	I	W	W	W	W	W	—	—	—	W
46	M. 43	3 months	Palpitation. Insomnia. Exhaustion. Headache	—	I	I	W	W	—	—	—	—	—	—	—
47	M. 15	2 ,,	Nervousness. Stammering. Night terrors	4 years	I	I	W	W	W	—	W	—	—	—	W
48	M. 43	3 ,,	Constant trembling. Fear of going back to work in coal mine. Hair gone grey rapidly	2 ,,	I	I	R	R	I	W	W	—	—	—	—
49	F. 40	3 ,,	Weakness. Headache. Insomnia. Confusion	10 years	I	I	I	W	—	—	—	—	—	—	—
50	F. 32	3 ,,	Exhaustion. Suffocating feelings. Dysphagia. Inability to concentrate	12 ,,	I	I	W	I	I	W	—	—	—	—	—
51	M. 38	2 ,,	Insomnia. Fear of being alone. Poor concentration	6 months	I	I	W	W	W	—	—	—	—	—	R
52	F. 23	9 ,,	Fear of spaces. Violent tempers. Alcohol addiction	4 years	I	W	—	Phthisis	—	—	—	—	—	—	—
53	F. 25	17 ,,	Vomiting. Anorexia. Extreme emaciation. (4 st. 3 lb.) Insomnia. Terrifying dreams. Amenorrhoea	10 ,,	I Gained 20 lb.	I	I	I	I	—	—	—	—	—	I
54	M. 28	12 ,,	Headaches. Globus. Pressure of head. Fear of meeting people. Cannot go out in the streets. Exhaustion	5 ,,	I	I	I	I	I	I	I	—	—	—	W
55	M. 24	2 ,,	Inability to read. Restlessness. Concentration poor, unable to play games properly. Idea that he does not get due recognition	2 ,,	I	W	W	—	—	—	—	—	—		—

56	F. 49	2 months	Exhaustion. Headache. Backache. Fear of everything. Flatulence. Abdominal pain	24 years	—	I	I	I	I	—	—	—	—	—	R
57	M. 44	4 ,,	Inability to concentrate. Poor sleep. Fear of disease, especially influenza. Depression. Exhaustion	15 ,,	I	I	W	W	W	—	—	—	R	—	R
58	F. 45	2 ,,	Insomnia. Dyspepsia. Grief at sudden death of husband	—	I	I	W	—	—	—	—	—	—	—	—
59	F. 39	3 ,,	Headache. Insomnia. Loss of weight. Poor memory. Worry	—	I	I	I	R	R	—	—	—	—	—	—
60	F. 37	6 weeks	Always tired. Pains in abdomen and neck. Insomnia	—	I	I	—	—	—	—	—	—	—	—	—
61	F. 33	2 months	Inability to cope with life. Pain in right side of abdomen. Exhaustion. Backache. Nervousness. Loss of weight	—	I Gained 13 lb.	I	R	I	W	W	R	R	—	—	R
62	M. 38	7 ,,	Loss of memory. Does not remember yesterday's occurrences. Violent hatred of relatives	—	I	I	R	R	R Organic cerebella degeneration	R	R	—	—	Dead	
63	F. 25	2 ,,	Cannot go out far. Giddiness. Peculiar sensations in head and neck. Fear of dark, omnibuses and trains	—	I	I	I	—	—	—	—	—	—	—	—
64	M. 22	1 month	Tired. Depressed. Giddiness. Inability to stick to anything. Aching in one leg	—	I	I	—	—	—	—	—	—	—	—	—
65	M. 23	5 months	Depression. Inability to work or to see people. Fulness of stomach after food. Colicky pains. Constipation. Never worked since school	—	I	I	R	R	R	R	R	—	—	—	R
66	F. 40	6 ,,	Exhaustion. Pains in head. Fear of fatigue, of cold. Insomnia. Depression	—	I	I	I	R	R	—	—	—	—	—	R
67	F. 29	1 month	Fears of company, of windows, of hurting someone	—	I	I	—	W	W	—	—	—	—	W	W
68	F. 45	2 months	Pains in left abdomen. Irritability	—	I	I	W	W	W	W	—	—	—	—	W
69	F. 39	2 ,,	Palpitation and tremors. Exhaustion	—	I	I	I	—	W	W	R	—	—	—	R
70	F. 30	7 ,,	Fears. Particularly in dark. Visual hallucinations. Tremor. Unsteady gait. Stammer	—	I	R	R	Re-ad	I	W Re-ad	—	In hospital	—	I	W
71	M. 43	1 month	Loss of self-control. Obsessed about wife. Fear of heights and death	2 years	I	I	W	R	W	W	W	—	—	—	W
72	F. 39	3 months	Depression. Exhaustion. Fears of being alone, of losing reason, of suicide, of heights	2 ,,	I	I	W	W	W	W	W	—	—	—	W
73	F. 39	11 ,,	Dysmennorrhoea. Headache. Depression. Loss of appetite. Constipation. Loss of weight. In bed for several months	—	I Gained 11 lb.	I	R	R	R	R	R	—	—	—	I
74	M. 56	4 ,,	Feeling of something going to happen to him. Pains in abdomen. Depression. Fits of weeping	—	I	I	I	I	I	I	—	—	—	—	R

1924. GROUP I, TABLE I (*continued*)

Case no.	Sex and age	Duration of stay	Symptoms	Duration of symptoms before admission	Result on discharge	Reports in 1925	1926	1927	1928	1929	1930	1931	1932	1933	1934
75	M. 42	2 months	Attacks of alcoholism. Fears. Self-reproach	—	I	I	—	—	—	—	—	—	—	—	—
76	M. 26	1 week and 1 month	Stammering. Sense of inferiority	—	—	I	I	—	—	—	—	—	—	—	—
77	F. 53	2 months	Insomnia. Headache. Constipation. Indigestion. Exhaustion	—	I	I	I	W	W	W	R	—	—	—	—
78	M. 26	6 months and 2 months	Out of sorts. Bilious. Nervousness. Sex worries. Lost both legs in the war	—	I	I	I	W	W	W	—	—	R	—	W
79	F. 30	2 month	Oppression on head. Frightened of everything. Giddiness. Impairment of vision, when the weather is dull. Horror of crowds	—	I	I	—	—	I	R	I	I	—	I	I
80	F. 57	3 months	Attacks of depression which last two or three months. They recur once or twice a year, accompanied by insomnia, fatigue and fears	12 years	I	R	R	I	W	—	W	—	—	—	W
81	F. 30	6 ,,	Sickness. Feelings of faintness	—	I	W	W	—	—	—	—	—	—	—	—
82	F. 64	2 months and 2 months	Pains everywhere. Unable to walk without sticks. Unable to bath herself	—	I	R	R	—	—	—	—	—	—	—	—
83	F. 28	5 ,,	Shortness of breath. Difficulty in swallowing. Headache. Sleeplessness. Constipation. Exhaustion	2 years	I	I	—	R	—	W	W	—	—	—	W
84	M. 19	4 weeks	Inability to concentrate. Excessive sexual desires. Feeling that he will smash furniture	—	W	W	—	—	—	—	—	—	—	—	—
85	M. 20	5 months and 3 weeks	Anxiety. Fears of crowds, of noise and of fainting	6 years	I	I	—	I	W	W	W	—	—	W	—
86	F. 27	2½ months	Dragging of left leg. Pains in hip. Depression. Headache	2 ,,	W	W	—	W	W	W	—	—	—	—	—
87	M. 38	7 weeks	Homosexual feelings. Superiority feelings	—	I	—	I	W	W	W	W	—	—	—	W
88	M. 28	1 year and 14 months	Fears. Fatigue. Palpitation	—	—	—	—	—	W	—	—	—	—	—	I
89	F. 35	3 ,,	Spasmodic torticollis after fright	—	I	I	I	R	I	—	W	—	—	—	W

1924. Group I, Table II. *Patients who state they are not any Better but who are at Work*

Case no.	Sex and age	Duration of stay	Symptoms	Duration of symptoms before admission	Result on discharge	Reports in 1925	1926	1927	1928	1929	1930	1931	1932	1933	1934
1	M. 52	2 months	Insomnia. Feeling of stupidity. Inability to think	—	ISQ	ISQ	ISQ	ISQ	ISQ	ISQ	ISQ	ISQ	—	—	—

1924. Group I, Table III. *Patients who are Better, but who do not admit that their Improvement is due to treatment at Swaylands*

Case no.	Sex and age	Duration of stay	Symptoms	Duration of symptoms before admission	Result on discharge	Reports in 1925	1926	1927	1928	1929	1930	1931	1932	1933	1934
1	F. 19	3 months	Noises in ears. Blepharospasm	1 year	I	R	—	—	—	—	—	—	—	—	—
2	F. 23	4 „	Fear of walking in sleep, of insanity, of never recovering	3 „	ISQ	W	W	W	—	—	—	—	—	—	—

1924. Group I, Table IV. *Patients who are no Better*

Case no.	Sex and age	Duration of stay	Symptoms	Duration of symptoms before admission	Result on discharge	Reports in 1925	1926	1927	1928	1929	1930	1931	1932	1933	1934
1	F. 18	2 months	Indigestion and constipation. Headache. Insomnia. Amenorrhoea. Loss of weight	—	I	R	—	—	—	—	—	—	—	—	—
2	F. 46	10 days	Exhaustion. Easily worried. Insomnia	—	ISQ	ISQ	—	—	—	—	—	—	—	—	—
3	M. 38	8 months	Attacks of unconsciousness, sometimes with epileptiform convulsions. Fugues. Alcoholism	8 years	I	R	R	R	R	—	—	—	—	—	—

1924. Group I, Table IV (*continued*)

Case no.	Sex and age	Duration of stay	Symptoms	Duration of symptoms before admission	Result on discharge	Reports in 1925	1926	1927	1928	1929	1930	1931	1932	1933	1934
4	F. 40	2 months	Tiredness. Backache. Depression. Indigestion. Insomnia. History of operations. Emaciation	—	ISQ	ISQ	ISQ	—	—	—	—	—	—	—	—
5	M. 32	1 month	Compulsions of staring at sun, of straining his body, of having to hurt himself some way	—	ISQ	ISQ	ISQ	—	—	—	—	—	—	—	—
6	F. 41	3 months	Exhaustion of mind and body. Belief that she is insane. Loss of memory	—	I	R	I	W	I	I	—	—	—	—	—
7	F. 60	2 ,,	Giddiness. State of emotional excitement	—	ISQ	ISQ	ISQ	ISQ	—	—	—	—	—	—	—
8	F. 33	7 ,,	Compulsive ideas and acts. Washes for hours. Cannot look at herself in a mirror. Obsession of hairs, of her shape being wrong. Insomnia. Outbursts of temper	—	ISQ	ISQ	ISQ	ISQ	—	—	—	—	—	—	—
9	F. 43	4 ,, and 2 ,,	General debility. Abdominal pains	—	I	R	R	—	—	—	—	—	—	—	—
10	F. 47	1 month	Insomnia. Fatigue. Failure of concentration. Dyspepsia. Noises in head	5 months	I	R	R	I	I	ISQ	—	—	—	—	ISQ
11	M. 36	2 months	Loss of appetite. Dyspepsia. Loss of sleep. Depression. Exhaustion	1 year	I	R	—	—	—	—	—	—	—	—	—
12	M. 31	9 ,,	Stress in head. Fear of killing wife. Ejaculatio praecox	4 years	I	ISQ	ISQ	I	I	W	W	W	W	W	R
13	F. 23	2 ,,	Exhaustion. Fear of meeting people. Feels well only after alcohol. Broken sleep	4 ,,	I	R	—	—	—	—	—	—	—	—	—
14	F. 75	1 month	Weakness. Poor sleep. Irritable and hypercritical. Depression	—	I	R	—	—	—	—	—	—	—	—	—
15	F. 50	7 months	Odd feeling in neck. Noises in ears. Bad smell in nose. Depression. Insomnia. Fear of insanity	15 years	I	R	R	R	—	—	—	—	—	—	—
16	M. 63	1 month	Irritation of dorsal spine. Mental excitability. Restlessness. Emotionalism	20 ,,	I	R	I	—	—	—	—	—	—	—	—
17	F. 45	2 months	Severe pain in vagina. Pollakiuria. Depression	4 ,,	I	R	W	—	—	—	—	—	—	—	—
18	F. 52	2 ,,	Depression. Fear of diseases especially duodenal ulcer. Pain after food. Insomnia	10 ,,	W	R	R	I	R	—	—	—	—	—	—
19	F. 69	4 ,,	Depression. Associated with religious fear of saying blasphemous words. Insomnia. Inability to read newspaper	15 ,,	W	R	R	—	—	—	—	—	—	—	

20	M. 56	5 months	Depression. Questions as to whether things happened really, whether he is himself. Insomnia. Fear	4 years	I	R	R	R	R	I	I	Well and at work			
21	F. 42	2 ,,	Exhaustion. Insomnia. Depression recurrent for the last six years	3 ,,	I	R	R	R	R	—	—	—	—	—	—
22	M. 65	4 ,,	Obsession that he will be sent to gaol. Pains and aches. Exhaustion. Poor sleep. Abdominal discomforts	1½ ,,	ISQ	ISQ	ISQ	ISQ	ISQ	—	—	—	—	—	—
23	M. 43	9 ,,	Complete exhaustion. Chilliness. Poor concentration. Anxiety. Done no work for 16 years	16 ,,	W	W	R	R	R	—	R	—	—	—	—
24	F. 64	2 ,,	Dyspnoea (subjective only). Choking sensations. Inability to walk	—	ISQ	I	Dead								
25	M. 25	8 ,,	Headaches. Pressure. Losing intellectual power. Poor sleep	—	I	R	—	—	—	—	—	—	—	—	—
26	F. 22	4½ ,,	Inability to meet people. Insomnia. Excessive blushing	—	I	R	R	R	R	—	—	—	—	—	—

1924. GROUP II. *Drug Addicts*

Case no.	Sex and age	Duration of stay	Symptoms	Duration of symptoms before admission	Result on discharge	Reports in 1925	1926	1927	1928	1929	1930	1931	1932	1933	1934
1	F. 51	1 month	Nervousness. Poor sleep. Poor appetite. Craving for alcohol	—	ISQ	ISQ	R	—	—	—	—	—	—	—	—
2	F. 32	4 months	Morphia addict. Takes 5 grains daily	—	I	R	R	R	R	—	—	—	—	—	—
3	F. 44	1 month	Insomnia. Depression. Pain in back when walking. Morphia addict	—	ISQ	I	R	—	—	—	—	—	—	—	—

1925. GROUP I, TABLE I. *Psychoneuroses. Patients who are Well or Improved*

Case no.	Sex and age	Duration of stay	Symptoms	Duration of symptoms before admission	Result on discharge	Reports in 1926	1927	1928	1929	1930	1931	1932	1933	1934
1	F. 32	3½ months	Hysteria. Incapable of looking after her children	—	I	R	W	—	—	—	—	—	—	—
2	F. 26	5 „	Epileptiform seizures	—	I	W	No attacks	—	—	—	—	—	—	W
3	M. 35	3 „	Lack of confidence. Inability to stick to work	—	I	I	I	I	W	W	—	—	—	—
4	F. 34	6 weeks	Sinking in abdomen. Fatigue. Loss of weight. Attacks of depression	—	W	W	W	—	W	W	—	—	—	—
5	F. 50	5 months	Exhaustion. Depression. Headaches	—	W	W	W	W	W	R	—	—	—	R
6	M. 43	2 „	Strain. Headache. Giddiness. Dyspepsia	—	W	W	W	W	W	W	—	—	—	—
7	M. 39	2 „	Headaches. Apprehension. Inability to work. Dyspepsia	—	W	W	W	W	W	W	—	—	—	—
8	M. 26	1 month	Violent nightmares	—	W	W	W	W	W	—	—	—	—	—
9	M. 24	2½ months	Depression. Inability to continue at any occupation	—	W	W	Returned for 5 days	W	—	—	—	—	—	—
10	M. 31	4 „	Odd feelings in head	—	I	W	W	W	W	—	—	—	—	I
11	M. 48	1 month	Dyspepsia. Insomnia	—	W	W	W	W	W	W	W	—	—	—
12	F. 40	1 „	Inability to mix with people	—	I	W	W	W	W	W	—	—	—	—
13	F. 43	1 „	Aphonia. Pain in chest	—	W	W	W	I	W	W	—	—	—	W
14	F. 23	9 months	Depression. Weeping. Lack of interest	—	I	I	W	W	W	W	—	—	—	—
15	M. 47	4 „	Great misery. Unable to concentrate. Homosexual thoughts	—	W Thoughts normal	W	W	W	—	—	—	W	—	W
16	F. 23	10 „	Insomnia. Emaciation. Depression. Hysterical attacks	—	W Gained 2 st.	W	W	W	—	Died (pneumonia)				
17	F. 25	6 „	Depression. Unreality feeling	—	I	I	I	I	W	W	R	R	R	I
18	M. 52	1 month	Depression. Suicidal thoughts. Lack of confidence	—	W	W	W	W	W	W	—	R	R	I
19	F. 29	3½ months	Nausea. Fear of vomiting. Loss of weight	—	W Gained 20 lb.	W	W	W	W	—	—	—	—	—
20	F. 24	6 weeks	Pain in leg. Depression. Fatigue	—	W	W	W	W	W	W	—	—	—	W
21	F. 20	3 months	Restlessness. Headache. Fears about sex	—	W	W	W	W	I	I	—	W	—	I

22	F. 33	3 months	Depression. Weeping. Fears. Pain in sacrum	—	I	I	I	I	I	I		—	—	—
23	F. 33	6½ „	Fears of insanity. Exhaustion. Insomnia	—	I	I	I	I	I	I	—	—	—	I
24	M. 57	1 month	Insomnia. Weakness	—	I	W	W	W	W	W	R	—	—	—
25	F. 29	3 months	Exhaustion. Headache. Agoraphobia	—	I	W	W	R	I	I	—	—	—	—
26	F. 35	4 „	Short attacks of depression every month	—	I	I	I	I	I	—	—	—	—	—
27	M. 43	10 weeks	Nervousness. Insomnia	—	I	I	At work							
28	M. 30	2 months	Agitation. Depression. Insomnia. Fugues	—	W	W	W	W	W	W	—	—	R	R
29	F. 60	8 „	Depression. Irritability	—	W	W	W	W	W	W	—	—	—	W
30	F. 30	5 weeks	Headache. Nervousness. Fatigue	—	I	W	W	W	—	W	—	—	—	—
31	F. 30	3½ months	Pain in left side of body. Feels she is going mad. Insomnia	—	I	W	W	—	W	—		—	W	R
32	F. 14	2 „	Anorexia. Loss of weight. Amenorrhoea	—	I Gained 21 lb.	W	—	W	W	W	—	—	—	W
33	M. 58	7 weeks	Apprehension. Fears of cancer. Unable to work	—	I	W	R	R	—	—	—	—	—	—
34	M. 30	6 months	Insomnia. Loss of will. Depression. Fear of diseases. (Invert.)	—	I	I	W	W	W	W	—	—	—	W
35	M. 27	3 „	Feeling of unreality. Fear of insanity	—	W	W	W	W	—	W	—	—	—	—
36	F. 61	6 weeks	Pains in head	—	I	I	W	W	W	W	—	—	—	—
37	M. 52	8 „	Insomnia. Indigestion. Tremors	—	W	W	W	W	R	R	At work		—	—
38	F. 36	7 months	Anorexia. Palpitation. Sickness	—	W	W	W	W	W	W	—	—	—	—
39	F. 29	6 weeks	Exhaustion. Dyspnoea. Pains	—	W	W	W	—	W	—	—	—	—	—
40	F. 37	2 months	Insomnia. Poor memory. Depression. Colitis	—	I	I	I	I	I	?	—	—	—	W
41	F. 44	4 „	Pollakiuria. Menorrhagia. Insomnia. Headaches. Exhaustion	—	W	W	W	W	R	R	I	—	—	R
42	F. 51	10 „	Fears on going to sleep. Fear of knives. Depression	—	W	W	W	W	—	—	—	—	R	W
43	F. 33	13 weeks	Easily tired. Headache. Fear of excitement	—	W	W	W	W	W	W	—	—	—	W
44	M. 43	3 „	Depression. Weeping. Talking of suicide	—	I	W	W	W	R	—	—	—	—	—
45	M. 47	1 month	Insomnia. Diarrhoea. Tremor. Giddiness. Sweating	—	W	W	W	W	W	W	—	—	—	—
46	M. 27	4 months	Loss of emotion. Loss of energy. Poor sleep	—	I	I	W	W	W	W	—	—	—	—
47	F. 47	2 „	Exhaustion. Fear of meeting people. Insomnia	—	I	W	W	W	—	—	—	—	—	—
48	F. 32	2 „	Fear of meeting people. Exhaustion. Insomnia	—	W	W	R	—	W	W	—	W	—	—
49	F. 29	7 „	Giddiness. Panics	—	I	I	—	I	—	—	—	—	—	R
50	M. 48	4 „	Depression. Numbness in legs	—	I	I	I	I	I	W	—	—	—	R
51	F. 34	4 „	Exhaustion. Dyspnoea. Agoraphobia	—	I	W	W	W	W	W	—	—	—	—
52	F. 28	15 „	Fears. Menorrhagia. Depression	—	I	I	I	I	—	—	—	—	—	—
53	F. 39	1 month	Brain in a whirl. Fear of insanity	—	I	I	W	—	W	W	—	—	—	—

1925. GROUP I, TABLE I (*continued*)

Case no.	Sex and age	Duration of stay	Symptoms	Duration of symptoms before admission	Result on discharge	Reports in 1926	1927	1928	1929	1930	1931	1932	1933	1934
54	F. 56	2 weeks	Exhaustion. Apprehension	—	I	W	W	W	W	—	—	—	—	W
55	F. 29	6 ,,	Fears of the dark. Nightmares, headaches	—	I	I	W	—	—	—	—	—	—	—
56	M. 26	3½ months	Headache. Afraid to meet people	—	I	W	W	—	W	W	—	—	—	—
57	F. 33	6 weeks	Nervousness. Exhaustion Worries over everything	—	I	I	—	—	W	—	—	W	—	—
58	F. 28	3 months	Fear that she is going to be sick. Fear of streets. Emotional and irritable	—	W	W	—	—	—	—	—	—	—	—
59	F. 48	4 ,,	Depression. Loss of energy. Panics	—	I	W	—	—	W	—	—	—	—	—
60	M. 28	6 weeks	Two fugues. Nervous. Hay fever	—	—	W	—	—	—	—	—	—	—	—

1925. GROUP I, TABLE III. *Patients who are Better but who do not admit that their Improvement is due to treatment at Swaylands*

Case no.	Sex and age	Duration of stay	Symptoms	Duration of symptoms before admission	Result on discharge	Reports in 1926	1927	1928	1929	1930	1931	1932	1933	1934
1	F. 62	14 weeks and 16 weeks	Emotionalism. Hysterical attacks	—	ISQ	Re-ad	R	W	W	W	—	—	W	W
2	F. 43	6 months	Fears. Insomnia. Headaches. Tinnitus	—	ISQ	ISQ	ISQ	I	I	—	—	—	—	—
3	M. 48	2 ,,	Depression. Poor sleep. Pressure on head. Fears	—	ISQ	ISQ	W	W	—	—	—	—	—	—
4	F. 55	6 ,,	Tinnitus. Giddiness. Deafness. Weakness	—	ISQ	ISQ	W Christian Science	W	W	—	—	—	—	—

1925. GROUP I, TABLE IV. *Patients who are no Better*

Case no.	Sex and age	Duration of stay	Symptoms	Duration of symptoms before admission	Result on discharge	Reports in 1926	1927	1928	1929	1930	1931	1932	1933	1934
1	F. 25	10 weeks	Exhaustion. Poor sleep. Fear of insanity. Headache. Shyness	—	W	W	R	R	R	—	—	—	—	—
2	F. 40	5 weeks and 8 weeks	Phobia of cancer of tongue. Obsessions about sex. Insomnia	—	I	ISQ	—	ISQ	—	—	—	—	—	—
3	F. 29	2 months	Pain in abdomen. Nausea. Indigestion	—	I	R	R	—	R	R	I	—	—	—
4	M. 47	1 month	Nervous tension. Loss of confidence	—	ISQ	—	ISQ	—	—	—	—	—	—	—
5	F. 62	1 "	Tinnitus. Headaches. Violent tempers	—	ISQ	ISQ	I	R	—	—	—	—	—	—
6	F. 46	2 months	Depression. Fainting attacks. Unable to concentrate	—	I	R	—	—	—	—	—	—	—	Not well
7	M. 41	2 "	Pain in abdomen. Insomnia. Depression	—	ISQ	W Appendicectomy	R	Not well	—	—	—	—	—	—
8	M. 48	3 "	Giddiness. Depression. Fear of impending death	—	ISQ	ISQ	ISQ	ISQ	ISQ	—	—	—	—	—
9	F. 23	4½ "	Phobias of travelling in trains and of being alone	—	ISQ	ISQ	ISQ	ISQ	I	I	W	—	—	—
10	F. 53	2 "	Loss of confidence. Stammering. Fear of suicide	—	I	I	R	R	R	R	—	—	—	—
11	M. 41	9 weeks	Exhaustion. Palpitation. Headaches	—	ISQ	ISQ	ISQ	ISQ	I	I	—	—	—	—
12	F. 67	5 "	Occipital pain. Loss of memory. Giddiness. Palpitation	—	ISQ	ISQ	—	—	—	—	—	—	—	—
13	M. 35	4 months and 9 months	Severe headaches. Amnesic periods. Violent tempers. Homosexuality	—	I	R	R	—	—	—	—	—	—	—
14	M. 59	3 "	Depression. Insomnia. Loss of weight. Homosexual inversion	—	I	R	R	R	R	R	—	—	—	—
15	M. 34	2 "	Fears. Loss of memory. Poor sleep	—	ISQ	I	—	—	—	—	—	—	W	W
16	F. 18	3½ "	Headache. Backache. Hysterical attacks. Loss of weight	—	W	R	Ill	Ill	—	—	—	—	—	—
17	F. 46	6 "	Pains and aches in arms and back. Headache. Poor sleep	—	I	R	Sometimes well		R	R	—	—	—	R
18	F. 32	6 "	Exhaustion. Poor sleep. Sexual obsessions	—	ISQ	ISQ	—	—	—	—	—	—	—	—
19	M. 30	4 "	Headaches. Weakness. Pains in back of neck. Weakness left side. Impaired vision	—	I	I	I	—	—	—	—	—	—	—

1926. GROUP I, TABLE I. *Psychoneuroses. Patients who are Well or Improved*

Case no.	Sex and age	Duration of stay	Symptoms	Duration of symptoms before admission	Result on discharge	Reports in 1927	1928	1929	1930	1931	1932	1933	1934
1	F. 36	10 weeks	Backache. Odd feelings in head	—	I	I	I	W	—	W	—	—	W
2	M. 34	3 months and 3 months	Depression. Loss of confidence. Magical beliefs	—	I	W	W	W	W	W	—	—	W
3	F. 29	13 ,,	Choreiform movements	—	W	I	R	I	—	—	—	—	I
4	M. 23	4 ,,	Palpitation. Faintness. Flatulence. Malaise	—	I	I	I	R	R	In asylum	W	—	Insane
5	M. 35	2 ,,	Self-conscious. Blushing. Insomnia. Headache. Palpitation. Sweating.	—	I	I	I	I	I	I	—	—	R
6	F. 33	3 ,,	Fears of insanity. Agoraphobia	—	I	W	W	W	W	W	W	—	W
7	M. 40	2 ,,	Exhaustion. Giddiness. Pain and tremor right side. Palpitation. Photophobia	—	I	W	W	W	—	—	—	W	—
8	F. 25	6 weeks	Anorexia. Insomnia. Constipation. Amenorrhoea	—	I	W	W	I	R	I	Re-ad	I	Re-ad
9	M. 46	10 ,,	Writer's cramp. Stutter in speech. Sense of inferiority	—	W	W	R	—	—	—	—	—	—
10	F. 39	10 months	Spasmodic torticollis	—	I	W	W	W	R	W	W	—	R
11	F. 27	10 weeks	Obsession that she is losing her good looks. Hysterical outbursts. Insomnia	—	I	W	W	—	—	—	—	—	—
12	F. 24	2 months	Untruthfulness. Stealing	—	—	W	W	W	W	W	—	—	W
13	F. 47	4 ,,	Headache. General pains. Insomnia. Exhaustion	—	I	W	W	W	—	W	—	—	W

14	M. 40	6 weeks	Agoraphobia. Fears of insanity. Chronic alcoholism	—	W	W Teetotal	W	R	I	I	I	—	W
15	F. 35	9 months	Headache. Fears. Dyspepsia. Spastic gait	—	I	—	—	—	—	—	—	—	—
16	F. 44	3 ,,	Exhaustion. Insomnia. Apprehensive	—	I	W	W	W	W	W	—	W	W
17	M. 36	1 month	Loss of confidence. Fear of insanity	—	ISQ	I	R	I	—	—	—	—	—
18	F. 27	6 weeks	Fatigue. Abdominal pain. Poor sleep. Fear of suicide	—	I	—	—	W	—	—	—	—	—
19	M. 45	2 months	Fatigued. Excitable	—	I	I	W	W	—	—	—	—	—
20	F. 40	9 ,,	Fears and terrors of the night. Insomnia. Nightmares	—	I	W	W	W	W	W	—	—	—
21	F. 42	1 month	Depression. Insomnia. Suicidal demonstration. Alcoholic excess. Homosexual tendency	—	—	—	—	—	—	—	—	—	—
22	F. 32	2 months	Awful feelings in head. Weeping. Homosexual friendship	—	I	—	—	I	—	—	—	—	—
23	F. 35	4 weeks	Fear of going off to sleep. Exhaustion	—	I	I	I	I	I	I	—	—	I
24	F. 44	4 months	Hysterical foot drop. Insomnia. Constipation fears	—	W	W	W	W	W	—	—	—	—
25	F. 25	1 year	Refusal of food. Emaciation. Unreality of day life. Reality of dream life	—	I	W	W	W	W	W	—	—	—
26	M. 47	3 months	Weakness of back and legs. Attacks of falling. Agoraphobia. Fears of insanity	—	W	W	—	I	W	W	—	—	—
27	F. 40	2 weeks	Fear of sleep. Horrors at night. Fear of suicide	—	I	W	—	—	—	—	—	—	—
28	F. 55	6 months	Dreads everything, illness, meeting people, etc. Exhaustion. Rigors. Pyelitis	—	I	W	W	W	W	I	—	—	W
29	F. 35	3 ,,	Noises in throat. Tremors. Backache	—	W	W	W	W	W	W	—	—	W

1926. Group I, Table I (*continued*)

Case no.	Sex and age	Duration of stay	Symptoms	Duration of symptoms before admission	Result on discharge	Reports in 1927	1928	1929	1930	1931	1932	1933	1934
30	M. 34	7 months	Fear of heights and trains. Palpitation. Impotence	—	I	I	R	—	—	—	—	—	—
31	F. 32	2 „	Insomnia. Unreality. Fear of insanity	—	I	W	W	W	W	W	—	—	—
32	M. 31	3½ „	Feels in a haze. Unable to remain alone. Depression. Exhaustion	—	W	—	W	—	—	—	—	—	—
33	F. 23	10 „	Insomnia. Malaise. Depression. Loss of weight	—	W	W	W	W	W	W	—	—	W
34	M. 20	5 „	Sense of detachment. Religious preoccupation. Nocturnal epilepsy	—	I	W	W	W	W	—	—	—	W
35	F. 17	4 „	Anorexia. Emaciation. Amenorrhoea	—	Gained 34 lb.	I	W	W	W	W	—	—	W
36	F. 40	2 „	Loss of weight. Indigestion. Agoraphobia. Headaches	—	I	W	R	W	W	—	—	—	—
37	F. 17	7 weeks	Loss of weight (2 st.). Loss of strength	—	W Gained 17 lb.	W	W	W	W	—	—	—	W
38	M. 45	3 months	Periodic drinking	—	W	W	W	W	W	W	R for 6 weeks	W	W
39	M. 19	7 weeks	Lack of confidence. Shyness. Feels different from others	—	I	W	W	W	W	—	—	—	W
40	M. 28	3 months	Insomnia. Terrifying dreams	—	W	W	R	R	—	—	—	—	R
41	F. 25	5 „	Dyspnoea. Headaches. Choreiform movements. Palpitation	—	I	I	I	I	I	I	—	—	R

42	M. 32	7 weeks	Pain in spine. Inability to concentrate. Syphilophobia. Nightmares. Frequent emissions	—	W	W	W	W	—	—	—	—	—
43	M. 32	2 months	Pain in head. Insomnia. Nervousness. Giddiness	—	W	—	—	—	—	—	—	—	—
44	M. 40	12 ,,	Depression. Insomnia. Inability to concentrate. Inability to sign his name	—	W	W	W	W	W	W	—	—	W
45	M. 37	1 month	Tremor, right hand. No money sense	—	W	I	W	—	—	—	—	—	—
46	M. 44	5 months	Tinnitus. Depression. Dull pain in head. Insomnia. Nightmares	—	I	I	I	I	I	I	—	—	R
47	M. 31	5 ,,	Blushing and sweating. Headaches. Chronic alcoholism	—	I	W	W	W	W	W	—	W	W
48	F. 47	6 weeks	Fear of meeting strangers. Deafness	—	I	—	—	I	—	—	—	—	—
49	F. 35	11 months	Spastic paraplegia. Depression. Insomnia	—	I	W	W	I	W	W	R	—	—
50	F. 36	4 ,,	Weakness. Tremor. Failure of concentration. Insomnia. Fears. Loss of weight	—	I Gained 17 lb.	W	W	W	W	—	—	—	W
51	F. 50	7 weeks	Exhaustion. Depression. Confusion	—	I	I	W	W	W	—	W	—	—
52	M. 45	10 months	Depression. Insomnia. Fear of people	—	I	W	W	W	—	—	—	—	—
53	M. 38	4 ,,	Alcoholic outbursts. Insomnia. Depression	—	No attack in hospital	At work R		I Probably relapsing					
54	F. 32	2½ ,,	Fear of cancer. Washing compulsion	—	I	—	—	—	—	—	—	—	—
55	M. 44	3½ ,,	Insomnia. Fatigue. Weakness in back	—	I	W	—	—	—	—	—	—	—

1926. Group I, Table I (*continued*)

Case no.	Sex and age	Duration of stay	Symptoms	Duration of symptoms before admission	Result on discharge	Reports in 1927	1928	1929	1930	1931	1932	1933	1934
56	F. 19	6 weeks	Anorexia. Amenorrhoea. Loss of weight. Feels well	—	Gained 10 lb.	—	—	—	—	—	—	—	—
57	F. 17	3½ months	Headache. Nausea. Fatigue	—	W	W	—	W	W	W	—	—	W
58	F. 44	10 "	Pain in neck. Insomnia. Constipation	—	I	I	W	—	—	—	—	—	—
59	F. 38	2 "	Giddiness. Dyspnoea. Palpitation. Insomnia	—	W	I	I	—	—	—	—	—	—
60	M. 49	1 month	Insomnia. Tinnitus. Apprehensive	—	W	W	—	W	W	W	—	—	W
61	M. 41	4½ months	Attacks of dyspnoea. Headaches. Fear of dark. Inferiority feelings	—	I	I	W	I	—	—	—	—	—
62	F. 36	4 "	Fear of going out alone. Exhaustion. Tremor	—	I	—	I	W	W	—	—	—	—
63	M. 35	3 "	Asthenia. Twitchings of body. Spasms of pain	—	W	W	W	W	W	W	—	—	W
64	F. 35	6 "	Exhaustion. Pains. Insomnia	—	W	W	W	—	W	W	W	—	W
65	M. 40	8 "	Agoraphobia. Depression. Headaches	—	I	W	—	—	—	—	—	—	—
66	M. 33	6 "	Weakness. Giddiness. Insomnia. Loss of confidence	—	W	W	W	W	W	W	—	—	R
67	F. 63	6 weeks	Anxiety about future. Fear of insanity	—	W	W	W	W	—	—	—	—	—
68	F. 35	3 months	Insomnia. Fatigue	—	I	W	W	I	—	—	—	—	—
69	M. 41	5 weeks	Attacks of loss of temper	—	?	W	W	W	W	W	—	—	W
70	M. 29	3 months	Tight feeling in head and eyes. Retardation	—	I	W	W	W	W	—	—	—	—
71	F. 52	3 "	Fatigue. Dyspnoea. Backache	—	I	W	W	W	—	—	—	—	—

72	F. 64	6 months	Headache. Pain in eyes. Inability to read. Exhaustion	—	W	W	W	W	W	W	R	W	W
73	M. 58	2 ,,	Palpitation. Giddiness. Exhaustion	—	I	I	W	W	R	W	—	—	W
74	M. 38	10 weeks	Headaches after taking meat. Fatigue. Apprehensive	—	I	W	W	I	W	W	—	—	W
75	M. 29	2½ months	Bouts of sweating in church and at meals. Poor concentration	—	W	W	W	W	W	W	—	—	W
76	F. 46	6 ,,	Abdominal pains. Constipation. Exhaustion	—	W	W	W	W	W	W	W	W	W
77	F. 32	3 ,,	Headaches. Fear of being alone. Indecisive	—	I	I	R	I	W	W	—	—	W
78	F. 35	6 ,,	Shuffling gait. Backache. Insomnia	—	I	I	R	—	—	—	—	—	—
79	F. 39	8½ ,,	Depression. Insomnia. Palpitation	—	ISQ	I	W	W	W	W	—	—	W
80	F. 16	—	Loss of appetite and weight. Amenorrhoea	—	Gained 2 st.	R Gained 15 lb.	W	W	W	W	W	W	W

1926. GROUP I, TABLE III. *Patients who are Better, but who do not admit that their Improvement is due to treatment at Swaylands*

Case no.	Sex and age	Duration of stay	Symptoms	Duration of symptoms before admission	Result on discharge	Reports in 1927	1928	1929	1930	1931	1932	1933	1934
1	F. 26	3 months	Nervousness. Fear of noise, of insanity and that she will die. Insomnia	—	ISQ	W	R	Re-ad I	W	W	W	R	I
2	M. 33	12 ,,	Unable to rest or sleep. Fear of being alive. Pressure in head. Spasm of arm	—	ISQ	W	—	—	—	—	—	Certified	
3	F. 26	6 ,,	Insomnia. Tight feeling in head. Exhaustion	—	ISQ	W After vaccines	W	W	R	—	—	—	R
4	F. 35	6 weeks	Nymphomania. Nerve storms. Depression. Unable to concentrate	—	I	—	W but from subsequent treatments	—	—	—	—	—	—

1926. GROUP I, TABLE IV. *Patients who are no Better*

Case no.	Sex and age	Duration of stay	Symptoms	Duration of symptoms before admission	Result on discharge	Reports in 1927	1928	1929	1930	1931	1932	1933	1934
1	M. 36	4 months	Depressed. Irritable. Sense of unreality. Jerkings of body	—	I	R	R	—	—	—	—	—	—
3	M. 54	3 "	Obsessive thoughts. Fear of insanity. Headache. Fear of homosexual assaults	—	Worse	Worse	In mental hospital						
4	F. 34	6 weeks and 2 weeks	Insomnia. Depression. Exhaustion	—	ISQ	ISQ	ISQ	—	—	—	—	—	—
5	F. 32	4 "	Headache. Insomnia. Fears of travelling alone	—	W	R	R	—	—	—	—	—	—
6	M. 30	6 months	Odd feelings. Tinnitus. Spermatorrhoea. Constipation	—	I	R	—	—	—	—	—	—	—
7	M. 30	2 "	Complete impotence	—	—	R	W	W	W	W	—	—	W
8	F. 36	6 "	Chronic alcoholism	—	I	R	—	—	—	—	—	—	—
9	F. 49	10 "	Spasmodic torticollis. Various phobias	—	ISQ	ISQ	ISQ	ISQ	—	—	—	—	ISQ
10	F. 44	2 "	Alcoholic outbursts	—	W	R	I	I	—	—	—	—	—
11	F. 47	8½ "	Giddiness. Weakness of legs. Pains in neck at meals. Feeling that body is light	—	I	R	R	R	—	—	—	—	Worse
12	F. 41	9 "	Exhaustion. Headache. Insomnia. Irritability	—	I	R	—	—	—	—	—	—	—
13	F. 54	2 "	Headaches. Concentration difficult. Dyspepsia	—	I	R	ISQ	R	R	R	—	R	—

14	M. 50	6 months	Obsessive thoughts and compulsive acts	—	ISQ	—	W	—	W	W	W	R	
15	F. 37	7 ,,	Exhaustion. Insomnia. Sexual sensation	—	ISQ	ISQ	—	—	—	—	—	—	—
16	F. 25	5 ,,	Fear of fatigue. Fear of heart stopping	—	I	I	R	R	—	—	—	—	—
17	M. 58	10 ,,	Headache. Insomnia. Giddiness. Depression	—	I	R	Ill	ISQ	—	—	—	—	—
18	F. 52	3 ,,	Agoraphobia. Dizziness. Lassitude. (B.P. 210)	—	ISQ	ISQ	ISQ	I	I	I	—	I	I
19	F. 35	3 ,,	Nervousness. Palpitation. Poor sleep	—	I	I	R	ISQ	ISQ	ISQ	—	—	—
21	F. 45	—	Spastic paraplegia	—	ISQ	—	—	—	—	—	—	—	—

1926. Group II. *Drug Addicts*

Case no.	Sex and age	Duration of stay	Symptoms	Duration of symptoms before admission	Result on discharge	Report in 1927
1	M. 55	2 months	Cardiac pain. Phobias. $\frac{1}{2}$ gr. morphia daily	—	—	Still taking morphia
2	F. 42	10 ,,	Morphia addiction	—	—	ISQ

1927. GROUP I, TABLE I (*a*). *Psychoneuroses. Patients who are Well or Improved. Anxiety States*

Case no.	Sex and age	Duration of stay	Symptoms	Duration of symptoms before admission	Result on discharge	Reports in 1928	1929	1930	1931	1932	1933	1934
1	M. 66	9 weeks	Headache. Unable to read	—	W	W	W	W	R	—	—	—
2	M. 35	10 ,,	Palpitation. Faintness. Phobias of heart disease and streets	—	I	W	Dead					
3	F. 29	4 months	Fatigue. Headache. Various phobias	—	W	W	W	W	W	W	—	W
4	M. 23	9 weeks	Headache. Tinnitus. Indigestion. Fear of insanity	—	I	W	—	—	—	—	—	—
5	F. 22	7 ,,	Aching in right eye. Headaches	—	W	W	—	—	—	—	—	—
6	M. 63	9 ,,	Fear that he may injure his wife. Hysterical outbreaks	—	I	W	—	—	—	—	—	—
7	M. 33	3 ,,	Giddiness in church. Odd sensations in body. Faint feelings	—	I	W	W	—	—	—	—	—
8	F. 29	2 months	Pressure and tension in head. Poor sleep. Depression. Panics	—	I	I	R	W	—	—	—	—
9	M. 42	2 ,,	Fears. Depression. Exhaustion	—	W	W	W	W	W	W	—	W
10	F. 39	3½ ,,	Loss of interest. Sleep poor. Headaches	—	I	W	—	W	W	I	—	—
11	M. 35	7 ,,	Headache. Lack of concentration. Fear of heart failure. Diarrhoea	—	I	I	I	I	I	I	—	—
12	F. 19	3 ,,	Fear of being alone, of fainting, indigestion	—	I	W	W	W	W	W	—	W
13	M. 47	2 weeks	Depression. Inferiority feelings. Pain in back. Flatulence	—	I	W	—	—	—	R	—	—
14	M. 38	3½ months	War dreams. Poor sleep. Numbness in limbs. Alcoholism	—	I	I	W	—	—	—	—	—
15	F. 50	15 ,,	Depression. Sense of unreality. Indigestion	—	I	W	W	W	W	—	—	W

16	M. 51	5 months	Depression. Difficulty of concentration	—	I	W	W	W	Re-ad	R	I	I
17	M. 37	2½ ,,	Eye strain. Giddiness. Insomnia. Fears. Indigestion	—	W	W	W	—	—	—	—	—
18	M. 24	3 ,,	Phobia about disease. Fear of company. Anxiety	—	I	W	—	—	—	—	—	—
19	M. 50	2 ,,	Palpitation. Indigestion. Loss of weight. Insomnia. Fear of cancer	—	I Gained 5 lb.	I	I	R	R	—	—	—
20	F. 29	2 ,,	Exhaustion. Headaches. Claustrophobia. Poor concentration. Epileptiform fits	—	I	W	I	Re-ad 2 weeks	W	W	W	W
21	F. 43	4 ,,	Agoraphobia	—	I	I	I	R	W	I	—	—
22	F. 37	2 ,,	Pressure on head. Pains in eyes. Many fears	—	I	W	W	W	W	W	W	W
23	M. 20	4 ,,	Inability to use brain. Fear of insanity. Shyness. Introspection	—	I	W	R	W	—	W	R	Re-ad
24	M. 24	11 weeks	Headaches. Depression. Irritability. (Post concussion)	—	W	W	W	W	W	W	W	—
25	F. 46	5 ,,	Odd sensations in stomach. Palpitation. Eye strain	—	I	W	—	W	I	R	—	R
26	F. 33	3½ months	Exhaustion. Unreality. Insomnia	—	I	W	I	I	R	I	—	—
27	F. 26	4 ,,	Depression. Unreality. Insomnia	—	W	W	W	W	W	W	W	W
28	M. 28	3½ ,,	Agoraphobia. Fear of dark. Unreality	—	I	I	W	—	—	—	W	W
29	M. 26	3 ,,	Exhaustion. Unable to concentrate. Headache. Asocial. Indigestion	—	I	I	—	—	—	—	R Re-ad	—
30	F. 38	8 ,,	Insomnia. Fatigue. Backache. Indigestion	—	W	W	W	W	W	W	—	W
31	M. 25	2 ,,	Nervousness. Weakness. Non-dissociated fugues	—	I	W	W	W	W	W	—	W
32	M. 42	7 weeks	Lack of concentration. Fear of insanity. Palpitation. Twitching	—	I	W	W	—	W	—	—	—

1927. Group I, Table I (*a*) (*continued*)

Case no.	Sex and age	Duration of stay	Symptoms	Duration of symptoms before admission	Result on discharge	Reports in 1928	1929	1930	1931	1932	1933	1934
33	M. 21	4 weeks	Self-consciousness. Shyness. Paraesthesiae	—	I	W	W	—	—	—	—	—
34	M. 20	4 ,,	Loss of appetite. Fatigue. Loss of concentration	—	I	I	I	—	—	—	—	—
35	F. 32	3½ months	Exhaustion. Neuralgic pains. Depression	—	W	W	W	W	W	W	—	W
36	F. 32	6 weeks	Insomnia. Worried about everything	—	W	W	W	—	R	R	—	R
37	F. 47	3 months	Pains in head and breasts. Nervousness. Giddiness. Exhaustion. Menorrhagia	—	I	I	W	R	—	—	—	—
38	M. 49	4 ,,	Fears of insanity, disease and knives. Depressed	—	I	I	W	W	W	W	—	R
39	F. 25	2½ ,,	Panics in the street	—	I	W	W	W	W	W	—	W
40	F. 35	11 ,,	Attacks of fear, especially of suicide	—	I	W	W	W	W	W	R	W
41	F. 33	11 ,,	Intolerance of noise. Photophobia. Headache. Bad temper	—	I	I	W	W	W	W	—	—
42	M. 29	5 ,,	Worry about everything. Loss of concentration. Insomnia	—	I	W	W	W	W	W	—	W
43	M. 33	2 ,,	Exhaustion. Poor sleep. Inferiority feelings	—	I	W	W	—	—	—	—	—
44	M. 53	4 ,,	Tremor on left side. Pressure on head and in mouth. Poor sleep	—	W	W	—	W	W	W	—	W
45	M. 38	5 ,,	Fear of knives, headaches. Insomnia. Exhaustion	—	I	W	I	I	W	I	—	W
46	F. 49	10 weeks	Unworthy thoughts. Terrors	—	I	W	W	W	W	W	—	W
47	F. 35	2 months	Exhaustion. Depression. Confused feelings. Hysterical attacks	—	I	I	I	—	—	—	—	—

48	M. 44	6 weeks	Fear of everything	—	W	W	W	W	W	W	—	W
49	M. 20	10 ,,	Fear of insanity. Unreality	—	I	W	W	W	W	I	—	W
50	F. 42	3 months	Headaches. Insomnia. Nausea. Exhaustion	—	I	I	I	I	I	—	—	—
51	F. 42	5 weeks	Exhaustion. Depression. Diarrhoea	—	W	W	W	W	W	W	—	W
52	F. 24	3 months	Attacks of terror in the street	5 years	I	I	W	—	—	—	R	I
53	M. 24	14 weeks	Fear of falling down dead. Palpitation. Poor sleep	—	I	I	I	—	—	I	I	W
54	F. 41	3 months	Insomnia. Fears of suicide. Has right optic atrophy	—	I	I	I	R	I	—	—	—
55	M. 41	4 ,,	Depression. Fear of crowds. Apprehension. Clonic movements of right arm and leg	—	ISQ	W	—	—	—	—	—	—
56	F. 33	2 ,,	Headaches. Exhaustion. Indigestion. Suspicious of husband	—	W	W	W	W	W	I	—	R
57	F. 42	3½ ,,	Palpitation on little exertion. Nervousness	—	W	W	—	—	—	—	—	—
58	F. 39	6 ,,	Phobias of snakes and knives Emotional attacks	—	I	W	I	I	I	I	—	W
59	F. 32	9 weeks	Exhaustion. Fear of heart disease. Loss of weight	—	W Gained 1 st.	—	—	—	—	—	—	—
60	F. 34	1 month	Fear of fainting. Faints. Depression. Claustrophobia	—	I	—	—	—	—	—	—	—
61	M. 37	10 weeks	Headache. Unreality. Apprehension. Giddiness	—	I	—	—	—	—	—	—	—
62	F. 30	9 months	Insomnia. Pains. Depression	—	I	—	W	—	—	—	W	W
63	M. 42	3½ ,,	Shy. Pain in back when eating	—	I	I	R	I	R	—	—	—
64	F. 26	14 ,,	Depression. Unreality. Faking temperature	—	W	Depressed	W	W	W	W	W	W

1927. Group I, Table I (*b*). *Hysteria*

Case no.	Sex and age	Duration of stay	Symptoms	Duration of symptoms before admission	Result on discharge	Reports in 1928	1929	1930	1931	1932	1933	1934
1	F. 22	7 weeks	Depression. Instability of moods	—	W	W	W	W	W	W	—	—
2	F. 46	11 months	Epileptiform fits. Insomnia. Pyelitis	—	W	W	W	W	W	W	—	W
3	F. 27	7 ,,	Pain in coccyx. Hiccups		W	W	W	W	—	W	—	W
4	F. 30	4 ,,	Vomiting. Retention of urine. Outbursts of temper. Suicidal demonstrations	6 months	W	W	R	W	R	—	—	W
5	F. 37	3 ,,	Flaccid paralysis left leg (12 years). Secondary talipes—organic. Pains in back	14 years	W	W	—	—	—	—	—	—
6	F. 22	2 ,,	Tic of shoulders. Attacks of unconsciousness	—	I	I	—	—	—	—	—	—
7	F. 50	12 ,,	Exhaustion. Confused feeling	—	I	I	W	I	R	I	Has diabetes	
8	M. 61	4 ,,	Spasticity and tremor of legs. Insomnia. Fatigue. Anxiety	—	W	W	W	W	W	R	—	R
9	M. 30	5½ ,,	Photophobia. Ideas of self-mutilation	—	I	I	—	—	—	—	—	—
10	F. 34	5 ,,	Depression. Suicidal demonstrations	—	ISQ	W	—	R	—	—	—	—
11	F. 33	3½ ,,	Headaches. Vomiting. Exhaustion	—	I	—	—	—	—	—	—	—
12	F. 45	3 ,,	Aphonia. Emotionalism	—	I	—	—	—	—	—	—	—

1927. Sub-Group. *Anorexia Nervosa*

Case no.	Sex and age	Duration of stay	Symptoms	Duration of symptoms before admission	Result on discharge	Reports in 1928	1929	1930	1931	1932	1933	1934
13	F. 20	5 weeks	Anorexia. Amenorrhoea. Loss of weight	—	Gained 14 lb.	W	—	W	—	—	—	W
14	F. 20	—	Anorexia. Amenorrhoea. Loss of weight	—	Gained 3 lb. Re-ad	I	I	—	W	—	—	W

1927. GROUP I, TABLE I (c). *Obsessive-Compulsive Neurosis*

Case no.	Sex and age	Duration of stay	Symptoms	Duration of symptoms before admission	Result on discharge	Reports in 1928	1929	1930	1931	1932	1933	1934
1	M. 48	6 months	Constant working of bowels. Fear of diseases	—	ISQ	ISQ	ISQ	ISQ	ISQ	ISQ	I	W
2	M. 20	5 ,,	Obsessions that testicles are too small	—	I	I	W	—	W	—	—	—
3	F. 17	3 ,,	Obsessional thoughts of sex. Compulsive acts of washing. Re-arranging things	—	I	I	I	I	R	R	—	R
4	F. 17	3½ ,,	Constant washing of hands. Constant thoughts about dirt	—	ISQ	ISQ	ISQ	ISQ	—	ISQ	—	ISQ

1927. GROUP I, TABLE II. *Anxiety States. Patients who state they are not any Better but who are at Work*

Case no.	Sex and age	Duration of stay	Symptoms	Duration of symptoms before admission	Result on discharge	Reports in 1928	1929	1930	1931	1932	1933	1934
1	F. 37	5 months	Nervousness. Exhaustion. Headaches	—	I	R	R	R	R	—	—	—
2	F. 44	2 ,,	Insomnia. Exhaustion. Anorexia. Depression	—	I	R	R	—	—	—	—	—

1927. GROUP I, TABLE III. *Patients who are Better, but who do not admit that their Improvement is due to treatment at Swaylands*

Case no.	Sex and age	Duration of stay	Symptoms	Duration of symptoms before admission	Result on discharge	Reports in 1928	1929	1930	1931	1932	1933	1934
1	F. 46	2 months	Giddiness. Pain in back and right knee	—	W	R (Spa treatment)	W	W	—	—	—	—

1927. Group I, Table IV. *Patients who are no Better*

Case no.	Sex and age	Duration of stay	Symptoms	Duration of symptoms before admission	Result on discharge	Reports in 1928	1929	1930	1931	1932	1933	1934
1	M. 32	5 months	Depression. Unable to concentrate. Worry about engagement	—	ISQ	ISQ	R	—	—	—	—	—
2	F. 31	2 ,,	Insomnia. Indigestion. Disgust at sex	—	ISQ	ISQ	ISQ	ISQ	—	—	—	—
3	M. 40	6½ ,,	Vertigo. Flatulence. Fear of strangers	—	ISQ	ISQ	ISQ	—	—	—	—	—
4	M. 49	10 weeks	Tremulousness. Insomnia. Palpitation. Fatigue. Cannot concentrate	—	I	R	—	—	—	—	—	—
5	M. 46	6½ months	Depression. Cloudiness in head. Loss of confidence. Insomnia	—	Worse	I	I	I	I	—	—	—
6	M. 43	2 weeks	Debility. Catarrh. Exhaustion. Faintness on right side	—	I	Being treated for abscess of liver	R	I	W	—	—	—
7	F. 46	4 months	Pains and weakness in legs. Tinnitus. Insomnia	—	I	R	—	—	—	—	—	—
8	M. 49	6 weeks	Insomnia because of fears on dropping to sleep	—	ISQ	ISQ	ISQ	—	—	—	—	—
9	M. 50	12 days	Loss of concentration. Insomnia. Indecision	—	ISQ	—	—	—	—	—	—	—
10	F. 57	4 months	Insomnia. No will power. Loss of memory. Worries	—	ISQ	ISQ	R	ISQ	ISQ	—	—	—
11	F. 33	3 ,,	Headaches. Depression. Fears of going out. Fear of swallowing	—	I	R	Re-ad	ISQ	ISQ	Dead		
12	F. 57	3 ,,	Indigestion. Pain in back. Insomnia. Tempers. Otorrhoea	—	ISQ	—	—	—	—	—	—	—

13	F. 41	3 months	Tachycardia. Exhaustion. Pains in shoulder	—	I	R	R	R	—	—	—	—
14	F. 57	2½ ,,	Tight feelings in head. Curious sensations in jaw. Lack of interest	—	W	R	Dead					
16	M. 22	11 weeks	Tics affecting chiefly the trunk	—	ISQ	—	W	—	—	—	—	—
17	F. 38	2½ months	Dimness of vision. Palpitation. Outbreaks of temper	—	ISQ	—	—	—	—	—	—	—

1927. Group II. *Alcoholics*

Case no.	Sex and age	Duration of stay	Symptoms	Duration of symptoms before admission	Result on discharge	Reports in 1928	1929	1930	1931	1932	1933	1934
1	F. 30	1 month	Bouts of alcoholism. Fear of facing people	—	ISQ	—	—	—	—	—	—	—
2	M. 28	6 months	Bouts of alcoholism	—	?	W	W	—	—	—	—	—
3	M. 36	2 weeks	Chronic alcoholism	—	?	?	—	—	—	—	—	—

1928. GROUP I, TABLE I (*a*). *Psychoneuroses. Patients who are Well or Improved. Anxiety States*

Case no.	Sex and age	Duration of stay	Symptoms	Duration of symptoms before admission	Result on discharge	Reports in 1929	1930	1931	1932	1933	1934
1	F. 40	5 weeks	Headache. Fatigue. Stuffiness in chest	6 months	W	W	W	W	—	—	—
2	M. 40	9 months	Panics in street. Impotence	2 years	W	W	W	W	W	W	W
3	F. 18	4 ,,	Exhaustion. Indigestion. Palpitation. Shyness. Loss of weight. Nightmares. Dysmenorrhoea	3 ,,	W Gained 17 lb.	W	W	W	W	W	W
4	M. 46	5 weeks	Pains in abdomen. Insomnia. Bad dreams	Many years	I	W	R	R	R	W	R
5	M. 43	9 ,,	Migraines. Fear of eating. Constipation. Emaciation. Mitral disease	33 years	Gained 12 lb. Fears gone	I	R	R	R	—	—
6	F. 60	1 year	Insomnia. Fear of insanity. Odd feelings in head	2 ,,	W	W	—	—	—	—	—
7	M. 34	3 months	Giddiness; fear of heart disease. Inferiority feeling	13 ,,	I	W	W	W	W	—	W
8	M. 38	5 weeks	Insomnia. Anxiety. Self-depreciation	2 months	W	W	W	W	W	W	W
9	M. 34	3 months	Fear of phthisis. Somnolence. Dyspepsia	1 year	I	W	W	W	Re-ad	W	W
10	F. 25	15 weeks	Insomnia. Trembling. Weeping. Worry	4 months	W	W	W	W	—	—	I
11	M. 33	9 months	Anxiety. Impulsive. Quarrelsome	3 years	I	W	R	R	R	R	R
12	M. 28	9 ,,	Fear of insanity. Self-consciousness. Inferiority feeling	14 ,,	W	W	R	R	R	R	R
13	M. 24	6 weeks	Fear of blood. Insomnia. Anxiety attacks	9 months	W	W	W	W	—	W	W
14	F. 45	5 months	Fatigue. Insomnia	22 years	W	W	W	W	—	—	—

15	F. 36	9 months	Agoraphobia. Sacralgia. Fear of insanity. Insomnia	6 years	I	I	I	R	R	R	R
16	F. 24	3 ,,	Recurrent thoughts against God. Visual hallucinations. Insomnia. Irritability. Hysterical weakness of legs	14 ,,	I	W	R	R	I	—	W
17	F. 56	4½ ,,	Headache. Fears of illness. Depression	8 ,,	W	W	W	—	—	—	—
18	M. 32	2 ,,	Epigastric distress. Anxiety. Alcoholism	4 ,,	W	W	W	W	W	W	W
19	M. 22	1 month	Pain in little finger on playing piano	15 months	ISQ	W	W	—	—	—	—
20	F. 36	15 months	Attacks of violent tempers. Sacrache. Loss of concentration. Constant worry	1 year	I	W	W	W	W	W	W
21	F. 31	2 weeks	Exhaustion. Weeping. Agoraphobia. Worries	3 years	I	I	—	—	—	—	—
22	F. 33	6½ months	Fear of insanity. Insomnia. Indigestion. Formication	3 ,,	I	W	W	W	—	W	W
23	F. 34	3½ weeks	Fear of knives. Depression. Insomnia	1 year	W	W	W	—	—	—	—
24	F. 31	3 months	Fears of all kinds. Depression	2 years	W	—	R	R	I	W	W
25	F. 38	10 weeks	Fear of bridges, water, gas taps. Fear of pregnancy	6 months	I	W	W	W	W	W	W
26	M. 34	4½ months	Worries. Depressed. Emotional. Feels world hostile	4 years	I	I At work	I	R	I	W	—
27	M. 35	4 ,,	Depression, weeping. Insomnia. Lack of concentration	6 months	W	W	W	—	—	—	—
28	F. 57	4 ,,	Giddiness, weakness. Poor sleep. Numbness of arm	3 years	I	W	R	W	I	—	—
29	M. 46	1 month	Fatigue	5 ,,	W	—	—	—	—	—	—
30	M. 24	1 ,,	Excessive day dreaming. Fears of future	3 ,,	I	W	R	I	I	R	R
31	F. 24	4½ months	Pain in back and head. Depression	18 months	I	W	W	W	W	W	—

1928. GROUP I, TABLE I (*a*) (*continued*)

Case no.	Sex and age	Duration of stay	Symptoms	Duration of symptoms before admission	Result on discharge	Reports in 1929	1930	1931	1932	1933	1934
32	M. 25	3½ months	Irritable heart. Rigors. Megalomania	5 years	I	I	W	W	—	—	—
33	M. 52	1 year	Depression. Insomnia	—	Died of influenza						
34	M. 22	5 months	Unreality. Depression. Restlessness	5 months	I	W	W	W	—	W	W
35	F. 45	1 month	Depressed, worried. Insomnia	5 ,,	I	I	I	I	—	R	R
36	M. 50	2 months	Anxiety in presence of other people	10 years	W	W	—	—	—	—	—
37	M. 24	1 month	Sense of unreality. Fear. Anxiety	1 year	W	W	W	—	—	W	W
38	M. 28	3 weeks	Sense of unreality. Doubts	18 months	I	W	I	I	—	W	R
39	M. 33	4 months	Loss of confidence. Fears of suicide	18 ,,	I	W	W	W	W	—	—
40	M. 45	5 weeks	Lack of energy. Unable to concentrate. Insomnia. Headache	18 ,,	W	W	W	W	—	—	—
41	F. 35	4½ months	Depression. Insomnia. Loss of weight	10 ,,	I Gained 7 lb.	W	W	W	W	W	W
42	F. 30	2½ ,,	Fear of vomiting. Insomnia. Headaches. Sensations in abdomen	—	I	—	—	—	—	—	—
43	F. 60	6½ ,,	Depression. Insomnia. Lack of concentration	5 years	I	I	R	R	Re-ad	ISQ	—
44	M. 33	6½ ,,	Depression. Pain in head and neck	3 ,,	I	I	W	R	R	R	R
45	F. 55	4 ,,	Depression. Indecision. Discontent. Insomnia	1 year	I	W	W	W	W	R	R
46	F. 35	3½ ,,	Difficulty in concentration. Depression	6 months	I	W	W	W	—	W	W

47	F. 33	4 months	Vasovagal attacks. Exhaustion. Anxiety. Homosexuality	1 year	W	W	W	—	—	—	—
48	M. 43	4 ,,	Feeling of impending illness. Unable to concentrate. Failure of memory	6 months	I	—	W	—	W	W	—
49	F. 28	6 ,,	Coarse tremor right arm. Fears of insanity and cancer	6 ,,	W	W	W	W	W	W	W
50	F. 23	1 month	Vomiting. Diarrhoea. Refusal to live in her own house or to consummate her marriage	—	I	W	—	—	—	—	—
51	M. 49	5 weeks	Fears of brain giving way. Distressing sensations in the penis	Many years	W	W	W	—	W	W	I
52	M. 53	3 ,,	Alleged loss of temper	—	—	I	—	—	—	—	—
53	F. 42	3 months	Lack of concentration. Claustrophobia. Feelings of incapacity. Loss of memory	2 years	I	—	—	—	—	—	—
54	F. 45	6 ,,	Depression. Insomnia. Loss of concentration	8 months	W	W	W	W	W	W	I
55	F. 34	6 ,,	Poor sleep. Depressed. Hysterical outbursts with screaming	Many years	W	W	—	—	—	—	—
56	F. 34	8 ,,	Crashing headaches—trephined twice. Outbursts of temper. Unhappiness	8 years	I	W	W	W	W	W	W
57	M. 24	3 ,,	Depression. Self-reproach and cannot face work but can play games	2 ,,	I	W	W	W	W	W	W
58	F. 30	9 ,,	Insomnia. Pains. Depression	—	I	W	—	—	—	—	—
59	M. 60	5 weeks	Loss of confidence	—	W	R	W	W	W	W	W
60	F. 35	5 months	Exhaustion. Pains everywhere	4 years	I	R	I	I	I	I	I
61	F. 30	4½ ,, and 7 ,,	Phobias of many kinds. Sensation of being strangled	8 ,,	W	R Re-ad	W	W	W	W	W
62	M. 56	3 ,,	Fear of being alone. Insomnia. Depression	—	W	R Re-ad	W	W	W	W	W

1928. Group I, Table I (*b*). *Hysteria*

Case no.	Sex and age	Duration of stay	Symptoms	Duration of symptoms before admission	Result on discharge	Reports in 1929	1930	1931	1932	1933	1934
1	F. 53	10 weeks	Attacks of loss of control of limbs. Spastic movements of limbs	10 years	Attacks much less	I	I	—	—	—	—
2	F. 27	10 ,,	Bad temper. Ideas that mother persecuted her. Attempts to malinger madness	—	I	I	R	—	—	R	—
3	F. 30	10 ,,	Weakness of legs. Exhaustion. Heats in skin. Insomnia	7 years	I	I	W	W	W	W	W
4	F. 58	2 months	Aphonia. Dyspnoea. Insomnia. Exhaustion	15 months	I	—	—	—	—	—	—
5	F. 34	3 ,,	Tinnitus. Depression. Anxiety. Spots in front of eyes	7 ,,	W	W	W	W	W	W	W
6	F. 22	4 ,,	Artefact rashes. Romantic tales. Erotomania	18 ,,	—	W	W	W	W	W	W
7	M. 21	3 ,,	Sense of inferiority. Thinks his chin is too small. Cannot stay long in any place	5 years	W	W	W	W	W	W	W
8	F. 50	2 ,,	Fatigue. Dypsepsia. Insomnia	Many years	I	W	—	—	—	—	—
9	M. 55	5½ ,,	Poor sleep. Worry. Lack of decision. Lack of sexual control. Depression	10 years	I	W	W	R	—	—	—
10	M. 26	7 ,,	Paraplegia with coarse tremor. Agoraphobia. Nightmares	2 ,,	I	W	W	W	—	—	—
11	F. 32	4½ ,,	Dysphagia. Paraplegic gait. Depression	9 months	W	W	Re-ad	—	I	I	W
12	F. 44	3 ,,	Demonstrations of suicide. Pains in neck. Tempers	9 ,,	W	—	—	—	—	—	—
13	M. 23	8 ,,	Unable to open mouth more than ½ inch. Insomnia. Constipation	2 years	I	W	W	W	W	W	W

14	F. 39	4½ months	Attacks of unconsciousness. Convulsive attacks	10 years	W	W	W	W	W	W	R
15	F. 60	2 „	Pains and weakness in leg. Stabbing pain in forehead	4 „	I	W	W	W	R	—	—
16	F. 42	3 „	Unable to stand or walk. Palpitation. Exhaustion. Emaciation	18 months	I Gained 12 lb.	I	W	—	R	I	I
17	F. 33	4 „	Headaches. Pain in spine. Jerkings of back and thighs. Exhaustion	10 „	W	W	W	W	W	W	W
18	F. 35	14 „	Inability to stand or walk. Insomnia. Tremors. Lack if concentration	3 years	I	W	W	W	W	W	W
19	F. 46	2 „	Hatred of noise. Insomnia. Pains all over body	1 year	W	W	—	—	W	W	W
20	M. 25	4½ „	Tremor of head and neck. Insomnia. Headache	—	W	R Re-ad	W	W	W	W	—

1928. Group I, Table I (*c*). *Obsessive-Compulsive Neurosis*

Case no.	Sex and age	Duration of stay	Symptoms	Duration of symptoms before admission	Result on discharge	Reports in 1929	1930	1931	1932	1933	1934
1	M. 48	4 months	Washing mania. Elaborate rituals against defilement	3 years	I	I	W	W	W	W	W
2	F. 20	6 weeks	Washing mania. Childish conduct	5 „	ISQ	I	—	—	—	—	—

1928. Group I, Table IV. *Patients who are no Better*

Case no.	Sex and age	Duration of stay	Symptoms	Duration of symptoms before admission	Result on discharge	Reports in 1929	1930	1931	1932	1933	1934
1	F. 24	8 months	Terror. Constipation	1 year	I	R	I	I	—	—	—
2	F. 58	3 ,,	Pains all over. Dazed feelings. Exhaustion. Palpitation. Tempers	10 years	ISQ	ISQ	—	—	—	R	—
6	M. 36	6 weeks	Soreness in penis. Exhaustion. Snapping in brain	6 ,,	ISQ	ISQ	—	—	—	—	—
7	M. 45	1 month	Fugue for 4 days. Depression. Insomnia and suicidal attempts	—	ISQ	—	—	—	—	—	Suicide
8	F. 57	10 weeks	Bad taste in mouth. Indigestion. Pains in legs, eyes and head	20 years	ISQ	ISQ	—	—	—	—	—
9	F. 47	5 ,,	Depression. Anxiety. Colitis	1 year	ISQ	ISQ	—	—	—	—	—
10	F. 36	2 months	Vomiting. Headache	24 years	ISQ	ISQ	—	—	—	—	—
12	M. 34	6 ,,	Emotionalism. Weeping. Full of grievances	3 ,,	I	R	I	—	W	—	—
14	M. 49	7 ,,	Generalized tremor. Agoraphobia	—	ISQ	ISQ	—	—	Dead		
15	F. 53	11 ,,	Polyuria. Spasmodic torticollis	—	ISQ	ISQ	Dead				

1928. Group II. (*a*) *Alcoholics*

Case no.	Sex and age	Duration of stay	Symptoms	Duration of symptoms before admission	Result on discharge	Reports in 1929	1930	1931	1932	1933	1934
1	M. 37	5 weeks	Boastfulness. Bouts of alcoholism	Many years	ISQ	—	—	—	—	—	W
2	M. 40	3 months	Insomnia. Irritability. Tremulousness	6 months	W	—	—	—	—	—	—
3	M. 33	10 ,,	Bouts of drunkenness. Megalomania	8 years	ISQ	W	—	Dead			

1928. Group II. (*b*) *Drug Addicts*

Case no.	Sex and age	Duration of stay	Symptoms	Duration of symptoms before admission	Result on discharge	Reports in 1929	1930	1931	1932	1933	1934
1	M. 42	3 months	Morphia addiction. 2 gr. per day. Alcoholism	—	Free from drugs for 2 months	R	—	—	—	—	—
2	F. 60	1 month	Bromidia addiction. Delirious attacks	—	ISQ	ISQ	ISQ	ISQ	Dead		

1929. GROUP I, TABLE I (*a*). *Psychoneuroses. Patients who are Well or Improved. Anxiety States*

Case no.	Sex and age	Duration of stay	Symptoms	Duration of symptoms before admission	Result on discharge	Reports in 1930	1931	1932	1933	1934
1	F. 34	4½ months	Feelings of wrong doing. Fear of suicide	2 years	W	W	W	—	—	W
2	F. 53	8 „	Depression. Headaches. Vomiting. Poor sleep	2 „	I	W	W	W	W	W
3	F. 58	10 „	Panics and fears	18 months	I	W	W	W	W	W
4	F. 43	10 weeks	Fear of insanity. Insomnia	9 years	I	W	W	—	—	—
5	M. 32	9 months	Hatred of sex. Solitary. Depressed. Terrors	5 „	I	W	—	W	W	W
6	F. 32	4 „	Depression. Feels unfit to be married. Insomnia	5 months	W	W Married	W	W	W	W
7	F. 33	15 weeks	Exhaustion. Failure of concentration. Outbursts of fury	5 years	I	W	W	—	—	W
8	M. 35	2 months	Loss of concentration. Suspicions. Sexual difficulties	6 months	I	W	—	—	—	W
9	F. 60	5 „	Agonizing pains in shoulder. Insomnia. Depression	2 years	W	W	W	W	R	I
10	F. 35	2½ „	Fears. Palpitation. Headache. Photophobia. Backache	1 year	I	—	—	—	—	—
11	M. 41	5 „	Compulsive flights without dissociation. Nervousness. Fears	Many years	I	W	W	R	W	W
12	M. 30	2 „	Depression. Feeling of inadequacy	5 months	W	W	W	W	W	W
13	M. 49	2 „	Anxiety lest he should fail in business and home life	3 years	ISQ	I	W	W	W	W
14	F. 40	5½ „	Anxiety attacks. Odd sensations in body	8 „	I	I	W	W	—	—
15	F. 50	1 month	Fears she will damage her grandchild. Intense jealousy. Depression	6 months	I	—	W	—	—	—
16	F. 29	2½ months	Dreads and panics	8 years	I	I	W	W	W	W
17	F. 23	4½ „	Depression. Lack of initiative. Suicidal demonstrations. Self reproach	1 year	W	W	W	W	W	W

18	F. 34	6 months	Inferiority feelings. Fear. Depression. Unable to cope with her work	6 months	W	W	W	W	W	W
19	M. 55	5 ,,	Depression. Worries easily. Shy. Headache. Tinnitus	4 years	I	I	I	W	W	W
20	M. 22	13½ ,,	Fear of travelling in trains, of exhibitionism, of death, of disease. Vomiting at meals	3 ,,	W	W	W	W	W	W
21	M. 38	10 ,,	Panics. Fear of insanity, of death, that he has ruined his life	1 year	I	W	W	W	—	W
22	F. 50	5 ,,	Pain in head and abdomen. Anxieties. Sinus disease. Operated on	Several years	I	W	I	—	—	—
23	M. 32	5 ,,	Nervousness. Headaches. Fears of insanity	18 months	I	W	W	W	—	W
24	M. 27	2	Loss of memory. Anxiety depression	2 ,,	W	W	W	W	W	W
25	F. 32	2½ ,	Diarrhoea. Exhaustion. Headaches	2 years	I	—	—	R	I	—
26	M. 21	2½ ,,	Fears of sex, of sin, of homosexuality. Has had confusional attack	18 months	W	W	W	W	W	W
27	F. 43	11 ,,	Depression. Loss of weight. Phobia of rabies. Occult ideas	3 years	I	I	W	W	W	W
28	F. 32	3 ,,	Pain in throat. Unreasonableness. Pains in limbs	—	I	W	W	W	W	—
29	F. 56	6 weeks	Headaches with vomiting (migraine). Fatigue. Failure of concentration	Many years	I	I	I	I	—	—
30	M. 25	5 months	Headache. Insomnia. Terrifying dreams. Fears of dark and diseases. Indigestion	2 years	I	W	W	W	W	W
31	M. 58	3½ ,,	Doubts concerning validity of ordination. Depression	6 months	W	W	W	R	R	W
32	F. 38	4½ ,,	Pains. Giddiness. Fears at night and of suicide	7 years	I	I	W	W	I	I
33	M. 16	3½ ,,	Unable to mix with people. Anxiety about eyes	Always	I	I	—	R	—	—
								Mental hospital		
34	M. 32	2 ,,	Fear of heart disease. Panics	15 months	I	I	W	—	—	—
35	M. 61	3 ,,	Fatigue. Lack of concentration. Poor sleep. Anxiety	18 ,,	W	W	W	Dead		
36	M. 37	2 ,,	Fatiguability. Loss of concentration	—	I	—	—	—	—	—
37	F. 60	2½ ,,	Insomnia. Exhaustion. Emotionalism. Fear of insanity. Nymphomania	Some years	I	I	W	—	—	—

1929. GROUP I, TABLE I (*a*) (*continued*)

Case no.	Sex and age	Duration of stay	Symptoms	Duration of symptoms before admission	Result on discharge	Reports in 1930	1931	1932	1933	1934
38	F. 45	4½ months	Dizziness. Headache. Fatigue. Insomnia. Bed-ridden for years	10 years	I	W	I	I	—	—
39	M. 43	6 ,,	Prostatic pain. Depression. Emotionalism. Sex fears	4 ,,	I	W	R	W	W	W
40	F. 42	6 ,,	Insomnia. Fatigue. Emotionalism	5 ,,	I	I	R	R	—	—
41	M. 42	5 ,,	Insomnia. Lassitude. Depression. Unable to concentrate. Flatulence	3 ,,	I	I	W	W	W	W
42	M. 44	2½ ,,	Morbid blushing. Feelings of inefficiency. Depression	2 ,,	I	I	I	I	—	—
43	F. 45	2 years	Depression. Loss of memory. Headache. Exhaustion. Tempers. Nymphomania	Some years	I	I	W	W	I	I
44	M. 54	6 months	Depression. Unable to use his brain. Headache. Poor sleep	1 year	I	I	I	W	W	W
45	F. 34	6 weeks	Weeping. Inability to go out alone. Insomnia. Fear of having children	6 months	W	W	R	—	—	—
46	M. 50	6 ,,	Always nervous about work. Fear of mistakes. Failure to consummate marriage	6 ,,	I	I	I	—	—	—
47	F. 40	2 months	Pains in arms and legs. Sweatings. Malaise	8 ,,	W	W	W	W	—	—
48	F. 48	2½ ,,	Vomiting. Indigestion. Constipation	3 years	I	I	W	W	R	—
49	M. 21	3 ,,	Odd sensations in head. Unreality. Fatigue. Cardiac sensations	18 months	I	W	W	W	W	—
50	M. 62	1 month	Inability to concentrate or make decisions. Poor sleep. Suicidal thoughts. Painful sexual ideas	1 year	W	W	W	W	W	W
51	F. 24	3 months	Terror. Fear of insanity. Religious doubts. Exhaustion	1 ,,	I	I	I	—	I	W
52	F. 27	4½ ,,	Never strong. Poor physique. Inferiority feelings	10 years	I	I	W	W	W	W
53	F. 27	10 weeks	Weeping. Attacks of anger. Anxiety about work	—	I	Re-ad	W	W	W	W
54	M. 56	2½ months	Anxiety. Depression about financial position	—	W	W	W	—	—	—

1929. Group I, Table I (*b*). *Hysteria*

Case no.	Sex and age	Duration of stay	Symptoms	Duration of symptoms before admission	Result on discharge	Reports in 1930	1931	1932	1933	1934
1	F. 32	10 weeks	Attacks of weeping, moaning, screaming. Suspicious	25 years	ISQ	W	W	—	—	—
2	M. 36	9 months	Complains that he has locomotor ataxia. Depression. Loss of concentration. Headaches	3 "	I	I	W	W	W	W
3	M. 40	5½ "	Anxieties. Fugues. Amnesias. One epileptiform attack. Insomnia	1 year	W	W	W	W	W	W
4	F. 19	11 "	Anorexia (Anorexia Nervosa). Amenorrhoea. Emaciation (5 st. 1 lb.). Untruthfulness	3 years	I 6 st. 8½ lb.	W	W	W	W	W
5	M. 37	3½ "	Spasmodic contraction of neck muscles pushing the head forward	1 year	I	W	R	R	R	R
6	F. 27	4½ "	Paralysis of left leg. General anxiety	2½ years	W	W	W	W	W	W
7	F. 58	4½ "	Vertigo with tinnitus. Falling; attacks of unconsciousness	9 "	I	I	I	W	—	—
8	M. 42	7 weeks	Tics and jerks of body every few minutes. Pressure on head	4 months	I	I	I	—	—	—
9	F. 34	2 months	Pain in spine. Depression	6 "	W	W	W	W	—	—
10	F. 18	4½ "	Sleep walking. Depression. Fits of starving herself. Suicidal demonstrations	2½ years	I	W	W	W	W	W
11	F. 40	2 "	Attacks of temper; breaking plates, etc.	3 "	W	W	W	W	—	I
12	F. 27	9 "	Ptosis. Imitation of other people's symptoms. Sexual fears	18 months	W	W	W	W	W	W
13	F. 34	11 "	Pains in back. Headaches. Agoraphobia	8 years	W	W	—	—	—	—
14	F. 41	5½ "	Fainting. Emotionalism. Insomnia. Depression	2 "	I	I	W	—	—	—
15	F. 38	1 year	Sense of unreality. Unable to concentrate. Ideas that her dead husband can hear her	—	I	I	—	—	—	I

1929. Group I, Table I (*c*). *Obsessive-Compulsive Neurosis*

Case no.	Sex and age	Duration of stay	Symptoms	Duration of symptoms before admission	Result on discharge	Reports in 1930	1931	1932	1933	1934
1	M. 36	6 months	Compulsion to count numbers; to make several attempts before he enters a door. Fears of children. Inability to read because of having to count. Occasional alcoholic bouts	7 years	I	I	I	—	R	W
2	M. 26	10 ,,	Obsession about clothes not being right. Various other obsessions	5 ,,	I	I	W	W	R	W
3	M. 19	2 ,,	Obsessions about fires, gas, doors; that he had swallowed things	9 months	I	—	W	W	W	W
4	M. 22	10 ,,	Obsessional thoughts and compulsive acts which vary	16 years	ISQ	I	W	W	W	W
5	F. 56	2 ,,	Obsessions of words. Depression. Insomnia	16 ,,	I	R	—	—	—	—
6	F. 55	3 ,,	Obsessions about words, about religious things. Unable to go to church	4 ,,	I	—	—	—	—	—
7	F. 45	3½ ,,	Compulsive acts. Arranging things endlessly. Outbursts of temper	Many years	ISQ	ISQ	—	—	—	—

1929. Group I, Table IV. *Patients who are no Better*

Case no.	Sex and age	Duration of stay	Symptoms	Duration of symptoms before admission	Result on discharge	Reports in 1930	1931	1932	1933	1934
1	F. 22	2 months	Lethargy. Bad tempers. Weeping. Depression	—	I	R	W	R	W	Dead
2	F. 32	15 ,,	Fear of knives. Depression. Fear of insanity	Some years	ISQ	ISQ	W	—	Certified	
3	F. 35	3½ ,,	Depression. Unable to manage her household	18 months	I	R	—	—	—	R
4	F. 53	5 ,,	Headaches. Palpitation. Exhaustion	Some years	I	R	I	—	—	—
5	F. 40	5 weeks	Headache. Exhaustion. Depression. Abdominal pains. Loss of weight	4 years	I	R	—	—	—	—

6	M. 30	3 months	Tremor at meals in public	10 years	I	R	R	—	—	—
7	M. 27	6 ,,	Inability to breathe. Loud retching. Fear of heart disease. Panics. Insomnia	4 ,,	ISQ	ISQ	I	R	I	I
9	F.	7 ,,	Violent tempers. Unable to live with her husband	2 ,,	ISQ	ISQ	—	—	—	—
10	F. 41	2 ,,	Weakness. Feelings of contraction	2 ,,	I	R	R	I	I	I
11	F. 46	10 ,,	Indigestion. Neuralgia. Insomnia. Loss of weight. Palpitation. Many operations	7 ,,	I	R	R	R	R	R
12	F. 32	10 ,,	Hatred of mother. Quarrelsome. Refusal of food. Sleep walking. Amnesias	3 ,,	ISQ	ISQ	ISQ	ISQ	Certified	
13	M. 31	4 ,,	Tremor of right arm in company. Desire to avoid company	20 ,,	I	R	R	I	I	W
14	F. 25	7 ,,	Anorexia. Insomnia. Recurrent cystitis. Bad dreams. Depression. Alcoholism	6 months	ISQ	ISQ	W	W	—	—
15	F. 35	4½ ,,	Fatigue. Lack of concentration. Depression	6 ,,	I	R	I	—	I	I
16	F. 55	2 ,,	Frequent sexual desire. Fear of sexual words	3 years	I	R	—	—	—	—
17	M. 39	6 ,,	Indigestion. Anxiety about trains, that he might be swept by a passing train. Fear of windows that he might fall out. Fear that he might kill his wife and children	—	Suicide					
18	M. 34	—	Fear of haemorrhage from an old wound. Fear of roads, of bulls, of the dark. Fear of marriage	10 years	I	R	R	—	R	—
19	F. 36	2 months	Anxiety about health. Fear of insanity. Pollakiuria	Always ill	ISQ	ISQ	—	I	I	R

1929. Group II. *Alcoholics*

Case no.	Sex and age	Duration of stay	Symptoms	Duration of symptoms before admission	Result on discharge	Reports in 1930	1931	1932	1933	1934
1	M. 40	6 weeks	Steady drinking. An epileptiform fit	—	No symptoms here	R Re-ad for 18 months	—	R	—	R

1930. GROUP I, TABLE I (*a*). *Psychoneuroses. Patients who are Well or Improved. Anxiety States*

Case no.	Sex and age	Duration of stay	Symptoms	Duration of symptoms before admission	Result on discharge	Reports in 1931	1932	1933	1934
1	M. 19	5 weeks	Poor sleep. Self conscious. Obsessive thoughts. Headaches	9 months	I	W	W	W	R
2	F. 43	5½ months	Fear of her father. Insomnia. Homosexuality	5 years	W	W	R	—	—
3	F. 35	3½ ,,	Fear of knives and of damaging other people. Suicidal thoughts. Insomnia. Nightmares. Tempers	10 ,,	I	I	W	R	W
4	M. 45	3 ,,	Anxiety lest he should commit a misdemeanour. Insomnia	18 months	W	W	—	—	W
5	F. 28	10 weeks	Outbursts of temper. Exhaustion	3 years	I	I	W	W	W
6	F. 48	3 months	Insomnia. Nightmares. Indigestion. Ornithophobia. Rages and hatred	10 ,,	W	W	W	W	W
7	M. 15	11 weeks	Attacks of depression. Visual hallucinations	Some years off and on	I	I	R	W	W
8	F. 39	3 months	Exhaustion. Depression. Headaches. Flatulence	10 years	I	W	R	I	I
9	F. 50	4 ,,	Exhaustion. Indigestion. Poor sleep. Rheumatic pains	5 ,,	I	W	W	W	W
10	M. 32	1 year	Phobias of many kinds. Homosexuality. Alcoholism	18 months	I	I	—	—	W
11	F. 36	8 months	Exhaustion. Malaise. Fear of impulsive acts	—	I	W	W	W	I
12	M. 17	4 weeks	Confused feelings. Fears of insanity. Depression. Poor sleep	18 months	W	W	W	W	W
13	F. 54	5½ months	Indigestion. Insomnia	18 ,,	W	W	W	—	W
14	M. 27	8 ,,	Poor memory. Unable to concentrate. Inferiority	18 ,,	W	W	W	R	—
15	M. 39	2½ ,,	Panics. Pain in eyes. Fear of people	—	I	I	R	I	—

16	M. 60	2 weeks	Fear of not sleeping. Fear of paralysis	9 months	W	W	W	W	W
17	M. 32	10 ,,	Dyspepsia. Depression. Fear of impotence. Homosexual	6 years	I	I	—	—	—
18	F. 42	5½ months	Fear of being left alone. Exhaustion. Feelings of impending death	Some years	I	I	I	W	W
19	F. 57	2 ,,	Insomnia. Disgusting dreams. Depression	3 years	I	I	I	—	I
20	F. 48	10 ,,	Ideas of reference. Poor sleep. Headache. Indigestion	6 ,,	I	—	—	—	—
21	F. 53	2 ,,	Pain in abdomen. Insomnia. Weeping	2 ,,	I	—	—	—	—
22	F. 54	7 weeks	Exhaustion. Failure of concentration. Insomnia. Nasal catarrh	1 year	I	W	W	W	—
23	M. 27	6 ,,	Exhaustion. Eyestrain. Fear of insanity and heart disease. Indigestion. Palpitation	2½ years	W	W	—	W	W
24	M. 42	3 months	Depression. Weeping. Inferiority feeling	—	W	W	W	W	W
25	M. 54	3½ ,,	Insomnia. Panics. Fears of insanity, that he will kill wife and family and commit suicide	9 years	I	W	W	W	W
26	M. 61	4 ,,	Anxiety about health. Fear of death. Obsessional reproaches	1 year	W	W	—	—	—
27	M. 62	4½ ,,	Inability to concentrate. Apprehensive. Fear of being alone	3 years	W	W	W	W	W
28	M. 44	10 weeks	Religious doubts. Depressed	9 months	W	W	W	I	—
29	F. 35	2 months	Panics. Agoraphobia	20 years	I	W	W	—	—
30	F. 39	5½ ,,	Voices which upbraid. Headaches. Bad dreams	6 months	I	W	W	I	W
31	F. 42	2 ,,	Panics in street, house, trains. Fears of insanity and heart disease	16 years	I	I	I	W	W
32	M. 53	5 weeks	Exhaustion—mental and physical. Poor sleep. Headaches. Indigestion. Sickness	2 ,,	W	W	W	R	W
33	M. 32	4 months	Agora- and claustro-phobias. Sex worries	6 ,,	W	W	—	W	W

1930 GROUP I, TABLE I (*a*) (*continued*)

Case no.	Sex and age	Duration of stay	Symptoms	Duration of symptoms before admission	Result on discharge	Reports in 1931	1932	1933	1934
34	F. 32	6 months	Anxiety attacks	18 months	W	W	W	W	W
35	F. 32	19 ,,	Idea that she had committed a crime	8 years	W	W	W	W	W
36	F. 40	4 ,,	Fatigue. Insomnia. Fears of serious disease	6 ,,	W	W	W	R	I
37	M. 34	4 weeks	Phobias in street and trains	15 ,,	W	W	W	R	R
38	F. 43	1 month	Fatigue. Depression. Fears	2 ,,	I	I	—	—	—
39	M. 25	4 months	Unable to concentrate. Dislike of indoor work	Many years	W	W	W	—	—
40	M. 56	2 ,,	Insomnia. Syphilophobia	6 months	W	W	W	W	W
41	M. 47	6 ,,	Fear of lingering death. Brain fatigue. Poor sleep. Wakened up by spasmodic movements	18 ,,	W	Re-ad W	W	W	W
42	M. 27	5 ,,	Lack of confidence. Sense of inferiority. Shuns all social intercourse	On and off always	I	I	W	W	R
43	F. 54	4 ,,	Exhaustion. Insomnia. Depression	2 years	W	W	W	W	W
44	M. 54	6 ,,	Fear of impotence, of some serious disease. Depression	2 ,,	W	W	—	R	R
45	F. 46	8 ,,	Urticaria. Dyspepsia. Weakness of legs	2 ,,	W	W	W	W	I
46	F. 37	2½ ,,	Depression. Loss of confidence. Insomnia	6 months	W	W	W	W	W
47	M. 21	4½ ,,	Fears of insanity and suicide. Agoraphobia. Bursting feelings in head. Panics	6 ,,	I	W	W	W	W
48	M. 32	3½ ,,	Debility. Impotence. Inability to concentrate. Poor sleep	18 ,,	I	I	—	—	W

49	F. 44	4 months	Depression. Remorse. Nightmares. Weeping. Pruritus vulvae	Many years	I Op. for pruritus	W	W	W	W
50	M. 35	1 month	Depression. Loss of interest. Wakes with a start at night	—	W	Died			
51	M. 54	4 months	Agoraphobia. Unable to concentrate. Depression	18 months	I	W	W	W	W
52	F. 45	4 ,,	Exhaustion. Insomnia. Indigestion	3 ,,	I	W	W	W	—
53	F. 23	3½ ,,	Inability to retain urine. Anorexia. Anxiety. Exhaustion	4 years	I	W	W	R	—
54	F. 45	2 ,,	Exhaustion. Unhappiness. Poor sleep	3 ,,	I	W	W	W	W
55	F. 26	10 weeks	Insomnia. Exhaustion. Excitability	4 ,,	I	W	—	—	—
56	M. 41	1 month	Indigestion. Insomnia requiring alcohol	11 months	W	—	—	—	—
57	M. 48	6 weeks	Indigestion. Insomnia. Depression	18 ,,	I	—	—	—	—
58	M. 32	3 ,,	Fear of responsibility. Alcoholism. One epileptiform fit	1 year	I	W	W	W	W
59	M. 24	3 months	Depression. Feeling of inferiority. Unable to concentrate	1½ years	I	W	W	W	—
60	M. 22	4½ ,,	Panics. Depression. Sees things "in two dimensions"	2 ,,	W but R and Re-ad	W	W	W	W
61	F. 28	4 ,,	Headache. Fear of becoming blind. General anxiety	1 year	I	W	W	R	—
62	M. 35	3 ,,	Sense of guilt. Bad dreams. Inability to concentrate. Feeling of superiority	1 ,,	I	I	W	W	W
63	M. 31	3½ ,,	Panics in trains. Unreality. Cloudiness in mind. Fear of marriage	2 months	W	W	W	—	W
64	F. 36	5 weeks	Vomiting. Insomnia	6 ,,	W	R	W	W	W

1930. Group I, Table I (*b*). *Hysteria*

Case no.	Sex and age	Duration of stay	Symptoms	Duration of symptoms before admission	Result on discharge	Reports in 1931	1932	1933	1934
1	F. 54	2 months	Flatulence. Feeling that heart would stop	4 years	I	—	—	—	—
2	F. 35	2 weeks	Fear of being responsible for father's death. Something snapped in head. Feels out of control	20 "	I	I	I	W	W
3	F. 47	4½ months	Pain in left arm and leg. Inability to walk. Insomnia. Lilliputian hallucinations	18 months	I	W	W	—	W
4	F. 23	5½ "	Pain in spine. Depression. Attempt at suicide by morphia	12 "	W	W	—	—	W
5	F. 50	4½ "	Indigestion. Eructation. Borborygmi	30 years	W	W	R	W	R
6	F. 25	6 "	Dislikes to people. Ideas of reference. Outbursts of temper	18 months	W	W	W	W	W
7	F. 43	4 "	Rigidity of neck. Unable to raise head from bed. Unable to feed herself. Pain in neck	18 "	W	W	W	W	W
8	F. 28	3½ "	Haematuria. Exhaustion. Sleep-walking. Fugues. Emaciation	3 years	I	I	W	—	W
9	F. 64	5 weeks	Indigestion. Flatulence. Pains over body	—	I	W	—	—	—
10	M. 48	3 months	Dyspepsia. Insomnia. Hallucinations. Exhausted. Every part of body out of order	—	W	W	—	R	—
11	F. 34	2 "	Headaches. Weakness of legs. Falling down. Fear of sex	2 years	I	I	I	W	R
12	F. 37	8 "	Severe headache. Photophobia	1 year	W	W	W	W	W
13	F. 44	6 "	Homosexual attachments. Jealousy. Suicidal threats	2 years	I	W	W	W	W

14	F. 32	6 weeks	Inability to pass water if anyone is near	18 years	W	W	W	W	W
15	F. 36	3 months	Attacks of screaming. General debility	2 ,,	W	W	R	W	W
16	F. 22	1 month	Amnesias. Two attempts at suicide. Visual hallucinations	3 months	W	W	W	W	—
17	F. 31	6 months	Pains in eyes. Fatigues. Fear of men. History of various paralyses	20 years	W	W	W	I	I
18	M. 24	6 weeks	Coldness in penis. Voices ridiculing him. Says that there is an "influence" against him	2 ,,	W	W	R	I	—
19	M. 39	11 ,,	Exhaustion. Panics. Feeling of numbness in legs and that they will give way. Unable to concentrate	16 months	W	W	R	R	I

Anorexia Nervosa

1	F. 17	4 months	Anorexia. Emaciation. Amenorrhoea. Insomnia. Suspicion of people	3 years	I Gained 1 st.	W	W	W	W
2	F. 19	3 months	Anorexia. Amenorrhoea. Loss of 2 st. in weight	—	Gained 23 lb.	W	W	W	W

1930. Group I, Table I (*c*). *Obsessive-Compulsive Neurosis*

Case no.	Sex and age	Duration of stay	Symptoms	Duration of symptoms before admission	Result on discharge	Reports in 1931	1932	1933	1934
1	M. 26	18 months	Compulsions of various sorts. Obsessive thinking. Anal erotism	13 years	I	W	W	W	W
2	F. 25	9½ ,,	Washing. Fears of diet	12 ,,	I	R	R	R	R
3	M. 23	4 ,,	Compulsive thinking about Christian Science. Depression. Weeping. Panics	1 year	I	—	—	—	—
4	M. 27	2½ ,,	Washing mania. Anxiety.	Many years	I	R	R	—	—
5	M. 20	16 ,,	Fear of dirt getting on his things. Compulsions to inspect them for hours. Infantile sexuality	2 years	I	I	I	I	I

1930. Group I, Table IV. *Patients who are no Better*

Case no.	Sex and age	Duration of stay	Symptoms	Duration of symptoms before admission	Result on discharge	Reports in 1931	1932	1933	1934
1	M. 23	3 months	Depression. Worries easily. Paraesthesiae of head	18 months	I	R	R	—	—
3	M. 35	4½ ,,	Depression. Agoraphobia. Fear of heart disease. Later, perforated duodenal ulcer	17 years	ISQ	ISQ	—	—	—
4	F. 45	10 weeks	Insomnia. Backache. Depression	6 months	W	R	W	W	R

5	M. 49	7 weeks	Phobias of crowds, trains, omnibuses. Insomnia. Alcoholic excess	2 years	W	R	R	—	—
6	F. 49	1 year	Depression. Fearful dreams. Aphonia. Exhaustion	—	W	R	—	—	—
7	M. 25	1 month	Insomnia. Exhaustion	3 years	ISQ	—	—	—	W
8	M. 49	3 months	Feelings of guilt and depression. Marital difficulties	Several years	I	R	R	R	R
9	F. 41	11½ ,,	Headache. Fear of insanity. Marital incompatibility	2 years	I	R	—	—	—
10	M. 40	6 weeks	Anxiety. Poor sleep. Pain in back	18 months	W	R	—	?	—
11	F. 50	6 months	Insomnia. Depression. Fear that she might do some-dreadful, i.e. kill people	1 year	I	R	—	—	—
12	M. 41	3 ,,	Fear of injuring his wife. Depression. Poor sleep	—	Suicide				

1930. Group II. (*a*) *Alcoholics*

Case no.	Sex and age	Duration of stay	Symptoms	Duration of symptoms before admission	Result on discharge	Reports in 1931	1932	1933	1934
1	M. 27	13 months	Agoraphobia. Indigestion. Alcoholic outbursts	14 years	ISQ	ISQ	ISQ	ISQ	Certified
2	M. 50	3½ ,,	Bouts of alcohol lasting five days	12 ,,	ISQ	ISQ	ISQ	—	—
3	M. 42	4½ ,,	Continuous over-drinking. Depression	12 ,,	W	W	W	W	W

1931. GROUP I, TABLE I (*a*). *Psychoneuroses. Patients who are Well or Improved. Anxiety States*

Case no.	Sex and age	Duration of stay	Symptoms	Duration of symptoms before admission	Result on discharge	Reports in 1932	Reports in 1933	Reports in 1934
1	M. 36	4½ months	Confusion on admission. Later anxiety and weeping	18 months	I	W	W	—
2	F. 20	5 ,,	Religious anxiety. Terrifying dreams when half asleep. Exhaustion. Failure of concentration	1 year	I	W	W	W
3	F. 48	19 ,,	Exhaustion. Insomnia. Headache. Dyspepsia. Rheumatism	5 years	I	W	W	I
4	F. 42	4½ ,,	Exhaustion. Pains in body. Twitchings. Headache Insomnia	18 months	I	W	R	—
5	M. 34	7 weeks	Fear of horses. Tremors of hands	3 years	W	W	—	—
6	M. 54	15 ,,	Exhaustion. Depression. Insomnia	4 ,,	I	I	R	—
7	M. 34	3½ months	Impotence. Dyspepsia. Nightmares	Some years	I	I	I	—
8	M. 22	18 ,,	Phobias of all kinds, especially of travelling in trains	5 years	W	W	W	W
9	M. 50	3 ,,	Lethargy. Exhaustion. Abdominal discomfort. Terror of bleeding from a duodenal ulcer	2 ,,	I	W	—	—
10	F. 28	4½ ,,	Depression. Fear of retching in public. Insomnia	9 ,,	I	I	—	—
11	F. 54	4 ,,	Exhaustion. Palpitation. Poor sleep	8 months	I	I	I	I
12	M. 42	2 ,,	Anxieties. Panics. Phobias. Depression. Feeling of unreality	1 year	I	I	I	I
13	F. 32	1 month	Emotional attacks. Insomnia. Anxiety	Always	I	W	—	—
14	F. 64	5 months	Depression. Loss of self-confidence. Agitation	1 year	I	I	I	—
15	F. 54	9½ ,,	Pain in back of head and neck. Lassitude. Weeping. Despair	1 ,,	W	W	W	W
16	M. 30	7 ,,	Vertigo. Panics. Loss of confidence	6 months	I	W	W	W
17	F. 36	16 ,,	Depression. Insomnia. Hatreds. Nightmares. Indigestion	3 years	I	W	—	—
18	F. 40	4½ weeks	Exhaustion. Insomnia. Indigestion. Constipation	1 year	I	W	W	W

19	F. 49	18 months	Rigidity. Tremors. Emotional storms. Excessive hates. Insomnia	18 months	I	I	W	W
20	F. 39	2 ,,	Anxiety. Restlessness. Fatigue	18 ,,	W	W	W	W
21	M. 31	3 ,,	Fatigue. Emotionalism	3 years	I	I	I	W
22	F. 21	2 ,,	Periods of depression	6 months	W	W	W	W
23	M. 54	6 ,,	Depression. Insomnia. Inferiority feeling	2 years	W	W	W	W
24	F. 33	7 ,,	Depression. Exhaustion. Fear of suicide and insanity	10 ,,	W	W	W	W
25	F. 23	9½ ,,	Sexual phobias	9 ,,	W	W	W	W
26	F. 37	9 weeks	Fear of insanity. Empty feelings in head. Palpitation. Flatulence	20 ,,	I	I	—	—
27	M. 55	2 months	Giddiness on right side of head. Brain exhaustion. Fear of cerebral tumour	3 ,,	W	W	—	—
28	F. 54	1 month	Fatigue. Sleeplessness. Fear of impulsive acts	Several years	I	I	W	—
29	F. 33	11 months	Phobias on road. Fears about marriage. Excessive sexual desires	6 years	W (Married)	W	W	Dead (childbirth)
30	F. 17	4 weeks	Fear of fainting in the road, in the bath, etc. Fear of death. Afraid to take exercise	2 ,,	I	W	—	—
31	F. 36	2 months	Exhaustion. Pain in back	6 months	W	W	—	—
32	F. 53	4 ,,	Pains in back and legs. Pin-pricks and heats. Other parathesiae	8 ,,	I	I	—	W
33	M. 58	2 ,,	Fear that he will murder his wife and commit suicide. Insomnia. Secondary alcoholism	11 ,,	W	W	W	W
34	F. 36	3 weeks	Exhaustion. Insomnia. Indigestion	1 year	I	W	W	—
35	M. 29	5½ months	Self-conscious. Remorse. Anorexia. Inability to hold a post. Homosexual	8 years	I	I	W	W
36	F. 54	6 weeks	Lack of concentration. Loss of memory	—	I	W	W	W
37	F. 48	4 ,,	Exhaustion. Severe headaches. Depression	18 months	I	W	—	—
38	M. 20	9 months	Lack of concentration. Panics. Difficulty in remembering	6 years	W	W	W	W
39	F. 42	3 ,,	Depression. Emotionalism. Anxiety	1 year	I	I	Re-ad	W
40	F. 38	8 ,,	Fatigue. Pains in head and face. Insomnia. Indigestion	18 months	I	W	I	I
41	M. 36	10 weeks	Depression. Brain feels numb. Loss of sexual desire	6 ,,	I	W	W	W

1931. Group I, Table I (*a*) (*continued*)

Case no.	Sex and age	Duration of stay	Symptoms	Duration of symptoms before admission	Result on discharge	Reports in 1932	1933	1934
42	M. 36	3½ months	Lack of confidence in church. Shyness. Sexual inversion	3 years	W	W	W	W
43	M. 28	3 ,,	Indigestion. Weakness. Anxiety about sex	1 year	I	I	W	W
44	F. 24	5 weeks	Giddiness. Sickness. Fear. Disgust	3 years	I	I	W	W
45	F. 39	4 ,,	Depression. Fear of her husband. Marital incompatibility	5 ,,	I	W	W	—
46	M. 47	5 ,,	Depressed and unhappy	9 ,,	I	W	I	I
47	F. 36	3½ months	Fear of injuring people. Depression. Anorexia	7 ,,	I	I	I	R
48	M. 29	5½ weeks	Worried. Unable to concentrate. Poor sleep. Nausea. Anorexia	16 ,,	W	W	W	R
49	F. 40	5 months	Exhaustion. Palpitation. Undue dependence on parents	5 ,,	W	W	W	—
50	F. 29	2½ ,, plus 1 month	Unable to manage her household. Irritable with her children. Considers that her husband should do nothing but attend to her. Epileptic fits	10 ,,	I	I	W	W
51	M. 46	4½ months	Palpitation. Instability in walking. Agitation. Anxiety	4 ,,	I	I	R	—
52	M. 40	1 week	Fear of heights, of trains, of insanity	14 ,,	W	W	—	—
53	M. 23	5 weeks	Depression. Anxiety. Fear of father	Always	I	—	—	—
54	M. 34	6 months	Depression. Fears. Headaches. Inability to write	15 years	I	—	—	—
55	M. 31	6 weeks	Fullness in stomach. Fears about gastric disease. Apprehensive	4 ,,	I	—	—	—
56	M. 44	7 months	Weeping. Loss of memory. Insomnia	Some years	I	—	W	I
57	M. 50	6 ,,	Throbbing in head. Anxiety. Lack of energy. Abnormal sex beliefs	10 years	I	—	—	W
58	F. 32	7 ,,	Insomnia. Excitability. Weeping. Headache	1 year	W	—	—	—
59	M. 28	3 ,,	Fatigue. Anxiety about heart. Fainting attacks	2 years	W	—	—	W
60	M. 50	9 ,,	Pain in abdomen. (Spastic colon.) Insomnia. Depression	10 ,,	I	—	W	W

1931. Group I, Table I (*b*). *Hysteria*

Case no.	Sex and age	Duration of stay	Symptoms	Duration of symptoms before admission	Result on discharge	Reports in 1932	Reports in 1933	Reports in 1934
1	F. 45	7 weeks	Functional hemiplegia. Insomnia. Periods of mental confusion. Depression	1 year	I	W	W	W
2	F. 48	4 months	Outbursts of temper. Maladaptation to home. Muscular twitchings	22 years	W	W	R	I
3	M. 38	6 ,,	Depression. Fears about disease of almost delusional intensity. Giddiness. Poor sleep	18 months	I	I	I	W
4	M. 48	$2\frac{1}{2}$,,	Intolerable at home. Throws the furniture about. Poor sleep. Depressed about work	18 ,,	I	I	R	R
5	F. 48	17 ,,	Outbursts of temper lasting for days	All her life	I	I	I	W
6	F. 29	5 ,,	Continuous abdominal pain, for which has had three operations. Anxiety. Insomnia. Sexual anaesthesia	$1\frac{1}{2}$ years	I	I	Has a baby	I
7	M. 58	$3\frac{1}{2}$,,	Aphonia. Insomnia. Indigestion. Difficulty with micturition	11 ,,	ISQ	ISQ	ISQ	—
8	F. 25	$5\frac{1}{2}$,,	Pain and paresis right arm. Fatigue. Blushing	9 ,,	I	W	W	W
9	F. 32	7 ,,	Exhaustion. Emotional attacks	—	W	W	W	—
10	F. 35	9 weeks	Aphonia. Flaccid paraplegia following spinal anaesthesia for appendicectomy	7 months	W	W	Nervous condition good but has T.B.	—

1931. GROUP I, TABLE I (*d*). *Anorexia Nervosa*

Case no.	Sex and age	Duration of stay	Symptoms	Duration of symptoms before admission	Result on discharge	Reports in 1932	1933	1934
1	F. 19	7 months	Anorexia. Amenorrhoea. Emaciation	18 months	Gained 2 st.	W	W	W
2	F. 18	2½ ,,	Indigestion. Anorexia. Loss of weight. Amenorrhoea	1 year	Gained 7 lb.	W	W	W
3	F. 22	3 ,,	Anorexia. Emaciation. Amenorrhoea	1 ,,	Gained 25 lb.	W	W	W
4	F. 14	5 ,,	Refusal of food. Violent tempers. Emaciation. Amenorrhoea	10 months	Gained 28 lb.	R Died in October		

1931. GROUP I, TABLE III. *Obsessive-Compulsive Neurosis*

Case no.	Sex and age	Duration of stay	Symptoms	Duration of symptoms before admission	Result on discharge	Reports in 1932	1933	1934
1	F. 40	2 years	Fears that she may have left poison lying about which may damage others. Compulsive acts to avoid this	Many years	ISQ	ISQ	ISQ	ISQ
2	M. 38	5 weeks	Compulsive staring at place of people's genitalia. Feeling of unreality. Outbursts of temper	3 years	I	R	R	R
3	M. 22	5 months	Washing compulsions	7 ,,	I	I	I	R
4	F. 54	6 weeks	Compulsions of tidying and washing. Obsessive ideas about sin	12 ,,	ISQ	ISQ	ISQ	ISQ
5	F. 32	2½ months	Compulsive counting of objects. Excessive times spent in dressing because of rituals	15 ,,	ISQ	ISQ	ISQ	—
6	M. 30	4 ,,	Compulsions of walking to the right. Obsessional thoughts about telling the truth and about stealing	3 ,,	I	—	—	—

1931. Group I, Table IV. *Patients who are no Better*

Case no.	Sex and age	Duration of stay	Symptoms	Duration of symptoms before admission	Result on discharge	Reports in 1932	1933	1934
1	F. 28	8 months	Agoraphobia. Depression. Inability to concentrate	3 years	ISQ	ISQ	—	—
2	F. 48	2 years	Exhaustion. Violent tempers. Depression	20 ,,	I	I	I	I
3	M. 33	9 weeks	Failure of concentration. Vacillation. Self-contempt. Fear of suicide	2½ ,,	W	R	W	W
4	F. 42	3 months	Fear of being alone. Sleeplessness. Fear of loss of power of legs	18 months	ISQ	ISQ	Re-ad	W
5	F. 40	5 weeks	Exhaustion. Poor sleep. Excitable. Emotional. Paralysed from polyiomyelitis. Walks with great difficulty	2 years	I	R	—	—
6	F. 25	2½ months	Sleeplessness. Day-dreaming. Cannot get rid of the past	6 months	I	R	W	—
7	M. 30	4 ,,	Weakness of ankle. Walks leaning heavily on stick	2 years	ISQ	ISQ	—	W
8	F. 35	18 ,,	Terrors coming on suddenly. Failure of concentration. Poor sleep. Exhaustion. Indigestion	—	I	R	I	I
9	F. 48	13 weeks	Pains in pelvis. Confusion. Loss of concentration. Fear of death	2 years	ISQ	ISQ	In mental home	
10	F. 52	2½ months	Fears. Headaches. Poor sleep	Some years	ISQ	—	—	—
11	F. 43	2 ,,	Indigestion. Nervousness. Depression. Weakness. Exhaustion. Pain in right leg. Anorexia	—	ISQ	—	Died	
12	M. 40	2 ,,	Nervousness. Weakness of left leg. Insomnia	1 year	W	R	R	—
13	F. 36	2½ ,,	Exhaustion. Agitation. Depression. Indigestion. Constipation	5 years	ISQ	ISQ	—	—

1931. Group II. *Alcoholics*

Case no.	Sex and age	Duration of stay	Symptoms	Duration of symptoms before admission	Result on discharge	Reports in 1932	1933	1934
1	M. 58	5 weeks	Alcoholic bouts. Homosexuality	—	ISQ	—	—	—

1932. GROUP I, TABLE I (*a*). *Psychoneuroses. Patients who are Well or Improved. Anxiety States*

Case no.	Sex and age	Duration of stay	Symptoms	Duration symptoms before admission	Result on discharge	Reports in 1933	Reports in 1934
1	F. 32	2 months	Fear of fainting, of paralysis. Feeling of guilt	18 months	W	—	—
2	F. 38	9 weeks	Fatigue. Anorexia. Abdominal discomfort. Headaches. Loss of weight	3 years	I	—	—
3	M. 45	7 ,,	Headache. Lassitude. Hatred of noise. Indigestion. Insomnia. Bodily pains	2 ,,	W	W	W
4	F. 36	4 months	Tachycardia. Loss of weight. Fine tremors. Excitability. Nausea	9 months	I	W	W
5	F. 48	3 ,,	Terrors. Awful feelings all over. Fear of cancer. Blasphemous thoughts	9 ,,	I	—	—
6	M. 23	10 ,,	Panics. Loss of confidence. Fits of weeping	1 year	W	W	R At work
7	F. 41	11 days	Attacks of giddiness. Objects whirl round. Pains on top of head	3 months	W	W	W
8	F. 44	4½ months	Insomnia. Anorexia. Indigestion. Depression. Exhaustion. Distressing dreams. Severe headaches	35 years	I	I	I
9	M. 49	2½ ,,	Inability to concentrate. Anxiety feelings. Poor memory. Slight depression. Loss of interest	6 months	W	W	—
10	M. 28	7½ ,,	Inability to meet people socially. Fear of responsibility. Superiority compensation	18 ,,	I	I	W
11	F. 29	10 ,,	Pricking feelings of vulva. Obsessive thinking. Pains in head	6 years	I	I	I
12	F. 40	3 ,,	Weeping. Loss of temper. Complains of hairs on face and legs. Loss of interest in her children	2 ,,	I	I	I
13	F. 36	2½ ,,	Pains in head. Unable to concentrate. Depressed	6 ,,	I	I	I
14	F. 38	6½ ,,	Drifting. Always worried. Inability to concentrate. Poor sleep. Exhaustion. Short paranoid period	2 ,,	W	W	W
15	M. 19	5½ ,,	Fear of men hurting and seizing his genitals. Pains in head. Choking feelings. Loss of confidence. Unsteady gait	—	I	W	W

16	F. 39	1 month	Insomnia. Fears of being alone in the dark. Exhaustion. Depression and suicidal thoughts	18 months	I	W	W
17	M. 30	4 weeks	Lack of confidence. Claustrophobia. Phobia of food	5 years	I	I	—
18	M. 48	3½ months	Inability to concentrate. Depression. Insomnia	3 ,,	I	I	I
19	M. 26	4 ,,	Depression. Insomnia. Lumbar pains	12 ,,	W	W	W
20	F. 42	6 weeks	Loss of confidence. Anorexia	3 ,,	W	—	R
21	F. 43	6 ,,	Tachycardia. Fear of sudden illness	18 months	W	W	W
22	M. 64	3 months	Feelings he may have made misstatements in legal documents and that he is being watched	16 years	I	I	I
23	F. 34	3 weeks	Weeping. Insomnia. Restlessness	1 year	W	W	W
24	M. 30	8 months	Depression. Restlessness. Loss of confidence. Unreality	1½ years	I	W	W
25	M. 17½	4 weeks	Loss of concentration. Loss of interest. Depression	3 months	W	W	W
26	M. 46	6½ months	Anxiety. Biting sensation in rectum	2 years	I	I	W
27	F. 32	4 ,,	Abdominal pain. Constipation. Loss of appetite	9 ,,	W	W	W
28	M. 27	4½ ,,	Panics in bus or underground. Inability to eat food in public. Suicidal thoughts	2 ,,	I	I	W
29	M. 21	3 ,,	Panics. Nervousness. Headaches	2 ,,	I	I	R
30	F. 63	3 ,,	Shakiness. Insomnia. Pains in head. Sleeplessness	2 ,,	I	W	W
31	F. 21	4½ ,,	Feeling of unreality. Depression. Insomnia	6 months	W	W	W
32	M. 54	11 weeks	Indigestion. Fatigue. Sleeplessness. Anxiety	18 ,,	W	W	W
33	F. 45	6½ ,,	Depression. Weeping. Sleeplessness. Feeling that people are against her	3 years	I	I	R
34	M. 33	5½ months	Depression. Disturbance of vision. Attempted suicide	6 months	I	W	W
35	M. 31	6½ ,,	Fears of infecting other people with syphilis. Pain in the tongue. Pain in abdomen. Insomnia. Depression	1 year	I	I	—
36	M. 44	6 weeks	Inability to work. Fear of insanity. Loss of confidence	9 months	W	W	W
37	F. 40	8 months	Complete exhaustion (in bed 5 years). Aphonia. Insomnia. Music in her head. Asthenopia. Agony in back	6 years	I	W	W

1932. Group I, Table I (*a*) (*continued*)

Case no.	Sex and age	Duration of stay	Symptoms	Duration of symptoms before admission	Result on discharge	Reports in 1933	Reports in 1934
38	F. 29	2 months	General anxiety. Indigestion. "Brain storms". Uncomfortable feelings in lower abdomen	2 years	I	I	I
39	F. 45	5½ ,,	Exhaustion (in bed 3 years). Insomnia. Fears of lonely places. Inability to concentrate	4 ,,	W	W	W
40	F. 31	9 ,,	Weakness (had to be carried into hospital). Insomnia. Indigestion. Constipation	18 months	W	W	W
41	M. 32	4 weeks	Loss of confidence and of concentration. Fear of authority. Bothered about approaching marriage	2 ,,	W	—	W
42	M. 51	4 ,,	Cardiac oppression, shortness of breath. Frequency of micturition. Anxiety feelings. Scruples	Many years	W	W	W
43	F 30	5 ,,	Panics. Fears. Tremors	6 months	W	W	W
44	F. 35	3 ,,	Agitation. Insomnia. Inability to concentrate. Deaf	3 ,,	W	W	W
45	M. 37	1 year	Amnesic attacks. Confusion. Depression. Apathy. Anxiety. Followed by periods of activity	4 years	W	W	W
46	F. 54	6 months	Loss of concentration. Irritable with family. Depressed and unhappy	18 months	I	I	I
47	F. 31	6 weeks	Loss of appetite. Sleeplessness. Irritability. Anxiety. Dyspeptic pains	2 years	I	—	—
48	M. 46	7 ,,	Nervousness and shyness of strangers, especially of people in authority	All his life	I	W	W
49	M. 46	1 month	Anxiety over everything. Fears that he would kill his family	2 years	I	—	—
50	F. 33	5 months	Exhaustion. Tremors. Palpitation. Vomiting. Fainting. Phobias	20 months	W	W	—
51	M. 39	3½ ,,	Panic in train and buses. Fear of epileptic fits. Insomnia	4 years	I	W	—
52	M.	3 ,,	Insomnia. Indigestion. Pains in the back and numbness in body	18 months	I	I	—

1932. Group I, Table I (*b*). *Hysteria*

Case no.	Sex and age	Duration of stay	Symptoms	Duration of symptoms before admission	Result on discharge	Reports in 1933	Reports in 1934
1	F. 29	11 months	Paraplegia (hysterical). Asthenopia. Loss of weight. Insomnia. Headaches	2 years	W	W	W
2	F. 27	9 ,,	Self-disgust, self-pity, self-reproach. Suicidal impulses. Feelings of disintegrated personality	1 year	W	W	W
3	M. 38	7 ,,	History of fugue lasting a week. Alcoholic bouts. Dissatisfaction with life	Many years	W	—	—
4	F. 30	4½ ,,	Epigastric pain. Coccyx pain. Emotional outbursts. Depression	2 years	W	W	W
5	F. 31	10 weeks	Unable to perform fine movements with right arm. Depressed. Insomnia. Abdominal pain. Dyspareunia	1 year	I	I	I
6	M. 35	9 ,,	Fears of disease one after another. Emotional lability. Tears. Self-pity. Insomnia	8 months	Worse	W	W

1932. Group I, Table I (*d*). *Anorexia Nervosa*

Case no.	Sex and age	Duration of stay	Symptoms	Duration of symptoms before admission	Result on discharge	Reports in 1933	Reports in 1934
1	F. 23	2½ months	Loss of appetite. Amenorrhoea. Loss of weight	3 years	W	W	W
2	F. 19	4 ,,	Anorexia. Amenorrhoea. Emaciation	18 months	Gained 19 lb. by October. Lost this, re-ad. Gained 17 lb.	—	W
3	F. 25.	2 ,,	Anorexia. Feels weak. Loss of weight	—	Gained 19 lb.	—	I

1932. Group I, Table III. *Obsessive-Compulsive Neurosis*

Case no.	Sex and age	Duration of stay	Symptoms	Duration of symptoms before admission	Result on discharge	Reports in 1933	Reports in 1934
1	F. 21	2 weeks	Fear of infecting others with venereal disease. Washing mania	—	ISQ	—	—
2	F. 50	2 months	Washing compulsion. Excessive time taken over everything	25 years	I	—	—
3	F. 44	6 ,,	Nosophobia. Washing compulsions. Depressions. Pains	20 ,,	ISQ	—	—
4	M. 21	5 ,,	Obsession that he will touch a man's penis. Compulsive attitudes to avoid this. Excessive interest in sex. Poor sleep. Headache	18 months	ISQ	ISQ	ISQ
5	M. 27	6½ ,,	Compulsive acts about lavatories. Masturbation in strange ways. High grade mental defect	—	ISQ	ISQ	ISQ

1932. Group I, Table IV. *Patients who are no Better*

Case no.	Sex and age	Duration of stay	Symptoms	Duration of symptoms before admission	Result on discharge	Reports in 1933	Reports in 1934
1	M. 43	2 months	Headaches. Pains in legs. Fatiguability. Depression. Failure of concentration	2 years	W	R	W
2	F. 42	11 ,,	Fear of sleep. Horrible dreams and visions. Exhaustion. Suicidal thoughts. Sense of sin	11 months	ISQ	ISQ	I
3	M. 35	2 ,,	Panics. Headache. Insomnia. Indigestion. Dyspnoea	Many years	I	R	R
4	F. 35	11 ,,	Fluttering of heart. Fear of sex and of life generally. Poor sleep	3 years	ISQ	ISQ	ISQ

5	F. 36	1 month	Hemiparesis. Hemiopia. Later these disappeared and were replaced by timidity	1 year	Left early on account of finance	ISQ	—
6	F. 36	2 months	Depression. Feeling of inadequacy. Sleeplessness. Frightened	18 months	ISQ	ISQ	—
7	F. 37	2 ,,	Weakness of legs. Unable to walk. Sundry disturbances	9 years	W	R	—
8	M. 29	9 weeks	Gastric discomfort. Nausea. Vomiting. Emotional lability	—	W	R	W
9	M. 64	7½ ,,	Horrid feelings when walking on bridges or travelling in trains or buses	2 years	I	R	—

1932. Group II, Table I. *Alcoholics*

Case no.	Sex and age	Duration of stay	Symptoms	Duration of symptoms before admission	Result on discharge	Reports in 1933	Reports in 1934
1	M. 23	4 months	Drinking bouts	4 years	W	W	W
2	M. 30	6½ ,,	Alcoholic bouts	—	W	W	W

1933. Group I, Table I (*a*). *Psychoneuroses. Patients who are Well or Improved. Anxiety States*

Case no.	Sex and age	Duration of stay	Symptoms	Duration of symptoms before admission	Result on discharge	Report in 1934
1	F. 28	2 years and 3 months	Fear of being alone. Unable to walk in corridor alone. Various other fears	14 years	I	I
2	M. 20	4½ ,,	Fear of illness. Weeping. Excitability. Erratic behaviour	1 year	W	W
3	F. 36	4 ,,	Loss of appetite. Abdominal pains. Terrors about epilepsy for her children	12 years	I	I
4	F. 32	3 ,,	Exhaustion. Various fears	4 ,,	W	W
5	M. 42	11 weeks	Difficulty in concentration. Depression. Insomnia. Trembling	6 months	I	W
6	F. 34	9 months	Lack of energy. Claustrophobia. Headache. Weeping	1 year	I	W
7	F. 34	8 weeks	Remorse over certain acts. Sense of inferiority	7 years	W	W
8	M. 32	9 months	Feelings of unreality. Depression. Inferiority. Ejaculatio praecox	4 ,,	I	I
9	F. 57	5 weeks	Insomnia. Distressing mental pictures	10 ,,	I	I
10	M. 28	2½ months	Tachycardia. Sweating. Disturbed sleep	—	I	I
11	M. 22	3½ ,,	Tachycardia. Exhaustion. Insomnia. Pains in eyes	6 years	W	W
12	M. 29	14 ,,	Panics. Depression. Fear of going out alone. Phobia of tube trains and closed spaces	4 ,,	I	I
13	F. 45	7 ,,	Fear of being alone. Fear of hurting her son. Sleeplessness and indigestion	—	I	Dead
14	F. 18	8 ,,	Sense of unreality. Insomnia. Fits of temper. Attacks of confusion	18 months	W	W
15	F. 35	2 years	Misery. Exhaustion. Sick headaches. Troubled sleep. Terrifying dreams. Tone deafness so that all music seemed a noise	3 years	W	W
16	F. 46	4½ ,,	Obsessional thinking that she must kill herself or her husband. Panics. Insomnia	Several years	W	W
17	F. 32	5½ months	Terrors. Poor sleep with bad dreams. Fear of insanity	3 years	I	I

18	F. 35	2 months	Suicidal thoughts. Idea that she was wicked. No initiative	5 months	I	W
19	F. 29	4 ,,	Indigestion. Tiredness. Diarrhoea. Fainting. Anxiety feelings	7 years	I	W
20	F. 30	6 weeks	Fatigue. Panic. Tremblings. Fear of return of a stroke	2 ,,	I	W
21	F. 57	12 months	Severe recurrent headaches lasting 4 or 5 days after emotional disturbances. Fits of anger	Since childhood	I	I
22	F. 24	6 ,,	Feelings of unreality. Idea that she ought to kill herself	12 months	I	W
23	M. 17	4½ ,,	Attacks of fear every few days that he has a serious bodily illness	Many years	I	W
24	F. 28	4½ weeks	Refusal to eat. Reluctance to go to bed and rest. Worried over physical pains	2 years	I	I
25	F. 21	10 months	Weeping. Fears. Weakness. Depressed	9 months	W	W
26	M. 43	3 ,,	Attacks of anxiety. Feelings of falling to the right. Dyspeptic symptoms due to adherent appendix	3 years	I	I
27	F. 54	2 ,,	Anxiety. Inability to concentrate. Insomnia. After an accident—illness subject to compensation	16 months	W	W
28	M. 21	6 weeks	Idea that he would have to take off his clothes in public	18 ,,	W	W
29	M. 21	11 ,,	Fear that he will lose control, that he will commit suicide	—	W	W
30	F. 31	3 months	Headache. Insomnia. Inability to concentrate. Depression	—	I	W
31	F. 53	7 weeks	Asthma. "Nervous feelings"	6 years	I	W
32	M. 54	4½ months	Failure of concentration. Restless. Pre-occupied about bowels	12 months	I	I
33	F. 29	6 weeks	Outbursts of temper nearly every day. Two attempts at suicide just before admission	15 ,,	W	W
34	F. 44	8 ,,	Exhaustion. Insomnia. Attacks of confusion. Hypersensitive to noise	3 years	I	I
35	F. 39	10 months	Depression. Tears. Restless. Sense of inferiority. Poor sleep	1 year	I	I
36	M. 33	6 weeks	Inability to eat in public. Shyness. Fear of father	3 years	W	W
37	M.	—	Under remand for exhibitionism. Romantic liar. Apparently actively homosexual	—	I	W
38	F. 43	3 months	Preoccupation with digestion. Abdominal pain. Insomnia. Tachycardia. Exhaustion	—	I	I

1933. Group I, Table I (*b*). *Hysteria*

Case no.	Sex and age	Duration of stay	Symptoms	Duration of symptoms before admission	Result on discharge	Report in 1934
1	M. 46	6 months	Torticollis (spasmodic). Weakness and athetoid movements of right arm. Tendency to compulsive washings	2 years	ISQ	ISQ
2	M. 20	2½ ,,	Asthma coming on to suit various purposes	4 ,,	?	W
3	F. 42	10 ,,	Insomnia. Fears of insanity. Compulsions. Anorexia. Later sore tongue	Always	ISQ	W
4	F. 36	7½ ,,	Constant choreic movements. Terror of dark. Insomnia. Terrifying dreams	10 years	I	I
5	F. 40	4 ,,	Fatigue. Tachycardia. Globus hystericus	3 ,,	I	I
6	F. 40	5 ,,	Spasmodic torticollis. Poor sleep. Emotionalism	6 months	W	Certified 6 months later W

1933. Group I, Table I (*c*), *Anorexia Nervosa*

Case no.	Sex and age	Duration of stay	Symptoms	Duration of symptoms before admission	Result on discharge	Report in 1934
1	F. 24	3½ months	Anorexia. Loss of weight. Dissatisfaction with life	4 years	Gained 20 lb.	W

1933. Group I, Table I (*d*). *Obsessive-Compulsive Neurosis*

Case no.	Sex and age	Duration of stay	Symptoms	Duration of symptoms before admission	Result on discharge	Report in 1934
1	M. 26	2 years and 8 months	Stuttering. Obsessions and compulsions about many things	14 years	Stuttering ISQ. Obsessions and compulsions M.I.	I
2	F. 35	2 "	Obsessive thinking mainly about God	4 years	ISQ	ISQ
3	F. 31	9 "	Must get furniture, pictures, etc. straight. Spends hours doing this. To put on her clothes takes 2 hours at least	8 years	I	I

1933. Group I, Table IV. *Patients who are no Better*

Case no.	Sex and age	Duration of stay	Symptoms	Duration of symptoms before admission	Result on discharge	Report in 1934
1	F. 28	1 year and 10 months	Fear of being alone. Thinks she hears voices. Afraid of the occult	2 years	I	R Later W
2	M. 27	2 years	Depression. Guilt. Self reproach. Sex phobias	3 "	ISQ	ISQ
3	F. 30	3½ weeks	Fears insomnia	15 months	ISQ	—
4	M. 34	1 year and 4 months	Anxiety. Insomnia. Depression	18 "	ISQ	W
5	F. 24	4 "	Dysphagia. Idea that people accuse her of immorality	3 years	ISQ	—
6	F. 30	13 "	Unreality. Afraid to be alone. Fear of cats	15 "	ISQ	Died of intestinal obstruction
7	F. 49	6 weeks	Palpitation. Anxiety. Fatigue. Insomnia	3 "	ISQ	ISQ
8	F. 35	4½ months	Fear of going out alone. Fear of insanity	8 "	ISQ	ISQ
9	F. 32	11 "	Agony in the back. Shuffling gait	20 "	ISQ	ISQ

1933. GROUP I, TABLE IV (*continued*)

Case no.	Sex and age	Duration of stay	Symptoms	Duration of symptoms before admission	Result on discharge	Report in 1934
10	F. 38	17 months	Pains in back and abdomen. Insomnia. Misery	10 years	ISQ	Died
11	F. 19	7 ,,	Hysterical weeping. Incoherent conversation. Depressed	Always	ISQ	ISQ
12	F. 42	3 ,,	Weakness. Sleeplessness. Feeling of something rising from stomach	6 years	W	R
13	M. 60	4½ ,,	Complete insomnia	3 ,,	ISQ	—
14	F. 31	1 year	Depression. Insomnia. Panics. Restlessness. Irritability	6 ,,	ISQ	—
15	M. 38	7 weeks	Train phobia. Headaches. Trying to get compensation	2½ ,,	W	R
16	F. 31	3½ months	Fear of being out alone, of collapsing. Fear of noise	2½ ,,	W	R
17	F. 31	3½ ,,	Attacks of inability to breathe. Fear of being alone	5 ,,	W	R
18	F. 46	2 years	Contracture of leg	2 ,,	ISQ	Re-ad
19	M. 30	10 months	Epileptiform attacks (petit mal). Phobias of suicide	3 ,,	ISQ	—
20	M. 24	4 ,,	Trembling sensations in muscles. Exhaustion. Feeling of inferiority connected with undescended testicles and hairlessness of face	2 ,,	ISQ	Suicide

1933. GROUP II. *Alcoholics*

Case no.	Sex and age	Duration of stay	Symptoms	Duration of symptoms before admission	Result on discharge	Report in 1934
1	M. 35	5½ months	Drinking bouts	—	—	R
2	M. 34	7 ,,	Alcoholic bouts	14 years	—	W
3	M. 53	3½ ,,	Alcoholic excess. Difficulty in concentration	8 ,,	—	W
4	M. 38	8 weeks	Alcoholic bouts. Disappears for days	3 ,,	Went off	—

INDEX

For EU product safety concerns, contact us at Calle de José Abascal, 56–1°,
28003 Madrid, Spain or eugpsr@cambridge.org.

www.ingramcontent.com/pod-product-compliance
Ingram Content Group UK Ltd.
Pitfield, Milton Keynes, MK11 3LW, UK
UKHW012345130625
459647UK00009B/551

* 9 7 8 1 1 0 7 4 5 5 8 8 7 *